The Habit Control Workbook

Nonie Birkedahl, M.S.W.

NEW HARBINGER PUBLICATIONS, INC.

Publisher's Note

This publication is designed to provide accurate and authoritative information in regard to the subject matter covered. It is sold with the understanding that the publisher is not engaged in rendering psychological, financial, legal, or other professional services. If expert assistance or counseling is needed, the services of a competent professional should be sought.

Copyright © 1990 by Nonie Birkedahl
      New Harbinger Publications, Inc.
      5674 Shattuck Avenue
      Oakland, CA 94609

Edited by Leslie Tilley and Patrick Fanning
Cover design by SHELBY DESIGNS AND ILLUSTRATES

ISBN: 0-934986-98-3 (paperback)
ISBN: 0-934986-99-1 (hardcover)

1st Printing January, 1991 7,000 copies
2nd Printing May, 1991 5,000 copies

For my Danish prince, my lifelong and eternal companion.

Acknowledgments

One person does not write a book. It is true that the lonely author sits in isolation bringing to life something within that demands expression, but he or she is not truly alone. A lifetime of personal experience, family relationships, and interactions with a great variety of people shape the book. Everything I have ever read, heard, experienced, or felt is somehow in this book.

No person is presented here factually. Although based on memories in some cases, names and personalities have been changed and blended to make several people one—in other words, the characters are fictional. I am indebted nonetheless to the clients who have strongly impressed me and contributed to my motivation to write. They have enriched my life in subtle and unbelievable ways.

I am indebted to my teachers as well. Fred Kolouch, who has departed this earth, was mentor, confidant, and friend. He schooled me sternly in living systems theory, never allowing me to trifle with the reality of my place in the system.

Richard Stuart, my teacher in graduate school, shaped my thinking about behavior, and I am still influenced by his writings.

Oliver Sacks set an example for me many years ago by treating me as a whole, unique person.

Ron Taylor, DDS, lent me his deep insights into the complexity of bruxism.

I want to express my appreciation for Leslie Tilley's precise attention to detail as copy editor, and a thank you to Gayle Zanca for her work as production manager.

And finally, I need to thank my editor, Patrick Fanning, to whom I am deeply grateful for meticulous appraisal of my work, his guidance through the intricacies of reorganization and rewriting, and for always providing just the right amount of support and encouragement.

Contents

How to Get the Most
Out of This Workbook

The underlying theme of this workbook is that habits are a response to tension caused by internal and external stresses. It has been well documented that people can learn to choose the way they handle stress. This means that you can change the way you behave by changing the way you think about events in your life. You can learn new ways to relieve tension.

This book can be used without the assistance of a therapist or teacher, but it is also designed so that a therapist can assist you. Alternatively, therapists and teachers can use the book as they work with people who struggle with habit control.

The habits covered in this book are overeating, compulsive spending, gambling, compulsive stealing, lying, fire-setting, hair-pulling, explosive temper, misuse of prescription drugs, irresponsible sex, overuse of TV and video games, teeth-grinding, and smoking. (These habits are covered in the same order in each chapter.) If your habit is not listed, you may still derive benefit from selecting one that is similar, and following the outlined program.

The habits presented here are those that have responded to a behavioral approach. More complex habits, such as anorexia, bulimia, self-mutilation, or pedophiliac behavior, are not addressed. These habits require skilled intervention from medical and psychiatric professionals.

The program includes self-evaluation on a living systems model, and exercises for determining the consequences of your behavior and recognizing the cues which trigger it. The self-treatment phase focuses on restructuring the way you talk to yourself, relaxation, and goal setting. Maintenance of replacement behaviors is encouraged by resolving conflict issues with other people, becoming appropriately assertive, and restructuring old memories. Negative reinforcements are included to prevent relapse.

The way to success in this program is as follows. Read Chapter 1 first to clarify what your habit is. Then continue the chapters in order. You can skip ahead to Chapter 6 if you need a head start on relaxation, but then go right back to Chapter 2 and work your way through. In each chapter you will be able to find examples for your particular habit. If you are tempted to jump into goal setting or dealing with people right away, bear in mind that the instructions in these chapters are built upon all that comes before. It's like building a house. The roof has to wait until the walls are in place. You've lived with your problems for a long time. They can wait a little longer.

Do every exercise thoughtfully, without haste. Practice what you've learned as you go along. Build your foundation firmly. Set aside a specific time for this work (and it is work) on certain days, just as if you had registered for a class at a university. You are going to be building new habits. You built the old habits by doing them over and over on a regular basis. Now you have to build new ones the same way. If you miss one of your scheduled sessions, make an appointment with yourself for a make-up session. Give yourself the same commitment and courtesy you give to your tennis coach or your doctor.

Let people around you know that you are working on a habit control program, and explain that you are unavailable during certain hours. It's about like the work I do. I write at home, and so I have to be firm about not accepting interruptions during my working time. The people important to you will respect you for wanting to change your habit, and they will cooperate when they know how important it is to you.

1

Identifying Your Problem

This book is about all kinds of habits, some mild, some severe, but all in some way destructive. These habits are, of course, different from "good habits" such as looking both ways before crossing the street and brushing your teeth after meals. Those are habits you should hang on to. The habits this book is concerned with are the ones that negatively affect your life and possibly the lives of others. The more severe of these habits are called *impulse control disorders* by therapists. But no matter what you call them, they are still habits, and they can be managed in the same way.

You probably bought this book because you, or someone you know, has a habit you would like to see disappear. In this book you are going to become your own therapist. You will teach yourself how to change your behavior.

What Is a Habit?

A habit is an acquired behavior pattern that becomes almost involuntary after many repetitions. I say "almost" involuntary because even when a habit seems automatic, there is thought behind it—a decision is made.

One characteristic of negative habits is that some anxiety or tension precedes the act, and performing the habitual behavior relieves that tension. For example, suppose your habit is hair-pulling and you have a job interview scheduled for Monday morning. On the Friday preceding the interview you feel calm, sure of your chances, and in control. Over the weekend, however, you gradually become more and more tense, playing out various scenarios of failure in your mind, until by Sunday evening the anxiety threatens to overwhelm you. Your hand goes to your head, pulls and twists, and you find yourself holding loose strands of hair. But the tension has abated; you feel relieved and calmer.

The more destructive the habit, the greater the amount of tension required to trigger an episode of your habit. But all negative habits follow this same pattern.

Unfortunately, there is also a price for this relief. With any negative habit, you feel regret and remorse about your behavior after it is over. Not so with good habits—you can feel pleased with yourself for having perfect teeth or a good credit rating. These negative feelings are the key to identifying the habits you want to lose.

It's Up to You

Whatever your habit is, and however you acquired it, you need to recognize that it is *your* habit. You are the one with the habit, and it doesn't help to blame your mother, your teacher, or your biochemistry for the problem. Even with a habit so severe that medication is required, you, not the doctor, are the one responsible for changing.

Drugs alone will not do it. Your therapist can't do it. And just reading this book won't do it. Get all the help you need, but recognize that you are entirely responsible for using medication as prescribed, for following therapeutic instructions, and for carrying out the program in this book.

The sections that follow discuss the habits covered in this book, in the following order:

Overeating	Explosive temper
Compulsive spending	Misuse of prescription drugs
Gambling	Irresponsible sex
Compulsive Stealing	Overuse of TV and video games
Lying	Teeth-grinding
Fire-setting	Smoking
Hair-pulling	

Find your habit in these pages and read carefully. Each section includes a description of the habit and a profile of a typical person with that habit. If you recognize yourself in one of these descriptions, this book may be what you need to help you to take charge of your behavior.

Overeating

Everyone overeats occasionally. Thanksgiving and Christmas are two holidays that beckon us to gluttony. The kind of overeating I'm talking about, however, is usually associated with chronic dieting. If you are constantly obsessed with your size or weight, and you are always on some kind of diet, then chronic dieting is a part of your overeating habit.

If you are an overeater, very likely you do not eat properly. Because your body does not receive a balance of nutrients, you are prone to binges. You are probably familiar with the aftermath of a binge: guilt, anger, and then big resolves to diet more stringently. You lose weight and gain back more, and you never seem to stabilize at the ideal weight you are seeking so frantically.

A word of caution: If you have lost a great deal of weight recently, if you go on binges and then make yourself vomit, or if you use laxatives on a regular basis to lose weight, you probably have a more serious disorder than overeating; you may have anorexia or bulimia. In this case, you need more help than this book can give. You need a behavioral therapist, and a doctor who will pay attention to the damage being done to your physical and emotional health. In addition, you should consult your dentist because the acids in vomit can contribute to tooth decay. Poor nutrition can also damage your teeth and gums. Once you get the proper help, this book can assist you in controlling your habit.

You Are Not Alone

Some researchers say that the incidence of destructive eating behaviors is about 75 percent of the population, with more women than men included. About 6 percent of these will have anorexia or bulimia. These statistics are questionable, however, since many studies have used the memberships of groups such as Weight Watchers and Overeaters Anonymous, in which the entire population being studied was already known to have eating problems. Other studies have been done on college students, a population known to have a high rate of eating disorders, and on groups of patients undergoing medical follow-up for obesity-related diseases. That may cause the population of overeaters and chronic dieters to be either under- or over-reported. Of those, some do not see their eating habit as a problem, and, in fact, it may not be.

What is clear is that overeating and chronic dieting are common habits. The good news is that they can be brought under control.

Randy

Randy was a muncher. He always had potato chips, cookies, and candy readily available. He ate whether he felt hungry or not. At meals he had several helpings of potatoes with lots of gravy, meat, and bread. He particularly relished dessert, and it was not unusual for him to devour three pieces of pie. He felt guilty about his eating, and then would eat more to assuage the feelings of guilt. Every overeater knows this feeling.

When he went grocery shopping, he would pick up a magazine that claimed a new, revolutionary diet, and he would try that for a few days. Then he would begin to feel irritable and suffer such dreadful hunger pains that he would abandon the diet. Randy's weight fluctuated—20 pounds up, 10 down, and 20 or more up again—until he was 85 pounds overweight. He tried a couple of weight loss clinics, losing as much as 70 pounds each time. Gradually the weight would climb back up, which served to discourage him further. Occasionally he would begin an exercise program, but being overweight made it hard to do, so he would abandon that, too. He was chronically depressed about his appearance and disgusted by his lack of will power.

Randy had a habit that was dangerous to his health. It takes time to change habits, but Randy was determined to develop better habits. The hard thing about eating is that you can't just quit, as you might do with smoking. You need to be very patient with yourself and stick to the program for a long time—the rest of your life. The result, however, will be good health and energy. You can be in control and still enjoy eating.

Compulsive Spending

If you are a compulsive spender, you often buy without regard for availability of funds to cover the purchase. You also buy things that are not really necessary. You simply like to spend money. What a wonderful feeling of power there is in being able to buy things. The ever-growing number of credit card users is a dramatic indicator of the spending habits of this country. If you have a good record of making the minimum monthly payment, you can be in debt for thousands of dollars—for the rest of your life. And because of this payment record, you will receive in the mail, at least once a month, an enticing offer for another credit card. You can wind up paying double or triple the purchase price for everything you buy.

Who Has the Habit?

It is estimated that 90 percent of credit card holders cannot pay off their bills each month—they charge more than they can afford. During one week, a therapist is likely to see from one to three people who have a spending habit. This may not have been the problem that brought them in, but it comes out as a major factor in the trouble the person is seeking treatment for.

June

June had only been married to Ned six months the day she opened a credit account at the local department store. She was browsing at the store with a friend when an account representative for the store stopped them and asked if they'd like to open accounts. He explained that with the credit card June would be able to take advantage of sale prices, even if she didn't have any money at the time. The bill could then be paid when she did have the money, and there would be no finance charge so long as the bill was paid in full each month. It sounded good to her. She and Ned needed a lot of things for their new house, and she had been disappointed when she couldn't buy the pretty towels and curtains she had seen on sale. June signed the application.

When she told Ned about it later, he was a little concerned because his personal ethic was that you didn't buy unless you had the money in hand. But he didn't want to deny June anything either, so he told her it would be all right to use the card, as long as the amount she charged was no more than they could reasonably pay at the beginning of the month.

Ned was an old-fashioned fellow. He paid the bills and didn't discuss financial affairs with his wife. This was fine with June. She didn't want to think about bills and money anymore. She had managed her own money before they were married, but now she was glad to have Ned take care of it.

At first June was very careful about the amount she charged. She always told Ned what she had bought and didn't spend more than they could afford. But then she began to see more and more things she would like to have, so she didn't always tell Ned. By not telling, she didn't need to really be aware of how much she spent.

After a while, June got tired of doing her shopping at just one store, so she applied for a Visa card. That would be much wiser, she thought, because then she could comparison shop and get the best buy. One Saturday she returned from a shopping trip, loaded with packages, to a red-faced Ned. He had just received very large bills for not one, but two, credit cards. The yelling match that followed left them tense and unhappy. Ned accused. June denied. It was an impasse. June felt guilty, but at the same time in need of defending her actions. Ned felt his trust had been betrayed, but he also felt bad about upsetting June. There was a chilly truce, and June did a little more shopping to ease her pain.

Eventually the day came when June tried to make a purchase and was embarrassed to be told that her card was already charged to the limit. She told the clerk there had been a mistake and she would check it out. June hurried from the store, face burning. That was the beginning of more stormy scenes with Ned, until June came to the realization that if she wanted to stay married to him, she would have to change her behavior.

Gambling

The excitement and risk of gambling are like an addictive drug, one that satisifies a craving that seemingly can't be met any other way. Whether you win or not is less important than getting that itch scratched. And there's always the hope of the big win. When you do win, it provides a powerful incentive to gamble again. When you lose, you want to make it up by winning next time. It's an endless cycle—unless, of course, you break it. And you can. Even if you've tried before and failed, you can stop gambling.

The Cost of Compulsive Gambling

Although the estimated prevalence of compulsive gambling among adults in the U.S. is only about 2 to 3 percent, the consequences of a single gambler's habit affect families, co-workers, and eventually society as a whole. The divorce rate among gamblers is 90 percent.

There are actually more gamblers than that 2 to 3 percent suggests, but they are professional gamblers and do not experience remorse. Gambling as a compulsive habit is different in that it serves to resolve tension. The guilt and regret that follow, however, wipe out any benefit. And that's only the beginning of gamblers' problems. Even apparently harmless forms of gambling, such as buying state lottery tickets, consume money that could be better spent in other ways, despite the percentage that goes for parks or schools.

Illegal gambling is risky not just because of the possibility of being arrested. Chances are the game is controlled by people who are going to be less than sympathetic if you've lost money you don't have. Even legal gambling can involve you with some pretty bad characters. When you are offered the chance to win big money and you don't have the stakes, thoughtful crooks will loan it to you at an exceptionally high rate of interest. The trouble is, the payment is due in a very short period of time. And the harsh reality is, if you don't win, you won't be able to pay, and your lenders are likely to resort to strong-arm tactics. What you see on TV is not all fantasy.

Greg

A few months ago I met a man who had no teeth. Greg told me the story of his gambling disaster.

It began when he got started betting at the race track. It seemed harmless at first, a $2 bet every week, which occasionally paid off. Then Greg began to want more money. His wife wanted a larger house, and the kids were getting older, needing things. He thought he could pick up extra money by getting into some of the poker games a fellow at work had told him about. He had twinges from his conscience, but he brushed them away. It was for the wife and kids, right?

Some of the guys he met in the games talked him into going to Nevada on the weekends to gamble. Greg took his winnings from poker games to Nevada. While he was there, it seemed that all his worries at work and the financial troubles at home disappeared. But on the way back home, he would start to feel let down and guilty. He was sorry about his family not actually getting all the things he dreamed of giving them, and he realized that his absence from home was affecting the whole family.

When he got home, he decided not to go again, but by Friday afternoon, he felt strongly drawn to the casinos. He thought he would invest more, make it pay, so his absence could be justified by all the nice things he would be able to provide for his wife and kids. Greg's wife was unhappy. She said, "It's worse than death or divorce. When he's home, he's irritable with all of us. He lives for the weekend, and we have no part in his life anymore."

The inevitable happened. Greg played for higher and higher stakes, borrowing heavily from loan sharks. Sure enough, the day came when he couldn't pay off a loan. For a while they just harassed him. Then they made threats against his family. When he still was unable to come up with the cash, even after putting himself in the humiliating position of begging and pleading, they knocked his teeth out and gave him a concussion that put him in the hospital.

Greg's habit gave him a lot of problems. His marriage was on the rocks, he was terrified about the safety of his children, and he had an intolerable financial burden. He now owed money to his parents, to his employer, and to friends who had come forward to help him out. Worst of all he felt humiliated and degraded because his uncontrolled habit had been made known.

Compulsive Stealing

We're not talking here about bank robberies, or planned, clandestine breaking into a house with intent to steal. Formally called *kleptomania*, compulsive stealing is when you take things from stores or friends' homes on impulse. Things you don't need. You don't take them because of their value. You do not intend to sell them or exchange them for something else. You just have the habit of taking things.

You don't feel very good about this stealing. When you see your friends, it's uncomfortable to look them in the eye. Each time, you resolve to not do it again. Then you get worried and tense about things, and there you are, slipping a lipstick into your purse. You want to stop. You can stop.

You Have a Lot of Company

It's difficult to get statistics on how many people steal compulsively. There are shoplifters, who steal things they want and can't pay for. They go into the store with the intent to steal. But they are different from people who steal compulsively and on impulse. Compulsive thieves often don't come to light unless they are caught. Sometimes when a person is very unhappy with this habit, he or she will tell a therapist or teacher. But these cases are seldom included in a data-gathering process. In short, there's an important difference between shoplifters and impulsive thieves, which statistics don't always show.

Anyone can have this habit. It's not just kids or bored housewives. Corporation presidents have been known to steal on impulse. The French composer Claude Debussy is said to have stolen things impulsively. He pocketed objects in shops and in the homes of friends. His habit was widely known, but was tolerated as the idiosyncrasy of an artist. While Debussy was treated kindly for his habit, this is not always the case.

James

I have known James, a young man in his early 20s, for four or five years and had no idea he had a stealing habit until he got into serious trouble over it. One of his fellow students who lived in the same college dorm had been complaining of small items missing from his room—things like an electric shaver, a small cassette player, pens, books, a shirt. One day he went into James's room when James wasn't there. He wanted to borrow a textbook. As he pulled the book off the shelf, he saw his shaver tucked in behind. He took down more books, and was outraged to find his cassette player and every other lost item.

Angry, the student went to the dorm manager, who then confronted James when he came in. Fortunately for James, his friend didn't want to press charges. He elected to let the matter be settled by college authorities. They went through James's room and discovered many items with price tags still on them hidden away in drawers and closet shelves. James was placed on disciplinary probation and required to return all the items to stores and dorm occupants. He then received counseling in controlling his habit. He suffered shame and embarrassment and had lost face with his friends and teachers. It took a long time to rebuild his confidence in himself and regain the trust of others.

Lying

If you lie consistently about things you have done, or didn't do, or you exaggerate and make things up just to be interesting, you have the habit of lying. As you well know, it is impossible not to be found out. What usually happens in the attempt to cover up a lie is that you have to tell another one, and then another, until you are caught in a web of deceit with no way out. Pretty soon no one believes anything you say.

Who Lies?

Liars are even harder to count than compulsive thieves. Lying is very common in childhood, and persists into adolescence in about one-fourth of the students seen by academic counselors. Therapists report chronic lying in about 2 to 3 percent of their adult clients. Probation counselors report 90 percent of their clients as being liars. Clearly, it depends on who is reporting. And it depends on what kind of lying is being talked about. Your kind of lying is not the same as that of most of the liars seen by probation counselors. It isn't productive to generalize from these numbers. The important thing is, if you are a compulsive liar, it affects your life adversely. It causes sorrow and grief for you and for others. That is more telling than a statistic. For you, it is 100 percent problem.

Barbara

Barbara, now in her 50s, has told lies virtually all her life. It began in early childhood, when she heard other children telling of exciting events in their lives. Her own family lived very quietly, on a modest income, and nothing much happened that she could talk about. So she did what a large percentage of preschool children do—she made things up. Her parents thought these stories were cute. As she progressed through school, she found that lying was a way to be included in group activities.

In high school she saw others getting a lot of attention because of skills they had developed. One friend was quite good at art, another in drama. Barbara's skill was in music, but in comparing her playing to the performances of others she felt that her own talent was inferior. So she lied about her musical accomplishments and avoided performing. Her habit thus became well established.

The trouble with lying about your accomplishments is that you cannot avoid being found out. Barbara was invited to play in a school competition. Everyone thought she must be very good. Now Barbara had to lie to get out of performing. She fabricated a trip to New York with her parents. One day a friend called while Barbara was not at home and said to her mother, "I bet you're really excited about going to New York." The jig was up. Very quickly everyone knew she had lied. Friends and teachers assured her that it was all right, they understood, but Barbara felt she had lost their respect. She was exposed and vulnerable, and her self-esteem was nil.

Did Barbara reform and never lie again? Of course not. She didn't know how to stop. It was a habit, and there was no one to teach her another way to cope. Well into adult life she continued to get herself and her family into hot water with her lies.

Fire-Setting

You have this habit, which is also called *pyromania*, if you have deliberately set fires on more than one occasion. This does not include fireplaces, wood stoves, or controlled campfires, of course. The habit of fire-setting is not the same as arson, although arson is what you will be charged with if you are caught. Arson is a crime involving the malicious and deliberate setting of fires for purposes of financial gain, or for retribution against the owner of the property.

See if the following description fits you. Before setting the fire, you experience a buildup of anxiety and tension, which then dissipates during the fire. You do not do it in anger or for retaliation, and you have not been hired to do it. You enjoy watching a fire, and you spend time thinking about fires. You are not a bad person. You simply have a habit that got started somehow, and you discovered that it relieved intolerable tension.

After the fire is over, and the damage is done, you feel remorse. You usually vow not to do it again. The problem is that setting fires is so effective in relieving your tension that you have not been able to stop before now. But you can overcome this habit.

How Many Fire-Setters Are There?

Since fire-setting as a compulsive habit may be confused with other kinds of fire-setting, such as arson or fire-setting that occurs as a result of a serious mental illness, there are no reliable figures on this habit. In the city where I live, the fire department reports that fire-setting comprises only 1 percent of all reported fires. This does not, however, differentiate between pyromania and arson. More important than a statistic is the fact that this is a *dangerous* habit. It threatens the lives of others and destroys property. Even one fire is one too many.

Bart

During the summer and fall of 1989, we had a fire-setter in our town. Bart's first fire was an empty school building. Fortunately, the burning happened at night, and no one was inside. Other fires occurred: a couple of businesses, a car, and a storage shed. People were frightened and kept their outside lights on at night.

This fire-setter, a young man, did not set the fires maliciously. He was not trying to get even with anyone. No one paid him to do it. He had nothing to gain except relief from his tension.

Another fire-setter, who was never caught, set fire to a beautiful church. The congregation went through a grieving period as real as if a loved one had died. They felt violated and displaced. The community at large resonated to their grief. Another church was burned, and other buildings. This fire-setter carries with him the lonely responsibility for what he has done. His remorse will eventually yield to tension that will demand he set another fire. I'm sure he isn't happy doing this.

Hair-Pulling

In mental health jargon this is called *trichotillomania,* which is hard to spell and harder to pronounce, so we won't use it. Hair-pulling includes yanking out hair on the scalp, eyebrows, eyelashes, beard, mustache, and anywhere else hair grows. There's no reason to do it; you simply do it compulsively. You feel nervous, anxious, or tense before you do it and excited and relieved while you are doing it and immediately afterward. Very quickly, however, remorse and guilt set in, and you begin to beat yourself up with words like "You're so stupid," "You're sick," or "You're worthless." Does this sound familiar? If so, you can begin right now to realize that you are not a sick person. Hair-pulling is just a habit.

A Common Problem

There are a lot of people with this habit. In fact, about 8 million people are out there pulling out hunks of hair.

This is not a habit that causes physical injury to others. The damage is primarily experienced by you, personally. Sometimes the bare places can be disguised with eyebrow pencil, false eyelashes, or wigs, but usually not effectively. Even if you do manage to fool others, you can't fool yourself.

This habit wreaks havoc with your self-esteem. It is hard to perform well in the world when you feel badly about yourself and your appearance. It's important to recognize that hair-pullers are not weird. They are normal, intelligent people, just like you, who simply have a self-defeating habit. A habit you *can* learn to control.

Catherine

Catherine is a beautiful young woman, a single mother of twin boys. When I first met her, she was wearing a blonde wig and had worn a wig of some kind since eighth grade. She knows more about hair than anyone I know, except a dermatologist.

She was, and still is, very achievement oriented. Her busy life includes her sons' scouting and sports activities in addition to her own graduate studies in biochemistry. Consequently, her life is full of stress, and as the stress becomes unbearable, her tension heightens until she finds herself standing in front of the mirror pulling out clumps of hair. She suffers depression, guilt, and remorse and vows she will never do it again.

Catherine's habit was so strong that she continued to do it even after her wig came off one night in a crowded restaurant. She was having dinner with a friend when a waiter brushed past, catching her wig on the button of his sleeve. It was a humiliating experience made worse by the fact that her friend was too embarrassed to call her anymore.

Explosive Temper

Everyone gets angry sometimes, even those who have trouble admitting it to themselves. Others erupt into rage at the least provocation. Somewhere in the middle is where most people operate.

You have an explosive temper habit if your temper flares quickly and you are unable to resist an impulse to do something that harms another person. The intensity of your rage is usually out of proportion to the seriousness of the event that triggered the flare-up. Afterward you regret what you have done and say a lot of negative things to yourself about what a terrible person you are. In between these attacks you are your normal self.

If anger is your habit, what's important is not how you developed it. While knowing the cause is of academic interest, it doesn't help you control the habit. It may, in fact, give you an excuse to continue. You could be using it as permission not to change.

A 12-year old, whose father habitually hit him in anger, said to me, "Well, I guess I'll be the same way." We talked about that for a long time. Eventually I think he understood that it did not follow that what dad did, son could do. We discussed ways for him to control his temper, so that when he had children of his own, he would be able to treat them the way he would have liked to have been treated. The angry outbursts you have do not need to go on into the next generation, but they will if you don't break the chain.

An Epidemic

Every day, in all parts of the world, there is increasingly more violent behavior toward those who are weaker. That means children and adults not strong enough to defend themselves. Any statistic about the incidence of explosive temper given today will change tomorrow. Today there are three times as many murders, assaults, and related crimes as there were 20 years ago. And these are only the violent acts that are reported as crimes. Unreported are the thousands of incidents occurring every day in homes and at work that are the result of the bad habit of explosive temper.

Cal

Cal was a chiropractor, but because of his temper, he can no longer practice. Cal had had a good reputation as a competent practitioner, but his uncontrolled habit of explosive temper changed his life in just a few seconds. One day, while examining an elderly man who complained of stiffness in his joints, Cal became angered by the man's resistance to Cal's attempts to straighten his leg. In an outburst of temper, Cal forcibly tried to unbend the knee. There was an crack and cry of pain. The shin bone had snapped. The man had osteoporosis, and his bones were extremely fragile.

Misuse of Prescription Drugs

Misuse means using your prescribed medication too often, too much, and for too long. Misuse of drugs is dangerous. All drugs have the potential for being toxic, which places you at risk for injuring your health. The condition for which you took the drug in the first place may be less serious than the effects of using the drug incorrectly.

No doubt this habit crept up on you in a very sneaky way, via a prescription from your doctor. You gradually began to take a little more, and a little more, until you were using too much, too often. Pain killers and tranquilizers are the most frequently misused drugs. These kinds of drugs are given for *acute* conditions—ones that are expected not to last very long. When symptoms become *chronic* (lasting or recurring) the use of these drugs is no longer appropriate.

What happened to you was probably something like this. You were given some medicine when you strained your back or experienced some other injury. You were afraid of the pain, of course, everyone is. When your prescription ran out, you still felt pain, so you called the doctor. He or she approved a refill, and that's when you began to believe you could not be comfortable without the drug. Fear kept you dependent. You didn't know any other way to control pain, and you certainly weren't willing to have pain. In the extremity of your fear, you may even have gotten prescriptions from several doctors, just to be sure you would always have something.

It isn't the doctor's fault. You had the complaint, and doctors are trained to respond to complaints. Unfortunately, doctors often resort to drugs when it would be better to offer another kind of therapy. But the fact remains that you asked for the drug, you accepted it, and you used it. You didn't do this with the thought in mind that you would develop a destructive habit. You didn't want to be addicted to drugs. You were simply frightened and needed help.

The paradox of pain is that even when you feel you can't stand it, you are, at that moment, "standing it," and have probably been doing so for quite some time. Pain is an unpleasant, but inevitable, fact of life. It would be more accurate to say, "This pain drains my energy, and I'm scared."

A Common Problem

Chronic pain and anxiety send more people to the doctor than almost anything else. Of patients with pain and anxiety, 75 percent misuse their prescribed drugs. Headaches are the most common complaint, with low back pain coming in a close second.

Larry

At age 32, Larry was unable to continue with his work as a truck driver because of pain in his lower back. Four years earlier he had fallen from his truck as he was loading a heavy piece of equipment. Surgery had been done, but the outcome was not good— Larry still had disabling pain. He had consulted several physicians, each of whom had given him prescriptions for pain killers, tranquilizers, and anti-depressants. The pain killers numbed the pain for short periods of time, and gradually, those periods became shorter and shorter. Larry was taking drugs at closer intervals than had been prescribed because he was afraid of the pain. Tranquilizers helped the anxiety he felt about his condition, but then he found it necessary to take more of those, too. The anti-depressants had unpleasant side effects.

Larry was concerned about taking so many pills and depressed that he could not work. He had thoughts of suicide. His wife, Jean, felt resentful because he didn't improve. She was tired of carrying the entire burden of providing for the family. Larry and Jean felt themselves growing apart. The children stayed away from their dad as much as possible because he was always cross with them. He never read stories or played games anymore. He was always telling them, "Dad doesn't feel good. Go play by yourselves." Larry was obsessed with his never-ending cycle of pain-drug-pain.

Irresponsible Sex

For the purposes of this book, irresponsible sex is defined as sexual activity in which there is risk of emotional or physical damage to one or both partners. We live in a time in which sexually transmitted diseases make having multiple or casual sexual relationships seem like playing Russian Roulette. Conflicting feelings about sex and its rewards and possible negative consequences may make it difficult to decide if your sexual habits are destructive. The fact that you are reading this would indicate that you are uncomfortable with what you've been doing. Answering a couple of questions may help you to sort this out.

Do you have genuine affection for your partner? Are you committed to his or her well-being?

Are your sexual behaviors congruent with the mental image you have of the person you'd really like to be?

"No" answers to these questions indicate you would like to change. You may think change is impossible, but it is not. You can change. It is up to you to make the decision.

Polly

Polly had been molested as a child. When she was 13, she started having sex with any boy who seemed to like her. By the time she was an adult, it had become a habit for her to relate to men sexually. It was automatic. She didn't know any other way to do it.

This is very common behavior in women who have been sexually abused, and it can have a high price. Polly had an abortion, a miscarriage, and surgery for pelvic inflammatory disease, all before she was 18.

As with most habits, there was comfort for Polly in doing what she had habitually done. And it was a difficult thing for her to accept the fact that having been molested was not reason enough to continue her self-destructive habits. At 13, she really didn't have control, she reacted out of anguish and emotional confusion. But as an adult, she did have that power, although it took time to recognize it.

There is a dreadful loneliness in feeling you haven't the power to change. And sometimes concentrating on the causes makes it seem that much more impossible. If you can step outside those causes, whatever they are, even for a moment, then you will be able to see that you too can change.

One further note: Therapists now consider sexual abuse to be far more common than previously thought. As many as one woman in four may have been molested or abused as a child, and the numbers are not terribly different for men. Sexual abuse has devastating effects on the victim. If you know or think that you may have been abused, I urge you to think strongly about consulting a qualified therapist or social worker.

Overuse of TV and Video Games

Television is a virtually inescapable force in contemporary life. From the magazines at the checkout counter to children's toys to conversations at work, TV's influence spreads far beyond the glow of the tube. But inside that glow is where problems can start.

People use television in many different ways. It may be less harmful for one person to have the TV on eight hours a day in the background than it is for another to spend two hours mesmerized by it. Children will probably be more negatively affected by a violent one-hour cop show than by three hours spent watching with an adult who monitors what they watch and explains what is going on.

To answer the question of "How much is too much?" it is necessary to consider your or your child's TV viewing or video game playing in the context of what it is replacing. How would that time have been spent if the TV were broken or Nintendo never invented? Among the things TV and video games take time from are family and social interactions, homework, physical activity, and recreational reading. Even people who spend no time watching TV (or playing video games) would like to have more time for at least one of those things. What are you giving up?

The bottom line is, if you feel you or your child is spending too much time staring at the box, then it's a problem. If you don't think so, why are you reading this?

Robert

After a ten-hour day as a telephone lineman, Robert retreated into the world of TV. He said that he was too tired to do anything else. When he came home from work, he washed up, gave his wife and kids a perfunctory greeting, and took a plate to his favorite chair in front of the TV. There he stayed until he fell asleep during the late movie.

His wife was hurt and angry. "It's like I don't have a husband," she said, "I just have a big silly creature who feeds his face and stares at that idiotic screen all night." It got worse. He began to forgo family outings to watch sports on TV. The children fell into the habit of staying home with him. It was only when his wife threatened to move out of the house that Robert began to understand that his habit was causing disaster.

Teeth-Grinding

Teeth-grinding, or *bruxism*, is often discovered through complaints of jaw pain and headache. You may not have been aware of your habit until you sought relief for the pain, or until your dentist noticed abnormal wearing of the molars. Once it was pointed out, you probably began to catch yourself clenching your teeth. If you look in a mirror, you will see that the muscles in your jaw are clearly visible when your teeth are clenched. This muscle tension is what causes the pain.

How Much of a Problem Is It?

Some dentists estimate that approximately 3 to 5 percent of all patients seen in a dental practice have the habit of teeth-grinding. However, since this data is based on the reports of patients themselves, it may not be entirely reliable. One thing is clear: the habit of teeth-grinding is not caused by dental problems such as under- or overbite. The consensus is that it is associated with stress and tension. Most habits are.

To get relief from the pain associated with teeth-grinding, you may already have been the round of dentists, physical therapists, orthopedists, and chiropractors. All may have had something useful to say or some treatment to offer, but you still have not overcome the habit. You will have to do that yourself. The following chapters will give you the necessary skills to do that.

Sam

The pain in Sam's jaw was puzzling. Sometimes it would get so intense that it spread upward to the top of his head and down through his neck and shoulders. Sometimes it felt more like an earache. He wondered if it could be associated with cello playing, since that is what he did six or seven hours a day. It didn't make sense, though, because it didn't start in the shoulder or neck, as one might expect with a cello player. It always started in his face and jaw. Other musicians in the orchestra had ideas about what it was and offered many suggestions. Some said he should get a longer end pin. Others told him to see a chiropractor. Everyone had advice.

Finally, the pain got so bad that he wasn't sleeping well. His wife suggested consulting their family doctor, which he reluctantly did. The doctor was puzzled at first. He had Sam bring his cello to the office in order to see what Sam did when he was playing. As he walked around Sam, he noticed the muscles in Sam's jaw standing out, rigid and hard. Running his fingers along Sam's jaw he found that Sam's teeth were tightly clenched.

That began a long process of trying various treatment methods: splints, diets, drugs, and physical therapy. All of these helped for a short time. Mostly they helped while he was having the treatment, but later the pain would return. When someone suggested exploratory surgery he decided to talk with his dentist. It was Sam's dentist who finally labeled the problem as a habit. He said it was stress related. At that point Sam realized he was going to have to become his own therapist.

Smoking

If you regularly smoke even one cigarette a week, you have a smoking habit. It's not likely that it will stay at one a week, either. Smoking tends to escalate. It is not too strong a statement to say that smoking one cigarette, period, is too many.

Since you are reading these words, it's likely you are thinking of quitting. You have probably tried before, and failed. You're not alone—this is a very difficult habit to get rid of. Seventy percent of smokers who give up the habit relapse in the first three month. Another 5 percent go back to the habit by the end of the first year.

The good news is that 25 percent are permanently free of their smoking habit, and you can be in that 25 percent. Also, recent studies have shown that quitting reverses the damage done by smoking. Of course, the longer you've been smoking, the longer the reversal takes. But there's no such thing as it being "too late to quit." And there's no time like the present. If you are ready to stop, you can do it.

Facts

In case you're not quite convinced, here's a little information to help you along. In 1980, 100,000 people died of smoking-related lung cancer. Cigarettes are now considered to be a direct cause of heart disease and chronic lung disease. Every year in this country smoking costs $28 *billion* in medical care, absenteeism, and accidents due to smoking.

Nicotine is absorbed through the respiratory tract and the mucous membranes lining the mouth, nose, gastrointestinal tract, and even through the skin. In concentrated form nicotine is a highly toxic poison. Nicotine and hydrogen-containing tars form particles that contain cancer-causing nitrosamines, beta-naphthylamine, radioactive polonium 120, and metallic nickel. Cadmium, lead, and fluoride are other ingredients carried by these particles. Free gases absorbed into the body during smoking are carbon monoxide, nitrogen dioxide, formaldehyde, hydrogen sulfide, ammonia, hydrogen cyanide, and acrolein. Sounds terrible doesn't it? Well, it is.

Ida

Ida, now 45, began smoking in her teens. Her friends were doing it. They all thought it was sophisticated. At first Ida just smoked when she was with her friends, but it wasn't long before she was smoking in her room, or in the bathroom. Her parents were outraged. "Don't you know what you are doing to yourself, young lady?" her father said.

"Don't worry, Dad, I can quit any time I want to," Ida replied. She really thought she could. Her mother banned smoking from the house, but Ida still sometimes sneaked a drag when Mom wasn't home. It got so she checked her purse for cigarettes before she went anywhere. She found herself becoming annoyed at people who didn't like smoking. "I have rights, too," she would mutter under her breath. One time her aunt heard her say that, and responded, "You don't have a right to contaminate the air I breathe." Ida went off in a huff.

After she married, she began to feel a little uneasy about smoking. She knew she shouldn't do it while pregnant, but she couldn't seem to stay away from it completely. After the baby was born, she got a stern lecture from the doctor. "Your baby is breathing in that smoke just the same as if you put the cigarette in his mouth." Ida felt guilty and vowed to quit. She did try, but it only lasted three months. She felt jittery and nervous when she quit. Through the years she tried several more times, either by trying to cut down on her own or by attending stop-smoking clinics. But she always went back to it.

As her children got older, they scolded her about it. "Mom, just quit," they would say. "We hate the way it smells. We don't want you to die." Finally, one morning as she was coughing and feeling sick from having smoked too much the night before, she made a decision. "I will quit," she told herself, "no matter what I have to go through." That time she was able to stick to her resolve and quit.

Unmaking the Habit

Unmaking old habits and replacing them with new ones starts with collecting information about yourself. Before you can start to change you need as much knowledge as you can get about your habit. For that you will need to keep some records.

Keeping the Record

The first step in record keeping is to determine just how severe your habit is. Using the Severity of Habit chart will enable you to "measure" your habit. Find your habit in the left-hand column and the frequency of your habit at the top of the chart. Then look down the frequency column to the row for your habit, and see whether your habit is mild, moderate, severe, or very severe.

If you find yourself in the category of very severe, you may want to enlist the help of another person. Professionals skilled in these areas would be clinical social workers, clinical psychologists, licensed behavioral counselors, and psychiatrists. When searching for a helper, find out first if they are licensed to do what they claim to do, and then ask if they do behavioral therapy. In rare instances medication is helpful.

The second step in record keeping is to record exactly what happens before, during, and after you do your habit. You need to keep a record faithfully every day for two weeks before proceeding to the next step. For this you will use the Habit Diary, at the end of this chapter. You may freely copy this chart for your own use. You may want to reduce. You will need 14 sheets for now.

No one can change your habit except you so you need to be diligent in your information gathering. As with all the materials in this book, the Habit Diary is only as effective as your diligence in using it.

Be honest. No one sees this record. It's a human tendency to want to make problems seem less than they are. But it is important for you to see clearly, in black and white, just

Severity of Habit

Habit	Once a Month or Less	Twice a Month	Once a Week	Two to Five Times a Week	Every Day	More Than Once a Day
Overeating to the point of discomfort: One event	No problem	Mild	Moderate	Moderate	Severe	Very severe
Compulsive spending: One event	Moderate	Moderate	Severe	Severe	Very severe	Very severe
Gambling, betting, buying lottery tickets: One event	Mild	Moderate	Severe	Severe	Very severe	Very severe
Stealing: One event	Moderate	Moderate	Severe	Severe	Severe	Very severe
Lying: One event	Mild	Mild	Moderate	Moderate	Severe	Severe
Fire-setting: One event	Moderate	Severe	Severe	Very severe	Very severe	Very severe
Hair-pulling: One event	Mild	Mild	Moderate	Moderate	Severe	Very severe
Explosive temper (verbal or physical assault): One event	Mild	Moderate	Severe	Severe	Very severe	Very severe
Drug misuse (exceeding prescribed dose or interval): One event	Mild	Mild	Moderate	Moderate	Severe	Very severe
Irresponsible sex: One event outside monogamous relationship	Moderate	Severe	Severe	Very severe	Very severe	Very severe
TV/Video overuse: More than two hours at one sitting	No problem	No problem	Mild	Moderate	Severe	Severe
Teeth-grinding: Awareness of clenched teeth	No problem	No problem	Mild	Moderate	Severe	Severe
Smoking: One cigarette, pipe, cigar, chew, snuff	Mild	Moderate	Moderate	Severe	Severe	Severe

how firmly entrenched your habit is. Alcoholics, for example, find it very hard to openly acknowledge that their drinking is not just "social." They have to be able to say with conviction, "I am an alcoholic." Then they have hope of changing. You need to be able to say, "I am a hair-puller," or whatever your habit is.

As you read the following example of record keeping, you will begin to understand how essential it is to have more information about yourself. When you do a meticulous job of recording everything on the Habit Diary chart, you are on your way to success. With a visible record of your habit you will be ready to learn more about control.

June

June was an overspender. She had been going on spending binges about once a week, so she could see on the Severity of Habit chart that her habit was severe. Her husband, Ned, said he thought *critical* was a better word. Nevertheless, June had made a decision to change, so she went on to the Habit Diary.

At first she was a little intimidated by the 24-hour record, but, recognizing the precariousness of her marriage, she was determined to try. Of course, she couldn't do much shopping in the middle of the night, which simplified her task a little. She just wrote the word *sleeping* across each hour of the night, with one exception. Thursday night she caught herself planning a shopping trip. She immediately turned on the light and recorded her feelings of guilt.

The hardest part of record keeping for June was remembering to keep the chart with her and making herself take time to record every hour. Even if she just went upstairs in her home, she took the diary with her. In meetings she found that recording in her notebook was no problem. People write themselves notes all the time.

June soon found she had a tendency to gloss over the truth. Seeing in black and white how often she was spending money irresponsibly was embarrassing. She mentioned this to Ned, and he pointed out that he received the black-and-white evidence every month in the form of statements from credit card companies. He said he was embarrassed, too. June realized that she had better face her embarrassment if she was going to learn to control this destructive habit. After that it was easier to be honest.

Look again at June's diary for Thursday. Notice that she was experiencing a good deal of anxiety most of the day. She also became tense and angry when she and Ned had a two-hour argument about money. Another interesting thing to notice is that there were two activities directly related to spending: planning a party and looking at catalogs. Add that to her hour of planning in the middle of the night, and you can see that June spends quite a bit of time thinking about spending money. At this point we don't know what her thoughts were while cleaning and ironing. It's quite possible she may also have been thinking of spending during those times.

Now look at her diary for Friday. Notice that the level of anxiety increases until she goes shopping. She spends a few hours shopping, during which time she feels happy and

Habit Diary

Date: *Thursday, May 5*

Time	Where are you?	With whom?	Doing what?	How do you feel?
7:00 a.m.	Kitchen	Ned	Eating	A little anxious
8:00	Kitchen	Alone	Cleaning	Less Anxious
9:00	Living room	Alone	Vacuuming	OK
10:00	Utility	Alone	Ironing	Anxious
11:00	Den	Alone	Talking on phone to Betty	Worried
12:00 p.m.	Kitchen	Alone	Eating lunch & planning	Excited
1:00	Car	Alice	Going to meeting	Happy
2:00	Community Center	Committee	Planning senior party	Excited
3:00	"	"	"	"
4:00	Car	Alice	Going home	Anxious, excited
5:00	Alice's house	Alice	Looking at catalogs	Anxious, excited
6:00	Kitchen	Alone	Cooking	Worried
7:00	Dining room	Ned	Arguing	Very tense
8:00	Kitchen	Ned	Arguing	"
9:00	Bedroom	Ned	Going over bills	Tense and angry
10:00	Bedroom	Ned	Watching News	"
11:00	Sleeping			
12:00 a.m.	"			
1:00	"			
2:00	"			
3:00	In bed	Ned	Planning to shop	Guilty
4:00	Sleeping			
5:00	"			
6:00	Bathroom	Alone	Showering	Sleepy

Habit Diary

Date: *Friday, May 6*

Time	Where are you?	With whom	Doing what?	How do you feel?
7:00 a.m.	Kitchen	Ned	Eating	Very anxious
8:00	Kitchen	Alone	Cleaning & baking	Nervous & anxious
9:00	Bedroom	Alone	Changing clothes	Nervous & anxious
10:00	Car	Alone	Driving to mall	Very anxious
11:00	Mall	Alone	Shopping	Excited
12:00 p.m.	"	"	"	"
1:00	"	"	Eating	Happy
2:00	"	Alone	Shopping	Excited
3:00	Car	"	Going home	Guilty
4:00	Bedroom	Alone	Hiding purchases	Guilty, worried
5:00	Kitchen	"	Cooking	Depressed
6:00	Dining room	Ned	Eating	"
7:00	Den	Ned	Watching movie	Depressed & tired
8:00	Bed	Alone	Crying	Hate myself
9:00	"	"	"	"
10:00	Bed	Ned	Watching news	Hopeless
11:00	Bed	Ned	Talking	Tense
12:00 a.m.	Sleeping			
1:00	"			
2:00	"			
3:00	"			
4:00	"			
5:00	"			
6:00	Bathroom	Alone	Showering	Worried

excited. But what happens on the way home? Guilt, depression, feelings of self-hatred, and finally hopelessness.

After keeping these charts for two weeks, the pattern of June's behavior became very clear to her. She was surprised that it was so obvious and yet she had never recognized it before. Having this information helped June see that her habit was *predictable*.

It is also going to be interesting for you, as you keep your own records, to see predictable patterns of behavior. The predictability appears in many forms. The first, which has already been referred to, are the consequences. Consequences of different kinds have a lot to do with how avidly you cling to your habit. In the next chapter you will learn to analyze the consequences of your habit and see how they keep it active. You also will be adding more information to your record. The best tool you have for helping yourself is this pattern of predictability.

A Note About the Habbit Diary Chart

This is a 24-hour record. For the hours you sleep, simply write the word *sleeping* in the first column, with a line across the other columns. Unless, that is, you do your habit in your sleep or wake up and do it, in which case you need to record that. It's important not to get discouraged and give up on the diary. While it is a bit tedious, it's the only way to get enough information to succeed in controlling your habit—not just for a while—for the rest of your life.

Further Reading

Denbo, Jay A "Maloclusion." In *The Dental Clinics of North America*. Vol. 34, No. 1. Philadelphia: W.B. Saunders, 1990.

Fanning, Patrick. *Lifetime Weight Control*. Oakland, Calif.: New Harbinger Publications, Inc., 1990.

Fredricksen, Lee, and Rainwater, Nancy. "Explosive Behavior: A Skill Development Approach" in *Violent Behavior: Social Learning Approaches to Prediction Management and Treatment*. Edited by Richard B. Stuart. New York: Brunner/Mazer, 1981.

Ramer, Elliot. "Controversies in Temporomandibular Joint Disorder." In *The Dental Clinics of North America*. Vol. 34, No. 1. Philadelphia: W.B. Saunders, 1990.

Segal, Bernard. *Drugs and Behavior*. New York, London: Gardner Press, Inc., 1988.

Habit Diary

Date:

Time	Where are you?	With whom?	Doing what?	How do you feel?
7:00 a.m.				
8:00				
9:00				
10:00				
11:00				
12:00 p.m.				
1:00				
2:00				
3:00				
4:00				
5:00				
6:00				
7:00				
8:00				
9:00				
10:00				
11:00				
12:00 a.m.				
1:00				
2:00				
3:00				
4:00				
5:00				
6:00				

2

Consequences

Positive versus Negative

The word *consequence* probably conjures up images of punishment or embarrassment. Because you dislike your habit, you may not be aware that some of the consequences of your habit are positive and rewarding. Positive consequences are like a paycheck or the praise and recognition that comes when you do a good job. These things keep you working and striving to do well.

Any job inevitably has its downside of course. You probably feel, at least sometimes, that you spend time working that could be profitably spent on personal matters or recreation. There is stress associated with work, and perhaps you don't always get along well with your boss or co-workers. These things are the negative consequences of the job. But the satisfaction you derive, and the paycheck, outweigh the negative aspects. Otherwise, no matter how miserable you may be, even if you feel you have no choice, you wouldn't continue in that job.

With your habit, the "paycheck" is the positive consequences that reinforce and perpetuate it. Negative consequences are what make your habit undesirable. As with the stress of a job, if the negative consequences had been stronger than the positive, you would have stopped doing your habit a long time ago. An examination of these opposing kinds of consequences will help you to understand why your habit is so hard to control.

Natural or Unnatural?

Consequences fall into two further categories: natural and unnatural. *Natural* consequences are predictable and obvious. *Unnatural* consequences are neither predictable nor obvious. They result from other people's reaction to the situation. For example, if Joe doesn't water his lawn, it will turn yellow and die. That is natural and therefore predictable. The unpredictable consequence is his wife's reaction to the death of the lawn. Jane will make a decision and take some action. Will she merely nag or hire someone else to care for the lawn? Will she do the job herself? Maybe she will simply shrug and do nothing at all.

Consequences occur on physical, social, and psychological levels. You are familiar with all of these, although you may not have sorted them out in quite this way. You are probably most aware of the physical consequences of your habit, although you may not fully realize their severity. On the social level are the consequences that result from others becoming aware of your habit. These consequences can range from disapproval to imprisonment, depending on your habit and its severity.

Psychological effects are less tangible than the other. The principal effect is a feeling of worthlessness or lowered self-esteem. These feelings are primarily the result of an especially uncomfortable kind of tension called *cognitive dissonance*. Cognitive dissonance means that what you do is discordant with the way you want to be. You have a mental picture of your ideal self—the person you feel you were meant to be. This picture includes attributes of physical strength and beauty, as well as qualities of kindness, wit, and intelligence. Anything that jars this picture of your ideal self will cause you to feel cognitive dissonance: tense, uneasy, and jumpy.

Find your habit in the following pages and see if you have experienced some of these natural and unnatural consequences. The descriptions won't match your experiences exactly, but there should be similarities. Even if you haven't experienced many of these consequences yet, you should be aware of the risks your habit entails.

Overeating

Natural Consequences

Some of the consequences of overeating have received attention in the media, primarily the health problems related to obesity. Those that can be life threatening include coronary artery disease, high blood pressure, and cancer. Certain kinds of cancer are specifically linked to obesity: colon, uterine, and breast cancers. Carrying too much weight will accelerate wear and tear on your joints as well as on your heart.

Many diseases are related less to the number of pounds you carry than to the kind of food you eat. Stuffing yourself on fruits and vegetables will not contribute to obesity. You might be a little uncomfortable until your stomach empties, but that is all. In fact, many fat people are not overeaters, per se. People who are truly seriously obese usually get that way because they eat too much of the wrong kinds of food. Foods high in fat, sugar, and salt, along with foods low in fiber, are the problem. The kind of food you eat is more important than how much you weigh.

Randy's ideal image of himself is not that of a man who is constantly shoving food in his mouth or one who can barely walk. He describes his ideal self as competent, productive, and well put together. He pictures himself as a tall, trim man. Every time he eats to the point of discomfort he is reminded of his habit of overeating. He then feels sorrow over the loss of his ideal self, and that begins the cycle of tension, habit, relief, tension, and on and on.

It is tempting at this point to say that all Randy needs to do to be his ideal self is stop overeating, but you know that is too simplistic. You've been trying for years to control your eating, and the harder you tried, the more you ate.

Unnatural Consequences

Feelings of self-worth are also lowered by the reactions of other people. Your tension is increased by the attitudes and opinions of others—by what people have said to you about your habit or just the way they seem to look at you. You feel bad because you don't measure up to your ideal, and then you feel worse because of someone's reaction.

There can be consequences in the workplace, too. Some companies, for example, have policies about health risk behaviors, obesity among them. Your employer spent time and money training you for the job. You are now at risk for heart attack and stroke—two events that will take you out of the workplace. On a less drastic level, overweight people have been shown to have a higher incidence of colds and flu. It sounds harsh, but your employer's goal is to get as much work out of you as possible with the least expense.

You know better than anyone what your negative consequences have been. It is important that you understand the difference between the natural and unnatural consequences of your habit. Once you have done your habit you can't stop natural consequences, but you can work with unnatural consequences to help you gain control of your habit. Next you will list your natural and unnatural consequences on the Consequence Record at the end of the chapter. Instructions for using the record begin on page 47.

Compulsive Spending

Natural Consequences

The first consequence of overspending that comes to mind is not having enough money to pay the bills. When you charge $400 worth of clothes and you only have $75 budgeted, the natural consequence is that you can't pay.

June denied the reality of this inevitable consequence every time she went shopping. The consequence was compounded as old bills were not completely paid before adding new charges. The bill grew and grew.

Unnatural Consequences

Unnatural consequences are those imposed on you by someone else. For example, your charge cards could be withdrawn so that you won't have credit when you really need it. The credit card companies could impose more severe consequences that will affect your credit rating and cause you to be harassed by a collection agency.

What has happened to you as a result of doing your habit? Which consequences were natural? Unnatural? What about feeling guilty every time you look at the couch that really isn't paid for? You need to define and organize all the consequences you have experienced. Turn to page 47 and read the instructions for recording your negative consequences on the Consequence Record.

Gambling

Natural Consequences

Loss of money is the inevitable result of gambling. Even if you win big, you've lost a lot of money before that. Most gamblers don't keep track of the amount of money they lose. Do you? It would probably shatter your illusions if you did.

Loss of time is another natural consequence. Gambling takes time away from other activities. If you have a family, you are losing precious moments with them. And they may feel they have already lost you. Depending on the frequency of your habit, you may lose time from work as well. Certainly you will not be concentrating on the job if you are obsessively thinking about how to win or worrying about losses.

Fear is a natural consequence of gambling if you have had to borrow money. Fear is a particularly vicious consequence because it drains your energy, disrupts your concentration, and alters your mood. Fear affects your physical well-being. The hormonal balance in your body is put out of kilter. Bursts of adrenaline make your heart beat too fast. You feel shaky and short of breath. Your immune system is also affected, so you are more prone to illness.

Fear acts like yeast in a lump of dough. It feeds and grows, and over time the dough begins to swell. If you let it rise too long, the dough will get frothy and full of holes. You get "frothy," too—your thinking process becomes full of holes. That's when you feel compelled to do your habit again. It's a vicious cycle, but you can learn to prevent it. You can learn to control your gambling habit.

Unnatural Consequences

The consequences imposed on you by someone else are usually related to the natural consequences. When you lose too much and can't make your mortgage payment, the bank forecloses on your home.

When you are too much away from your family, your spouse may decide to file for divorce. Your children will likely begin to act out and get into trouble because you aren't there to teach and guide them. They may even decide to try gambling, too.

If you have borrowed money from a legitimate source and can't make payments, the lending party may decide to take you to court. That will cost more money, as well as shame and embarrassment.

If the money you borrowed came from a loan shark, you could wind up like Greg; in a hospital, bruised and broken. Or dead. Or your family could be harassed, threatened, and injured.

You have probably experienced some of these consequences. Your consequences may have been worse or less bad. Turn to page 42 now. In the section "Understanding Your Habit—The Consequence Record," you will record your consequences, both natural and unnatural.

Compulsive Stealing

Natural Consequences

The obvious consequence of stealing is loss. The people or stores you steal from take a loss. Predictably, prices in the store will go up to compensate for the loss. If you steal from individuals, their loss is even greater. They may not be able to replace stolen items and you will have lost something else that is harder to replace—their trust.

Once the stealing episode is over you have to deal with feeling of guilt and remorse. Actually, these responses are healthy—they could lead to repentance, which would prevent you from stealing again. But it hasn't worked that way, has it? Instead, the guilt and remorse have turned into more tension, which is the biggest factor in triggering your habit. Until now, you have not had the skills to interrupt this cycle.

Unnatural Consequences

Getting caught may or may not be a natural consequence of stealing, but the decision about what action will be taken against you if you are caught is an unnatural consequence. In James's case, no charges were made, so he did not have to go through the embarrassment of an arrest. If you get caught stealing in a store, you will most likely be arrested. Perhaps this has already happened to you.

The decision, in James's case, was humiliating in a different way. Having to face his friends and confess to his habit was extremely difficult. For a long time after that James suffered from the loss of their trust.

If you are arrested, society imposes heavy consequences—expulsion from school or loss of your job—events that can drastically alter the course of your life.

If charges are made against you, there will be hearings and possibly jail, probation, restitution, and /or community service. All of this erodes the quality of your life, including relationships with others.

Knowing that you steal when you can afford to pay is very hard for other people to understand. You cannot understand it yourself, and the things you say to yourself are generally not uplifting. You begin to believe that you are a psychiatric basket case.

Which brings us back to the cycle of tension and relief. James had an internal dialog that was destructive. He would say things to himself like, "Stupid jerk," or No good bus." He would even look on the mirror and say, " I hate you...no one could like you...you're nothing but a dumb jackass." Every statement intensified his anxiety and deepened his depression. Pretty soon, he couldn't stand the way he was feeling. The tension had to be relieved. That was when he would find himself stealing, an act that seemed automatic.

Before you get totally depressed from reading this, turn to page 42. Read the instructions there and then record the consequences you have experienced on the Consequence Record. Sort your consequences between natural and unnatural. This is one more bit of information that will help you learn to control your habit.

Lying

Natural Consequences

In the words of Sir Walter Scott, "Oh, what a tangled web we weave, when first we practice to deceive." Being found out is a natural consequence of lying. It follows as the night the day that you will get tripped up. The key word in that phrase is practice. You have a lot of practice in lying. But the more you practice, the more complicated it gets, until it is impossible to escape detection.

Another consequence is what happens to you physiologically. One example is the principle behind lie detector tests. A polygraph machine measures changes in your skin. If you put your finger on the sensor and tell a lie, the stylus that makes the printed graph will move widely out of the normal pattern. There is a change in the tension of tiny muscles in your fingers and in the amount of moisture on the surface of your skin. These things can only be picked up by very sensitive electronic equipment.

Although there is controversy about the profundity of physiologic changes in your body when you are stressed, it's undeniable that you get a "funny feeling" when you've told a lie—an uneasiness that is uncomfortable and hard to dismiss. This feeling is the cognitive dissonance discussed at the beginning of the chapter. It is not only that you lied, it is that you were untrue to your ideal self. That dissonance alters your perception of yourself. As your self-opinion goes down, you react to people differently. Consequently, they behave differently toward you, too. How you are treated by others, however, is actually an unnatural consequence arising from a natural one.

Unnatural Consequences

We all make decisions about how we will treat others. Most of the time we are unaware of this decision-making process and think that our behavior occurs naturally or spontaneously. But think about a time when you found yourself drifting out of a friendship. If you can reverse the film in your brain that allows you to remember this, you will find that at some point you began to say some things to yourself about that person and how you were going to behave toward him or her.

As Barbara became more and more uncomfortable with her lying habit, she found that her friends did not call her as often. She didn't receive invitations as she once had. A long time after Barbara had overcome her habit, an old friend confided to her, "Barb, you just stopped being fun. It was like you were trying too hard to make us like you. I can remember saying to myself, 'I don't want to be around Barbara anymore,' and that's when we stopped being friends." Being abandoned by her friend had reinforced for Barbara the low regard she had for herself.

You can't erase a lie. The words, once said, make their mark. Omar Khayyam said it best: "The moving finger writes; and, having writ, moves on; nor all your piety nor wit shall lure it back to cancel half a line, nor all your tears wash out a word of it." That's a beautiful statement of a harsh truth—one that's tough to handle. A brighter thought for you to cherish now is that you can change. You can grow out of and overcome this unhappy habit. While growing, you will gain respect.

Turn now to page 47. There you will find instructions for using the Consequence Record to record the natural and unnatural consequences that have resulted from lying.

Fire-Setting

Natural Consequences

Destruction is the natural consequence of starting fires. Burned wood, molten metal, and ashes of fabric cannot be reconstructed. Badly scarred skin can never be returned to normal. A dead child won't ever run or laugh. Fire-setters have a way of defending themselves against such grim thoughts. When awareness does dawn, guilt and remorse set in. Sometimes it is a relief to be caught. Sometimes you think you deserve to be punished.

Unnatural Consequences

Destruction leads to consequences imposed upon you by others. Society views fire-setting with horror and imposes severe penalties. Usually no one bothers to determine whether you are an arsonist or the slave of a habit. Those who are criminals and those who have habits get the same sentence as a rule. In prison you may get treatment, but it isn't always the case.

Perhaps you have already been apprehended and incarcerated. Even if you were lucky enough to receive therapy in prison, you probably didn't receive much help after your release. If you have not learned to handle the tension that triggers your habit, you are likely to do it again. In fact, the anxiety will be worse because people treat you differently. You don't feel good about yourself and you communicate this to others in nonverbal ways. You are keenly aware of the lack of respect from others.

The consequences are ongoing until you take charge and make changes. Even if you have a therapist, you are the one who has to change. No one else can do it for you. The good news is that others have done it. And what they have done, you can do, too. The Consequence Record at the end of the chapter has been developed to enable you to become more knowledgeable about your habit. Take time now to analyze consequences you have experienced. Which were natural? Unnatural? Turn to page 42 and 47 for specific instructions about using the record.

Hair-Pulling

Natural Consequences

Some habits, like smoking, can be life threatening, but hair-pulling is not. Temporary bald spots are the usual consequence. When hair-pulling goes on for a long period of time scarring of the scalp may occur, which would prevent growth of new hair. Sometimes the hair that replaces what's been pulled out is coarser than the rest of the hair. Pulling eyebrows and beards has similar consequences. Eyelashes can be a more serious matter. Infection can occur, and then the lashes may not grow in again.

Unnatural Consequences

The unnatural consequences may be more distressing than the natural ones. Your habit is often viewed by others as bizarre. People don't know how to handle it. Mostly they wish you would stop. People close to you try various ways of coercing you into quitting, and it is humiliating to have your habit discussed by others. It can get worse than that. Catherine was threatened by her parents in the hope that fear would make her stop. At times they would tell her that they would shave her head. More damaging were threats of putting her in the state hospital for her craziness. They viewed her habit as a symptom of serious mental illness. If you have wondered that yourself, I hasten to assure you that it is not.

When you do your habit you punish yourself in myriad ways. You do it because of the dislike you have for yourself. You probably call yourself names or deprive yourself of a treat or event that would have given you pleasure. This can go on endlessly, perpetuating the tension that made you pull out your hair in the first place. Or it can all change. Every person is capable of change. Why should you be an exception?

Turn to page 49 now and use the Consequence Record to write down the consequences you have experienced, both natural and unnatural.

Explosive Temper

Natural Consequences

Most people lose their tempers occasionally, but some people seem to have continual temper tantrums. If you habitually lose your temper over unimportant things and feel out of control, then it is a problem.

The natural consequences of an explosive temper are injuries inflicted upon another person, or an animal, or destruction of inanimate objects. Outbursts of anger are quickly followed by feelings of remorse and sorrow. You're generally a nice person between attacks, aren't you? These violent outbursts just don't fit your ideal self.

The child's bruises, the friends who avoid you, the puppy that cowers at the sight of you, are hideous reminders of your loss of control. Basically you feel terrible a lot of the time because you have not been able to stop doing your habit.

Unnatural Consequences

Other results of your temper are imposed upon you by others. Charges of assault may be bought against you. That can mean a few days in jail and one or more court hearings. You might be admitted to a hospital for psychiatric evaluation, which is not a bad thing, but you might not like it very much.

The worst of these unnatural consequences is the disruption in family and social relationships. If you have hurt your child, you may lose your children. Society takes a dim view of allowing a child to remain in a home where there is risk of injury. The tidal wave of your temper makes you dangerous. Your spouse may leave you, which might be for the best.

Further repercussions are felt by children who have been placed in foster care. They have already suffered intimidation and terror as well as physical harm. Now they have to face life in a strange house, which may itself be abusive. In any case they will miss all the familiar things: friends, siblings, toys, food. Even worse, they will believe it is their fault—that somehow they have caused and deserve both the physical pain and your abandonment. And they will grow up with that image of themselves.

They will also grow up believing that it is OK to vent their anger on others. They will abuse their own children. Unless your explosive outbursts of temper stop now, it could go on through many generations.

Your children can mend if you mend yourself. It takes a long time, and it is not easy. But I know many people who have learned to control their habit of explosive temper. Believe me, it is worth the effort. Just decide to do it now. Take a look at the instructions on page 42 and 47 and write the consequences that have happened to you on the Consequence Record at the end of the chapter. This is a strong step toward mending yourself.

Misuse of Prescription Drugs

Natural Consequences

All drugs are toxic at certain doses and using too much, too often, is a proven path to a toxic condition. *Toxic* means poison, and it is a good idea to remember that when taking drugs. The liver and kidneys do their best to keep the blood pure, but when overwhelmed by too much of any chemical, the cleaning factory breaks down. That includes over-the-counter drugs, too. People have had serious kidney damage from too much aspirin.

There is also the issue of dependence. Any drug has the potential for being habit forming in some way. Physical dependence occurs with many drugs, which means that your body has a physiological need for the drug. If you don't get your drug, you will experience withdrawal symptoms: shakiness, anxiety, and intestinal cramps. Other symptoms may follow, some very serious, which require special treatment. No drug should be abruptly discontinued without a physician's advice.

Psychological dependence can occur with anything, even pills that contain no active ingredients. If you believe the pills helped you to sleep, or if they relieved pain and anxiety, then you could begin to fear that you cannot do without them. This is called the *placebo response*. Later you will learn to use this response to control your pain. Your psychological dependence is responsible for the ever present thought that without the drug you will suffer unbearable pain, intolerable anxiety, and nights of staring at the ceiling, wide awake and desperate.

This fear itself can create symptoms of withdrawal, but they are not life threatening, as those that accompany physical dependence can be. However, do not take it upon yourself to determine the difference between the two sets of symptoms. Consult a doctor before discontinuing any medication. Once that is done, you can safely use the techniques in this book to overcome your drug habit.

Drug misuse can diminish your ability to think logically and to make love. It stifles creativity and can even change your personality. Those nice prescription drugs, which you thought were harmless, can upset every system in your body. The good news, surprisingly, is that it is not a terribly difficult habit to change.

Unnatural Consequences

Unnatural consequences are those imposed on you by other people in your life. When your employer sees that you can't function on the job with necessary alertness, you may be demoted, or even fired. That results in financial strain, greatly compounding your problems.

When you try to get your driver's license renewed, you could be refused. Many prescription drugs carry a warning about not driving while using that drug. For example, some people are refused license renewal because of anti-depressants and hay fever drugs, to say nothing of tranquillizers and pain killers. People on drugs do drive, of course. You probably do. But it can be as dangerous as drinking and driving.

You notice that the term *drug* rather than *medication* is used here. This is because it is too easy to fool yourself about the dangers when you think of your habit as medication, which sounds benign and beneficial. It is important to remember at all times that the medicine you take is a drug. It may even be for sale on the street right now as a black market drug.

Marriages are put at risk when drugs are misused. Many times the consequence is divorce. When there is divorce, the children get hurt. There are books about creative divorce, friendly divorce, family divorce, and so on, but the bottom line always is that the children get hurt. Even if the hurt isn't apparent at the time, it's in there. Drugs can be the source of such injury, and yet you can't blame the drugs. Who puts them in your mouth every couple of hours? But you can learn to control your habit. On page 42 and 47 you will find instructions for making a record of your consequences.

Irresponsible Sex

Natural Consequences

As mentioned in Chapter 1, the consequences of irresponsible sex are legion. AIDS is a life-threatening disease, as is syphilis. Several other sexually transmitted diseases can cause permanent damage if undetected. I urge you to have a medical examination, including an HIV test, and then follow the guidelines for sexual behavior recommended by the health department in your area. The best course is to combine these precautions with the self-management program outlined in this book.

The psychological effects of irresponsible sex can also be devastating. If you're reading this book, you probably aren't feeling very good about yourself. You may feel remorse, guilt, or fear. What you're doing doesn't fit the image of the person you like to be.

Whether these feeling arise out of religious or moral values or simply from a feeling that you deserve better, the outcome is the same. You worry and berate yourself, growing more tense and anxious, until the tension is intolerable. Then you do your habit. That is the way you have learned to release tension. But now you can learn better ways to handle tension.

Unnatural Consequences

Your habit of irresponsible sex affects other people. And those people react to your habit. Depending on where and with whom you do your habit, you may be arrested. If you are not discriminating in your choice of a partner—and most people with this habit are not—you could be beaten or murdered. Irresponsible sex has nothing to do with love. It can become violent in an instant. It can turn out to be rape.

Irresponsible sex is frequently a totally self-serving act, and because of that, other people can get hurt. Your impulsive and irresponsible act can result in another person being scarred emotionally and even physically, for life. And you may never see that person again, never have a chance to make amends.

One of the things you can learn from this book is how to see sex as an *interaction*—something two people do together, because they care for one another—not as something you do simply to feel better. When you learn to think beyond the boundaries of your inner tension, you will be on the way to controlling your habit. What you need to do first is record all the consequences you can think of that have come about because of your habit. The Consequence Record, which you will learn about on page 42, is designed to help you do this. Turn there now.

Overuse of TV and Video Games

Natural Consequences

The natural consequences of watching too much television or spending too much time playing video games include poor physical condition resulting from inactivity. You probably neglect schoolwork or housework and other jobs around the house to watch television. Your performance at work may even suffer.

Excessive viewing can also cause you to become increasingly isolated from other people and removed from day-to-day reality—you may begin to see what's on screen as more true than real life. Your imagination and creativity may suffer as well.

There is also evidence suggesting that people who watch violent programs on TV may become more violent themselves, or at least more accepting of violence. Other studies have shown that, rather than being relaxing as you might think, TV can actually raise levels of arousal—not what you need after a stressful day at work, perhaps.

Unnatural Consequences

If you prefer video games or television to other people, other people are likely to prefer someone or something else to you. The more you use video to insulate yourself, the more isolated you will probably become. Your family and friends will find other pursuits. Eventually, you might lose them altogether.

The exception to this is children. Children are particularly vulnerable to television as it is, and seeing a role model installed in front of the set gives them the message that this is a perfectly acceptable way of spending their time. As a result, they too neglect homework and chores, don't get enough exercise, and spend less time interacting with others. None of which is going to improve their lives in the long run.

So you've decided it's time to stop; you want to come back into real life. The next step is to write down how your habit is affecting your life. Turn to page 42 and 47 now, to learn how to use the Consequence Record at the end of the chapter.

Teeth-Grinding

Natural Consequences

One natural consequence of teeth-grinding is wear and tear on the teeth and to the temporomandibular joint, if the habit continues long enough. Pain occurs much sooner and can be quite extensive, involving the large muscles in the upper back, shoulder, neck, and back of the head. Muscles along the side of your face can also become tender and painful.

Unnatural Consequences

The unnatural consequences of teeth-grinding are less severe than those of other habits, but they can still affect your life. If you grind your teeth in your sleep, you may keep your spouse awake, which will not make him or her happy, and he or she will find a way to let you know about it. If you're in pain from your habit, you are probably also impatient and short-tempered. Your irritability affects other people and will come back to you. People may avoid you or simply be more wary around you. In either case, it won't make you feel any better.

There is only one person who can get you to stop grinding your teeth—you. Although pain relief can be obtained through several treatment methods, in the long run the only truly effective treatment is to organize your environment so that you will not be disposed to continue your habit. Read the instructions on page 42 and 47 now and write down the consequences you have experienced on the Consequence Record at the end of the chapter.

Smoking

Natural Consequences

The complete list of natural consequences of smoking would be a long one, starting with smelling bad and ending with dying of cancer or emphysema. None of us like to accept consequences that are terribly negative. We are inclined to say to ourselves, "Sure, that happens, but it hasn't happened to me." It's hard to get hold of the idea that you really could die in a horrible way if you continue to smoke.

You probably know what an artery looks like: a tubular structure that carries blood through important places, like your lungs, heart, and brain. Arteries do that year after year, day and night, with no thought from you at all. They will do that your whole life through, unless years of smoking have clogged and constricted them so badly that the blood can't get through. Then you have a stroke. Or a heart attack.

Nicotine is a very potent toxin. A dose of 90 milligrams would kill you in a few minutes. A filter cigarette contains about 2 milligrams—a not insignificant amount. The tars in tobacco build up in the respiratory system, causing grievous damage. In addition, carbon monoxide, a byproduct of combustion, displaces oxygen in your hemoglobin. In sufficient quantity, it causes a heart attack.

Unnatural Consequences

Our society is becoming increasingly aware of the dangers of sidestream, or passive, smoking. That is, the person sitting near you, breathing your secondhand smoke, also risks being poisoned. Because of this awareness, some important decisions are being made with regard to smoking. It is now common to find restrictions in the workplace and in public areas. You may be barred from the lunchroom if you smoke there. Some people will not allow you to smoke while riding in their car. Other people will refuse to ride in your car. You have probably been offended by this. There have likely been times when you have said, "I have rights, too." Think about this: suppose you sat down at a table in a restaurant, and the waiter came around putting arsenic in everyone's water. Does he have a right to poison people? Do you? Because your illness and death can affect many other people, it's questionable whether you even have a right to poison yourself. Your smoking habit can be lethal to yourself and others. You can impair your baby's development. You can give your children asthma, emphysema, or cancer. Worse, you can teach them to smoke, to poison their own bodies. I know one young boy who had to go to court on a marijuana charge. When asked why he smoked the stuff, he said "Mom smokes." You teach by example.

I admire you for wanting to quit. You can quit. It will be hard, but you can do it if you decide to decide. Use the instructions below and the Consequence Record at the end of the chapter to help yourself come to terms with the consequences of your habit.

Understanding Your Habit—
The Consequence Record

From the records you have been keeping so far, you have learned a good deal about how severe your habit is and the pattern of its repetition. The following exercise examines the consequences that happen to you.

Your consequences will not be the same as anyone else's You need to be specific about the consequences you have experienced. Don't bother with generalized statements like, "People are disappointed in me." Instead, think about the last time you did your habit. What happened? Who did what? Who said something? Who turned away? What did you do afterward? How did you feel, emotionally and physically? Tell in detail what happened during the days or weeks after your habit. Take a look at the following chart to see how one person recorded her consequences.

A blank Consequence Record appears at the end of the chapter. Make copies of it so that you can have an ongoing record. When scientists want to learn about the dolphin's behavior they don't just record the behavior for one day. They keep a continuous record for a long period of time so they can see if certain things happen over and over. You must do the same for yourself. You'll notice that the Consequence Record has space for positive consequences as well as negative ones. Work on recording the negative consequences for now, and then, after reading the next section, you can begin to record positive consequences as well.

Positive Consequences

With all this talk of negative consequences, it makes you wonder why people continue with their habits. That's the interesting thing about habits—they do reward us, in spite of the punishments we receive. You do your habit because you get something from it. If that's hard to understand, read the following story about Jimmy.

Consequence Record

Use one copy for each occurrence of habit.

Date: _____ *Feb. 20* _____   Time: _____ *3:00 p.m.* _____

I was with _____ *Annie* _____ at _____ *sidewalk sale downtown.* _____

This is what happened: *Annie called and asked me to go to the sidewalk sale. I told myself I wouldn't buy anything—just look. When we were walking around it seemed like I just started buying things without thinking. It was almost like I watched myself do it and couldn't stop.*

Just before that I had been *making phone calls for the garden club party*
_____

and I felt *tense, edgy, irritable—like I was going to explode.*
_____

Afterward I felt *stupid. I didn't need those things, but while I was buying them it felt fun and exciting. It made me feel relaxed—not so grouchy*

and I did *housecleaning. All the closets, scrubbed the floors, and cried the whole time.*
_____
_____

The negative consequences I experienced were (natural) *most of the grocery money was gone.*
_____

(unnatural) *Ned is taking my checkbook away.*
_____
_____

The positive consequences were _____
_____
_____
_____

Jimmy

Jimmy was having a lot trouble at school. His teacher kept sending notes home that Jimmy stood on top of his desk and disturbed the class. He refused to remain in his seat. Jimmy's mother lectured him sternly about not standing on his desk. She went to school and saw that Jimmy did indeed stand on his desk. When he did it the teacher would come over to him, grasp his hand, and say, "Jimmy, get off that desk and sit down right now!" The kids would laugh, and Jimmy would sit down—for a few minutes. Then he was back up on the desk, and the whole routine would be repeated.

Jimmy's mother could tell that the teacher was almost ready to give up teaching altogether. She yelled at Jimmy all the way home. Finally, the teacher asked the school social worker to visit the class and observe Jimmy. The social worker enjoyed the same performance Jimmy's mother had seen. When the children had all gone home, the teacher and the social worker sat down to talk.

"What am I going to do?" the teacher said, wringing her hands.

The social worker laughed. "You are certainly doing a good job of giving Jimmy the attention he craves."

The teacher looked at the social worker. "Were you in the same classroom I was?"

"Oh yes," said the social worker, "Jimmy has learned very well how to control your behavior. When he wants your attention he knows that all he has to do is stand on the desk. He also gets a bonus when the children laugh." The teacher saw that this was so. Then they got down to business and formed a plan.

The teacher called Jimmy's mother and asked her to keep Jimmy home one day. On that day the teacher made the other students her co-therapists. They talked about the good things about Jimmy, and how he would probably be fun to be with if he wasn't always showing off and teasing. The children agreed to the plan, which included their promise to keep the plan secret for a while. They could tell their parents, but that was all. The teacher called Jimmy's mother that night to tell her about the plan. She agreed to help out at home by not saying anything to Jimmy about his behavior at school. Instead, she was to be interested in what Jimmy had to say and take extra time with him.

The next morning Jimmy stood on his desk. The teacher was talking to another child about an art project and didn't notice. The other students were all busy doing their work. No one noticed. Jimmy stomped his feet a little, but nothing happened. He made funny noises, but still no one noticed. After a while he began to feel silly, so he sat down. Immediately, the teacher came over and said, "How nice you look, Jimmy. Thank you for sitting quietly at your desk." She touched his shoulder before moving on. Some of the children looked at Jimmy and smiled. The boy next to him slipped him a piece of gum.

Jimmy stood on his desk more that day than ever before, but no one paid any attention. After recess the children all came in and sat down. Jimmy was feeling good because some boys had asked him to play Batman with them. Without even thinking about it, Jimmy sat down at his desk. The teacher looked around the room and said, "I see Jimmy, Carl, and Dan are all sitting quietly. Will you three please come into the hall and help me roll the piano in?" Jimmy had never, ever been asked to do anything like that before. He walked with pride. He felt strong.

That's an abbreviated version of the story because, of course, Jimmy relapsed into his old habit of standing on the desk when he felt worried or unhappy. But over time he did it less and less, until finally he never stood on the desk at all.

Rewards and Reinforcement

Seemingly negative consequences can actually be positive and reinforce a habit. Jimmy needed someone to pay attention to him. The only way he knew how to get it was by standing on his desk. He needed to have the teacher call him by name, touch him, and make him feel special. The negative consequences of being yelled at and rejected were acceptable because the reward of the teacher's attention meant so much more.

Reward carries more weight than punishment. The reward of being released, even temporarily, from tension is much stronger than all the negative consequences put together. Ida knew smoking was dangerous. She didn't like hacking and coughing, and she didn't like the rejection she felt from others because of her habit. But Ida was more miserable from her constant state of tension than she was from coughing or from fear. The comfort she derived from the cigarette was more compelling than the negative consequences.

For example, eating too much sugar can cause tooth decay. That means a trip to the dentist. Most people don't like to do that. They fear discomfort, and they don't want the expense. Yet most people continue to eat sugar. Why? Because it is sweet and tastes good. It has an effect on the amount of adrenaline being released into the bloodstream. It is usually just enough to make the person feel energetic for a short period of time. The reward in eating sugar outweighs the unpleasantness of going to the dentist.

Are you saying, "Believe me, there is nothing positive about my habit. I'll do anything to be rid of it."? Do yourself a favor—keep the record. Let it tell you if there is anything that keeps you doing a habit you hate. Finding reward in your habit is no cause for shame. You are a normal person. Normal people behave in whatever way rewards them. It is necessary for you to understand this about yourself so that you will be free to learn better ways to relieve your tension.

As a child I missed a lot of school because of illness. Sometime during high school I began to notice that I got sick when there was something happening at school that made me feel frightened and tense. This insight embarrassed me because I thought such behavior was abnormal and neurotic. As I struggled with this unpleasant awareness, I developed a new behavior. Instead of getting sick, I just started cutting classes whenever I felt uncomfortable. I didn't like this habit. I knew it wasn't a good solution to my problem, so I began to worry about myself. Then I started listening to what other people were saying about school. When they talked about getting sick or cutting classes, they sounded just like me. Gradually, I came to believe that people just do that. They devise ways to get out of things that make them uncomfortable. It's not neurotic. It's a way of coping. When I accepted that, I was ready to accept that avoidance or escape is not the best way to cope. As I tuned into my thoughts and feelings I could catch myself getting too tense to handle things, and then I would figure out more acceptable ways to cope. As a result, I got along better at school and didn't need my habit to protect me from tension.

Physical Factors

As you have seen, there are both emotional and biological reasons you repeat your habit. The tension you feel when you do your habit, and the relief from that tension, affects you physically, at a cellular level. Negative feelings, such anxiety and depression, have profound effects on vital systems in the body. Positive feelings of reward and satisfaction have equally profound effects.

When you are in a stressful situation, even something as routine as having too much to do in too little time, your body reacts as if it is in danger. Adrenaline is released into the bloodstream. In a truly dangerous situation this would give you the energy and strength to either run away or fight. In day-to-day life, however, all that happens is that you feel shaky and jumpy—your heart may even beat faster. Your body is prepared for a burst of physical activity, but you may be stuck at a desk or in a car. Wherever you are you feel the need to do *something*. Your habit is the something you've come up with.

After you've taken action—fleeing, fighting, or doing your habit—endorphins are released into your system. Endorphins are the body's natural equivalent of narcotics like morphine and heroin. Although not addictive in the same way as those drugs, they have a pleasant, relaxing effect. They are also natural pain relievers. The soothing feeling caused by endorphins in effect becomes a reward for having done your habit.

These rewards are kind of sneaky. You know all the while that your habit is not good for you, and you even know the reasons why, but a little voice in your head keeps rationalizing your behavior. "Just this once," it says, "I'll quit after this." and the most deceitful message of all is, "Maybe it's normal for me to be this way. It's just me. So who cares, anyway?"

You have probably been labeling your feelings of tension as "uncontrollable," "intolerable," and "incurable" for a long time now. These labels put you in the position of being helpless. Then you justify the helplessness by saying, "I can't stand it." In this way you maintain and intensify your tension and anxiety. You give yourself permission to continue your habit.

The Consequence Record...Again

At the bottom of the Consequence Record, where it says, "The positive consequences were," record whatever you think keeps you doing your habit. Refer back to your Habit Diary. Analyze the events around your habit to see what may have served as a reward in the past months. Could it have been something to do with other people? Perhaps an activity? A certain place? How about feelings? For help in understanding how to do this analysis, take a look at another example Consequence Record, on the next page.

The Consequence Record is essentially an expanded version of the Habit Diary in Chapter 1. It enables you to look at the component parts of your habit, including negative and positive consequences. Look for patterns. Also think about the strength of the consequences. Remember that negative consequences are what make habits undesirable—something you want to get rid of. Positive consequences are what keep you doing your habit in spite of the negative consequences.

There are many ways to relieve stress and tension that are better than your habit. You can learn new behaviors, and now is the time to make the decision to do so. But you need the record—the black-and-white picture of what things reward you enough to maintain your habit.

The Courage to Change

It took some courage to buy this book, and since you are still reading it, it follows that you have the courage to work hard at changing. You may doubt it, but you have the ability to change. Once your habit is controlled you will find yourself changing in many other positive ways. You will have a better opinion of yourself, because you won't be plagued all the time by the tension of cognitive dissonance. You will be free of the restrictive bonds of your habit. Then you will experience the wonderful consequence of actual improvement in your physical health and appearance. People will notice that you look better. They will respond to your lighter spirit and spontaneity. You will bask in the acceptance and respect you deserve.

No matter what your habit is, you will need to carry out all the exercises described in the following chapters on internal and external cues. These additional bits of information will complete the puzzle of your habit. After that you will be ready for treatment—ready to make the changes for overcoming your habit. You are on the threshold of realizing your ideal self. You have the hope of becoming the person you were meant to be.

Consequence Record

Use one copy for each occurrence of habit.

Date: _____ *Feb. 22* _____   Time: _____ *10:00 a.m.* _____

I was with _____ *alone* _____ at ___ *Samuels dept. store* _____

This is what happened: *I went to Samuels to buy a dress for the garden party. They were having a sale, and I wound up with over $300 worth of clothes, towels, and makeup. All charged to MasterCard.*

Just before that I had been *working for 3 days on the party decorations.*

and I felt *worried about the party and insecure about how I look. I had been tense and edgy for a couple of days. On that day it was intolerable.*

Afterward I felt *At first I felt kind of high and at the same time peaceful and calm. On the way home I began to feel uneasy. After I got home I felt terrible, guilty.*

and I did *I cried, and then I wrapped up one of the blouses and mailed it to my sister. Then I cried some more. What I did didn't help my problem.*

The negative consequences I experienced were (natural) *anxiety about what would happen when the bill came. When it did come, there was a note saying no more could be charged.*

(unnatural) *Ned was so angry. He said I have to go to consumer counseling.*

The positive consequences were *the feeling of excitement I have when I'm shopping. I feel carefree and happy. I guess I feel important, too, and I imagine how much I will enjoy the things I bought. It's a terrific feeling, and it makes all my tension and uneasiness go away for a little while.*

Consequence Record

Use one copy for each occurence of habit.

Date: _____   Time: _____

I was with _____ at _____

This is what happened: _____
_____
_____

Just before that I had been _____
_____

and I felt _____
_____

Afterward I felt _____
_____

and I did _____
_____
_____

The negative consequences I experienced were (natural) _____
_____

(unnatural) _____
_____

The positive consequences were _____
_____
_____
_____

3

Internal Cues

Talking to Yourself

An orchestra conductor has 65 or so musicians in front of him playing many different parts. Although the musicians have music to read, they keep an eye on the conductor to see his beat, facial expressions, and other signals he gives to help them play together. These signals are cues. Frequently, when things get ragged in the orchestra, the conductor will say to the clarinetist or the first violin, "Watch me, I'll cue you."

The conductor's signals are *external cues*—reminders from someone else to behave in a certain way. The musicians also have cues inside themselves—*internal cues*. These cues are the rhythm they feel in their own bodies and the counting they do in their heads. Other cues are words they say inside, such as, "Here comes a crescendo," or "Remember the key change at letter A." These internal instructions are going on all the time.

You also have internal cues. You talk to yourself, and you answer back. When I was growing up, people used to say, in jest, that it was OK to talk to yourself, but when you started answering it was time to worry. The truth is, both talking *and* answering are an important part of the thinking process. As your mental impressions rise to the surface they are verbalized. You express them to yourself, silently, and to others, out loud. This dialogue is healthier than a monologue would be because it enables you to consider a problem from different angles.

In the musical *Fiddler on the Roof*, for example, the main character, Tevye, is faced with the challenges of survival in a hostile land (Russia), where poverty and threat of pogroms against the Jews are everyday concerns. To add to his worries he has three daughters of marriageable age who show signs of breaking with age-old traditions. Tevye handles these problems by talking to himself. While ploughing a field one day he agonizes about one of his daughters. He stops in the middle of a row and says, "I can't let my daughter marry a gentile," then, with a sigh, he answers, "On the other hand, she says she loves him." In this manner he has a dialogue with himself over every crisis. His life is hard. One tragedy after another comes to assault him. But out of Tevye's dialogue comes an affirmation that he speaks directly to God. He looks heavenward and declares, "Even a poor man is entitled to some happiness." His internal dialogue helps guide him in his changing world. It's a tool you too will learn to use.

Managing Your Self-Talk

The purpose of this chapter is the discovery of the events, people, and places associated with your habit, and your reaction to them. It is an exploration of how you talk to yourself.

You think about the events happening around and to you all the time. Your thoughts are words you say to yourself. Whatever happens just before you do your habit is called an *antecedent event*. Antecedent events are cues, like the markings in a musical score—they trigger your habit. By becoming aware of these events, thoughts, and feelings, you can change. You may be able to change certain antecedent events themselves. Others, which are not under your control, can be avoided. All can be handled by changing your reaction to them.

In this chapter you'll learn that the most important part of the antecedent event is what you say to yourself. Your tension, and the accompanying feeling of depression, is caused by your interpretation of these antecedent experiences and what you say to yourself about them. You'll learn to talk back more effectively by refuting negative statements and incorporating positive affirmations.

Managing your self-talk is a three-step process, consisting of

1. Identifying your antecedent events and self-talk

2. Analyzing your self-talk for quality

3. Changing your self-talk

How Self-Talk Works

Let's observe one of the violinists in the orchestra. Suddenly, in the middle of a technically difficult passage, he sees the conductor looking directly at him. He thinks, "Why is he looking at me?" and then proceeds to make himself tense by saying, "He doesn't like the way I play." With pounding heart and sweating palms, the player escalates this with, "You never were any good." Predictably, this unfortunate violinist is miserable the rest of the rehearsal, and his performance deteriorates. After the rehearsal he bums a cigarette. He has none of his own because he had resolved to give up his habit.

The violinist had made assumptions about what the conductor was thinking. His assumption led him into negative and self-demeaning thoughts. Thus his habit was triggered.

Martha had a gambling habit. She had been hooked on gambling since high school when she learned to play poker. Later, she went to Las Vegas with an aunt, and couldn't tear herself away from the slot machines. If the machine poured out coins she immediately put them all back in. She eventually went home with a very dismayed aunt.

In college Martha researched ways to beat the house and wrote a sociology paper on the gambling personality. Thinking about gambling all the time led to a drop in her grades. Eventually she quit school, thinking she could earn enough money to keep up with her insatiable urge to gamble. When she eventually realized she would never achieve the success and happiness she wanted in life if she continued with her habit, she decided to change.

The first thing Martha was able to recognize was the feeling of irritability she had when she wasn't gambling. Then she began to connect the irritability with things she said to herself when she was under stress in her job or at home. She would say something like, "You've got to get on top…you're a loser." Gambling made her feel that she was doing something to get on top. She kept telling herself that eventually she would be rich.

Everyone's antecedent events are different. Your task in this chapter is to track the events that lead to your impulsive act. In the sections that follow you will practice identifying and analyzing these events so that you can change. At the end of the chapter, you'll learn a new way to talk back. You'll begin to compose positive affirmative statements that refute your negative self-talk. These new self-statements will become your automatic response to certain events.

Step 1: Identifying Your Antecedent Events and Self-Talk

Take a look now at the Self-Talk Record at the end of the chapter. Notice that it includes everything from the Consequence Record in Chapter 2 and has additional spaces for recording what you thought (what you said to yourself), both before and after doing your habit. Xerox the record and carry it with you. Make enough copies to keep records for three weeks. You will discover a pattern of certain places or specific people that trigger your habit.

For example, one man I know lost his temper whenever a co-worker was commended for excellent work. He did not vent this anger on the co-worker, or on the boss.

He went out and kicked the car. One time he kicked it hard enough to dent the car and break his foot. Unfortunately, he had also been so angry he failed to notice that it was someone else's car.

Before going on to work on your self-talk, let's take a minute to define what is meant by "events," "thoughts," and "feelings."

Events

An event is anything that happens—planned or unplanned. It is the activity you are doing at any given time, such as shoveling snow, shopping, or being interviewed for a job. You might be talking to your spouse, taking the children to school, or reading a letter. Sometimes the event is just ruminating about life's problems, as was the case with Tevye. It will be interesting to see what kinds of events triggered your behavior. This kind of detective work is fun.

Thoughts

At the time of the event you said something to yourself. You verbalized a thought. Maybe you said, "How could you be so stupid?" or it may have been a single word like "Idiot." More often than not your self-talk is negative and self-demeaning. Like the violin player in the orchestra, you make assumptions that are not true, logical, or helpful.

You will probably have to sweat a little as you try to identify what you said to yourself at the time of your habit, because you aren't used to making a deliberate effort to monitor your self-talk. At first you may think, "I didn't say anything," and then you will realize that at that very moment you were verbalizing a thought. You said, "I didn't say anything." Taking a mental trip back to the last time you did your habit will put you in the proper mental state to remember your self-talk. Instructions for doing this are given later in this chapter. Recognizing self-talk is an essential prelude to change.

Feelings

People generally think that feelings come first, self-talk second. On the contrary, here is clear evidence that self-talk precedes feeling and that feelings are the product of the self-talk. When you tell yourself something derogatory such as, "You're stupid," bad feelings follow. The bad feelings are created by a biochemical response in the brain.

Brain chemistry is not a stable condition. What you say to yourself can alter it. When Norman Vincent Peale first wrote *The Power of Positive Thinking* 40 years ago, he didn't know about brain chemistry. He only knew from experience that people who had a positive attitude and said kind things to themselves were happier and better able to solve problems in life.

Norman Cousins, former editor of *Saturday Review*, studied the effects of self-talk in himself when he was suffering from a disabling illness. With the help of his doctors he learned that negative thoughts would not only produce unpleasant feelings, but also measurable changes in his medical condition. Negative thoughts brought negative emotions.

Many scientists have studied the brain and what happens under positive and negative conditions. Unpleasant emotions such as fear, anger, and depression constrict blood vessels and increase the amount of chemicals in the blood that affect behavior. (For a deeper understanding of brain chemistry, you might enjoy reading Richard Restak's book, *The Mind*, the companion volume to a PBS television series on the fascinating workings of the brain and central nervous system.)

Physical symptoms can also act as internal cues. Feelings of muscle tension, shakiness, nausea, rapid heart beat, pain, hunger, and others are all cues that prompt you to behave in a certain way. The question is, which came first—the symptoms or the self-talk? With or without organic illness, quite often self-talk precedes symptoms. Less often, physical symptoms arise spontaneously. In that case, interestingly, the physical symptom will often lead to fearful or negative self-talk.

You need to find out for yourself what your sequence is. One method is this: every time you feel an uncomfortable sensation, stop what you are doing for a few seconds and ask yourself what you were just thinking about. Identify the self-talk. Then you can talk back by saying, "This feeling is distressing but not dangerous."

If you can develop enough self-discipline to do this consistently, two things will happen. One is that you will be able to identify the effects of your thinking on your physical body. The second is that you will stop following up the symptoms with more fearful and negative self-talk. Remember, self-talk creates the tension that produces your habit.

Step 2: Analyzing Your Self-Talk

One of the 20th-century pioneers in the treatment of depression was Aaron Beck. He found that seriously depressed people could overcome depression by changing what they said to themselves. They learned to examine their self-talk for self-demeaning statements and statements that expressed hopelessness and negativity. Beck defined a circular process of thoughts causing feelings, which in turn triggered certain actions that then resulted in negative thoughts and so on, like this:

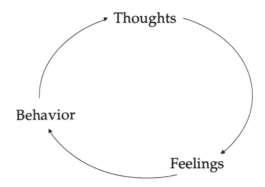

The antecedent events you have been recording on your chart are meaningless until you have formed an opinion about them. At that point the meaning of the event is expressed in self-talk. As you read this, you are talking to yourself. What are you saying? Are you expressing doubt that any of this will work for you? Or fear, perhaps, that your habit is so ingrained that simply talking to yourself could not change it? Stop and say something else to yourself. Say, "Now, now, don't jump to conclusions. Keep trying."

Albert Ellis is another significant contributor to theories about why people are depressed and how states of mental health are maintained. He helps his patients by teaching them to see that what they said was not logical or rational. One way to examine your self-talk is to look for the truth in your statements. Catherine, for example, became able to look at her statement, "I'm bad, I'm stupid. No one loves me." She looked for evidence of her badness. While it was true that she, like everyone else, had made unwise decisions at times, there was really nothing about her attitude or behavior that could logically be defined as bad. Pulling her hair was not bad, nor was it good. It was a habit that caused her unhappiness.

Similarly, there was no reason to believe she was stupid. She was a college graduate, a hard-working student, and a capable mother. A stupid person could not do these things. Was it true that no one loved her? No—in fact there was ample evidence to the contrary. Her children expressed their love daily, and she had recently met a man who wanted to marry her. Catherine realized that people did in fact love her very much, but that she was having trouble loving herself. She was then able to formulate new self-talk, which was based on a more realistic appraisal of herself.

Listening to Your Self-Talk

The quality of your self-talk is important. Is it positive or negative? It is negative when you do your habit. Self-talk is often accompanied by images as well. These images remain in your mind and can be called up during the process of remembering and analyzing self-talk. One way to do this is to relive the experience in your mind, slowly, so every detail becomes clear. Some people are more visual than others, so don't get discouraged if you don't see pictures right away. This process can also be quite painful. Try to stick with it, though.

Find a quiet time and a place where you will not be disturbed for 15 to 30 minutes. Imagine that you are putting a tape into the VCR of the last time you did your habit. Turn it on and let it play. Don't worry if things are not clear. When the entire scenario of your habit has finished, rewind it, and set it for a very slow speed. Now play it again. In slow motion the self-talk will become clearer. Fragments of sentences and flashes of color begin to emerge as complete sentences and well-developed scenes. When you become very good at this you will reexperience all the feelings you had before, during, and after doing your habit. Those feelings are always preceded by a thought or an image. Your task is to sort out the self-talk and analyze it. Soon you will begin to see the sequence of thoughts, self-talk, and images leading to negative feelings, which in turn produce a behavior—your habit.

You are already experienced at keeping track of events and responses around the time of doing your habit. Now, as you record your behavior, you will be aware of what you were saying to yourself.

Sharon

Sharon and her husband had a disagreement in the morning about whether or not their daughter should have ballet lessons. Jim thought that it was frivolous. Sharon believed it to be a necessity. Later, Sharon began to think about the word *frivolous*, and said to herself, "Jim thinks I'm an airhead." Then she felt depressed and worried about her self-worth. She went to the mall to look for bath towels, becoming increasingly tense with every minute. As she passed the perfume counter she picked up a tester to try the scent, put it down, picked up a bottle of another scent, and found herself slipping it into her purse. Apparently no one noticed. She had a moment of feeling relieved, even exhilarated, but as she left the store, without the towels, she felt ashamed and degraded. At home, the perfume went into a drawer, never to be used. Whenever she saw it there she felt unhappy and berated herself for doing such things.

Are you beginning to see how the things people do are directed by self-talk? Here's and example of how you can tune into yours.

Peggy

My young friend, Peggy, like most people, was not really aware of her thoughts. It had not occurred to her that her thoughts were words. She thought her habit of explosive temper happened by itself. It seemed as if she found herself spontaneously exploding for no reason and with no forethought. The first task for Peggy was to learn to listen to the words her thoughts were made of. She started with a simple assignment: every morning she was to record what she said to herself in the first few moments of being awake. At first, she didn't hear anything, but after a few days she caught herself thinking; "Oh no, I hope today won't be as bad as yesterday. Probably will. Always is." She was surprised at this negative expectation she had of her daily life. Then she began to record her thoughts at other specific times, such as while brushing her teeth, driving to work, and preparing the evening meal.

Peggy always felt extremely tense before she did her habit, and although she had some awareness of what her thoughts were, she needed to pinpoint her self-talk. At this point she had already gained some control over her habit, but when unusually stressed she would still do it. As she kept her self-talk record she learned that she often said, "I have too much going on in my life. I can't handle it. Something's got to give." In that statement she was using words that both exaggerate and denigrate. "Too much" says that it is more than anyone can handle. "Can't" says that Peggy lacks the ability to control her life. Remember how your brain believes what you say, and your body acts accordingly? "Something's got to give" was a statement that gave her permission to do her habit.

By analyzing her self-talk, Peggy was able to stop her thoughts as they began to form and give herself new messages. She decided that the next time she caught herself saying words like that, she would switch to this: "I have a lot going on right now. I can handle it if I drop some of the less important activities until things slow down." This is a rational statement that recognizes the reality of her stress and offers a solution. Of course, Peggy has many solutions in her repertoire. She might have decided to practice relaxation, or divert herself with a pleasant activity.

Finding the Right Words

For a few years I was director of a pain clinic. The most difficult part of the job was teaching people to talk about their pain in realistic terms. When a person said, "This is the worst possible, most unbearable pain anyone has ever had, and I can't stand it another minute," I knew self-talk training had to take place before other pain control techniques could be effective. The patient was on the way to recovery only when I heard these words: "Although I've had [past tense] pain for six months, I am [present tense] handling it as well as I can [refutes 'can't stand it']."

Negative Permissions

Beware of words that make ominous predictions. When pain patients say, "I can't stand it," they are predicting they will not do anything to help themselves. If you say about your habit, "I'll never be able to stop this, I've been doing it too long," you are programming yourself to believe that you are too weak and ineffectual to overcome it. That statement can't possibly be true, however. You have proven that in many ways. You do many things in your life that are difficult, and you do them well. You take care of yourself and most likely other people as well. Clearly you are neither ineffectual nor weak. In addition, you are working your way through this book, and you have already made changes. That indicates strength. You will have setbacks, but you will pick yourself up and go on because your self-talk is going to be logical, rational, and self-affirming.

Negative permissions clutter up the self-talk of everyone who has an uncontrolled habit. They also clutter up the self-talk of everyone else at times. It is extremely common. You have an advantage, however. You have some control now, and learning to spot negative permissions will enable you to increase that control. Words that alert you to the fact that you are uttering a negative permission are, *can't, never, won't, unable*, and similar words and phrases that bring you down enough to make you go ahead and do your habit.

The Importance of Tense

A violin student who says, "This piece is too hard. I never get this part right. I just can't do it," has guaranteed for himself and his teacher that he cannot play this piece. Instead of this, he could learn to say, "I have had [past tense] some trouble with this spot. I need suggestions about how to master it [permission to be in control]."

The tense you use in speaking to yourself is important. There was a time when it was necessary for you to say, "Yes, I am a fire-setter" (or whatever your habit was), but now you can say, "In the past I had a habit of..." Whenever you use present tense, you are instructing yourself to continue in your habit.

Young children are often heard to say, "I'm going to be a fireman," or, "Someday I'll be a famous artist." There are a number of interesting things about that. The child has not yet been filled with self-doubt. She knows she can become whatever she wants to be. It would be most strange and tragic to hear a 3-year-old say, "Aw, I'll never be anything when I grow up." It is very, very rare for a child to have that kind of negative expectation, although it can happen in children who have been badly mistreated. As an adult, you already are something, and you can be something else, if you wish. Be realistic. What you are now is not the same as what you have been. Who you are now is not the person you will become.

Putting Words in Others' Mouths

There is yet another piece in the puzzle of analyzing your self-talk. How often do you find yourself thinking about what someone else thinks? Peggy became depressed after an evening with friends. She found herself saying, "I know they think I'm stupid. They probably wish they hadn't invited me." Does that sound familiar? Can you really know what someone else is thinking? Of course not. The only thoughts you are privileged to know anything about are your own. When you catch yourself talking about what someone else thinks, say to yourself, "Stop! You don't know what they are thinking" and then, "If I feel uneasy about something that happened, I can ask my friend what he was thinking." Another option is to say, "I can laugh at my irrational thinking and forget it." Asking people questions is a good way to keep your thinking on a rational plane.

The following story about my friend Clark is similar to many I have heard over the years from people who hate their habits.

Clark

Clark has been pulling his hair for many years. He knows he began to do it when his mother died, but knowing this has not helped him to stop. Clark began to record and analyze everything he heard, did, felt, and experienced when he did his habit. Then he began the analysis of his self-talk. At first he was mainly aware of the intense degree of his tension before pulling his hair. Then he began to catch fragments of self-talk. Sometimes he would have a fleeting picture of himself looking lonely and defeated. Other images were of himself standing before a mirror, bald. Once in awhile there was an image of her mother in the casket at her funeral. Phrases flashed through his mind: "tearing my hair," or "creep," "no good," and "wretch." Clark wrote all these things down. It wasn't long before he began to have an awareness of complete sentences.

One particularly trying day, as he was standing before the bathroom mirror, his hand in his hair, pulling out small clumps, he heard himself say, "You ugly toad." A feeling of sadness washed through him, bringing tears and more unhappy thoughts. He was shocked to discover that during this process his hand was still busy pulling out hair. He stood for a moment, looking at the hairs, fascinated by the bulbous roots, until finally he flushed them. At that point he was saying to himself, "You're disgusting. You'll never change." Then he was overcome with remorse and self-hatred. He was frightened by his lack of control.

Clark sat down on the edge of the tub. He said to himself, "It's true. What I think makes me pull my hair." Clark was then able to look at how he was handling stressful events. Earlier that day he had seen his girlfriend in a restaurant with another man. Clark was devastated and went home crying. He began to imagine what his girlfriend was thinking. "She never did love me. The whole time we've been going together she's been laughing at me, using me. She thinks I'm a boring, neurotic slob." First thing he knew, his hand was in his hair again, but this time he said, right out loud, "Stop!" Then he went a step further, "I don't know what she's thinking," he said to himself, "I'm not a slob. I have a habit, it's true, but I'm working on it, and I'm getting better. I'm not going to jump to conclusions."

His girlfriend called a little later, and she and Clark talked about the episode in the restaurant. "It's true I was there with someone else," she said, "but it was National Secretary's Week, and each of us took one of the secretaries to lunch. Denny's a very good secretary." Then Clark remembered having seen the man in her office and having read the newspaper story about Secretary's Week. "OK," he said to himself, "It makes sense, and I'm going to give her a chance. I'm going to take care of my own thoughts after this, and not worry about what other people are thinking."

Using Your Self-Talk Record

If you keep your Self-Talk Record faithfully every day for three weeks, you will have a sufficient amount of information to do an analysis. You will need pencils or pens in several colors. Go back to the beginning of your Self-Talk Records and underline the following things in red:

- Self-statements that are derogatory and demeaning to you ("You ugly toad.")

- Self-statements that predict failure ("I'll never win.")

- Self-statements that are judgmental ("You are a bad person. You deserve to be punished.")

Now, using your blue pencil, mark statements that are

- Exaggerations ("Worst pain in the world.")

- Negative statements that are in present or future tense ("I'm stupid, always will be.")

Many of these statements will already have been red-lined. Blue-line them as well.

How about an orange pencil for underlining statements about what other people are thinking? Again, some of these will already be underlined, but mark them now, anyway.

Green is said to be a healing color, so let's use that for underlining the following:

- Positive statements in the present tense

- Statements about your habit that are past tense

- Logical, rational statements that are true and positive

Next, go back over the chart and look for events, people, or places that occur more than once in connection with your habit. Circle those in black. That's for future use, but it is good to be aware of these patterns now.

Step 3: Changing Your Self-Talk

Just as Clark was able to say "Stop!" when he heard himself making assumptions about his girlfriend's thoughts, you can learn to stop negative self-talk, and you can replace such statements with positive affirmations.

Using Affirmations

To affirm something means to declare unequivocally that it is true. Patrick Fanning, author of *Visualization for Change*, defines affirmation is "a strong, positive, feeling-rich statement that something is already so." He further equates "strong" with short and simple. Positive, of course, means there would be nothing derogatory, pessimistic, or demeaning spoken or implied. The words *feeling-rich* tell us that it is an emotional statement.

Feelings are sometimes hard to name, especially if you are not used to describing your feelings. Here's a list of words describing feelings you've probably had:

Angry	Depressed	Frustrated	Lonely
Satisfied	Cheerful	Free	Eager
Mad	Sad	Confused	Unhappy
Tranquil	Delighted	Conflident	Secure
Furious	Blue	Disturbed	Isolated
Centered	Comfortable	Focused	Pleased
Enraged	Down	Panicked	Unloved
Peaceful	Happy	Calm	Super
Livid	Bum	Frightened	Sick
Relaxed	Fulfilled	Competent	Accepted
Appalled	Discouraged	Insecure	Unworthy
Intelligent	Energetic	Elated	Excited
Uncertain	Hyper	Shaky	Desperate
Strong	Capable	Vigorous	Peaceful
Relieved	Crazy	Dumb	Nervous
Rotten	Apathetic	Lethargic	

Finally, an affirmation needs to be in the present tense in order to reinforce that the statement is true *now*.

Through the following exercises, bear in mind that what you say is what your brain believes. Self-talk governs how you feel and dictates what you do.

Now before tackling your own statements, take time to practice on someone else's. For each statement given in the examples below, ask yourself these questions:

1. If I heard someone else make this statement would it make sense?

2. Is there evidence that this statement is not entirely true?

3. How can I restructure this statement so that it is true, logical, and rational?

Example 1

Let's look at the violin student's statement:

> "This piece is too hard. I never get this part right. I just can't do it."

Does it make sense? Of course not. Violin pieces are graded for difficulty. The teacher would not have given him a piece that was not at his level of ability. It also doesn't make sense that the student "can't do it." He has mastered every assignment thus far. He has the technical skills to do it.

Is there evidence that this statement is not entirely true? None of it is true. The piece is not too hard. *Never* is clearly exaggeration. In practicing anything, some trials will be right, and some will be wrong. "I just can't do it" is negated by the evidence of many pieces learned.

How can you restructure this statement to be true, logical, and rational? You need a statement that is positive, self-affirming, and in the proper tense. Write your new statement here:

Can you make it better by making it shorter? Is one statement enough? Does it contain a positive affirmation in the present tense? Does it contain a feeling word? Work on it some more in the space below.

Here is a new statement I concocted:

> *This is a challenging piece. I'm working most on this part right here. I play all of my pieces well, so I know I can play this well, too. I am happy with my progress.*

Example 2

Larry, who suffers chronic pain, says,

> "I'm of no use to my family. I've become a worthless bum."

Analyze Larry's statement and write a new one below that is positive and in the present tense.

Here's my attempt:

> *I am a good person. I am available to my family for listening and sharing. My life has value and joy.*

When you compare your statements and mine, you will see that they each reflect our own perceptions of being disabled by pain. One is not more right than the other.

Example 3

How about one for James, the compulsive thief? He said,

> "I'm a jerk. No one could like me."

James needs a strong statement of affirmation. Go ahead and give it a try.

This is what I thought of:

I'm OK. I'm gaining more control every day.

Rewriting Your Self-Talk

You are ready to work on your own self-talk now. Pick one of the statements from your chart that is underlined in red or blue. Say it out loud. It feels awful, doesn't it? One at a time, write out the statements you have underlined, and ask yourself the three questions. Now write new statements—statements of positive affirmation. Use words that are strong and powerful to you. In James's statements I could have said, "I love myself," rather than "I'm OK." Choose words you are comfortable with.

When you have reconstructed your statements, read them out loud. How does that feel? Better than the old statements I'll bet. When you say positive affirmations out loud, you are breaking the cycle of negative self-talk and bad feelings. This alone will decrease the number of times you do your habit.

Constant Companions

You know from experience that when you get down on yourself you don't succeed at things. You get discouraged and depressed. In this kind of mood it is no wonder that you do not perform as well in work or school as usual. You create your own tension.

To counter these moods you need to develop a repertoire of positive affirmations that will continually remind you of your worth. Here is a partial list of some that have been helpful to others:

- I love myself.

- I am intelligent.

- I always do the best I can.

- I am pretty.

- I am following God's plan for me.

- I am becoming the person I was meant to be.

- I care about others.

- I am friendly.

- People respond to me.

- I have a great smile.

- I am a good parent.

- I am happy with what I do in life.

- I am good at handling crises.

Maybe some of these will work for you. Using someone else's statements is fine for a start. They act as kind of a springboard to stimulate your thinking about the good things you can honestly say about yourself. But even better would be for you to make up some statements that reflect truths about yourself.

If I could wish something wonderful for you, it would be that you could be as spontaneous in your affirmative self-talk as you were with negative statement—as children are. Children's affirmations have no strings attached. They never say, "Except that," nor do they say to themselves, "Oh yeah?" What they say comes from the heart and they believe it.

One affirmation that makes me warm and happy whenever it comes to mind was made by my 4-year-old grandson at his first piano lesson. As he happily climbed down at the end of the lesson, he said, "I'm a great pianist." He believed his statement totally. You could see it in his dimpled smile and shining eyes. Even more telling, though, is the fact that he believes it so much that he practices every day, on his own, with no reminders from anyone. You would do that too if you believed you were a great pianist. Your feelings and behaviors will change as you come to believe your affirmations.

A Noteworthy Technique

Begin collecting affirmations. Start with 3x5 cards, cut in thirds. On each write an affirmation—a positive statement about yourself that is true. Make several cards for each affirmation. Put these notes all over the house: on the refrigerator, on mirrors, inside the medicine chest, in drawers. Use them for bookmarks. Put some in your billfold or loose in your purse. Place them in the glove compartment of the car and on the dash. Put them in your lunchbox and inside the cookie jar.

Whenever you see one, read it, aloud if possible, and reflect on the truth in the statement. If the card says, "I am a nice person," then take time to think about the ways in which you are nice. There is one important rule that goes with this game. Whenever you read the card, or make an affirmative statement, you are not allowed to say, "Oh, yeah?" That's sabotage. It is mandatory that you find the truth in what you say. Affirm it, reinforce it, believe it, rejoice in it. You know it's true, or you would not have written it.

Each week, maybe on Sunday evening as you prepare for the week, write out new cards to replace the old ones. Some of your affirmations will change. Others will remain perfect for you for a long time. Rewriting affirmations is the kind of reinforcement that makes positive thinking automatic.

You also can prompt affirmations by putting colored dots or stickers in various places. When you see the dot, you should stop to say an affirmation and accept it as truth. Stickers with pictures or words are fun. I have one on my telephone right now that says, "Bravo." When I pick up the phone it reminds me of my affirmation: "I can handle it, whatever it is." A pretty good affirmation for someone with nine grandchildren who are constantly falling out of trees, getting into poison ivy, and suffering the other mishaps of childhood.

Put It on Tape...

After you have gotten into the habit of making cards and using them, you can add another way to teach yourself to think and speak positively. Buy a loop tape and record several affirmations over and over until the tape is full. These tapes come in various lengths, from the 15-second answering machine tapes to 30 minutes or more. Use your tape in the car where you can hear the affirmations over and over as you drive. This is a proven method used by music students for memorizing pieces and by language students for mastering vocabulary and pronunciation. It works for making affirmations automatic. Make some statements that begin with "I am..." Another tape could be "You are..." statements.

...Or in Your Shoe

For some, a tactile reminder is helpful. Put a dime in your shoe, and keep it there, changing it to other shoes as needed. A lot of the time you won't even be aware of that thin dime, but once in awhile it will get in a place under your foot where you will feel it. When you feel the dime, immediately direct your thoughts to an affirmation. It could be the first one that pops into your head, or you could look at one of your cards. Think about that affirmation for several minutes, and let yourself feel the security that comes from knowing the truth.

Jill craved sweets whenever she got anxious. She was careful never to keep any in the house, but at work it was more of a problem. She always kept a dime in her shoe, though, and found she noticed it most when she would get up to go to the candy machine or the cafeteria. When she felt the dime, she would stop and say, "I'm a good person. I'm loved by others, and I love myself." As she said this, her tension faded and she no longer wanted to indulge her sweet tooth.

Jill began to include affirmations in her conversations with others. When greeted by another in that meaningless ritual of "Hi, how are you?" she no longer said, "OK, and you?" Instead, she answered, "I'm just wonderful, the best I've ever been. And how are you feeling this morning?" Not only did she actually feel much better as she said this affirmation, but she noticed that the other person relaxed and often responded with a genuine statement of his or her feelings. Affirmations are not only good for the one who says them. They are uplifting to everyone around you.

One Final Task

You've done a lot of work in this chapter. But you need to do one more thing before we move on:

Transfer the new affirmative statements you wrote earlier in this chapter to 3x5 cards. Choose those that clearly refute your most common negative statements. Keep these, along with your completed charts, for use in later chapters. You will also need to continue to work on correcting negative self-talk as you begin to focus on your external cues, in the next chapter.

Further Reading

Beck, Aaron. *Cognitive Therapy and Emotional Disorders*. New York: New American Library, 1979.

Cousins, Norman. *Anatomy of an Illness as Perceived by the Patient*. New York: Bantam, 1983. (Cousins has also written a number of related books.)

Ellis, Albert. *A New Guide to Rational Living*. Hollywood, Calif.: Wilshire Books, 1975.

Fanning, Patrick. *Visualization for Change*. Oakland, Calif.: New Harbinger Publications, Inc., 1988.

Peale, Norman Vincent. *The Power of Positive Thinking*. Englewood Cliffs, N.J.: Prentice Hall, 1987.

Restak, Richard. *The Mind*. New York: Bantam Books, 1988.

Self-Talk Record

Record each occurrence of habit for three weeks.

Date: _____   Time: _____

I was with _____ at _____

This is what happened: _____

_____

Just before that I had been _____

_____

I said to myself _____

_____

and I felt _____

_____

Afterward I said to myself_____

_____

I felt _____

_____

and I did _____

_____

The negative consequences I experienced were (natural)_____

_____

(unnatural) _____

_____

The positive consequences were _____

_____

4

External Cues

External cues can be people, things, or events. The orchestra conductor, the music, and the audience are visual and auditory cues for the musicians. Other cues that are equally strong are the smell of rosin and valve oil, heat from the lights, and the taste of a reed. For you, also, there are many cues. Some of them are common to nearly all people with your habit, but others are unique to you. External cues are things you can see, hear, touch, smell, and taste.

Common Cues

Overeating

The sight of your mother, in her apron, stirring something on the stove may be a strong cue for overeating. Even if it's only a memory flash it works the same way. Walking past places where the smell of food is strong can cue tremendous hunger pangs. Some food smells seem to be particularly enticing, such as pizza, chocolate, or pastries baking. Every time you see your son's batting helmet it may remind you of the orange sign over the root beer stand at the ball park and make you yearn for a root beer float.

Compulsive Spending

Catalogs! Those wonderful, glossy pictures of chic clothes and gadgets should be banished from the home of every overspender. Before you know it, you're phoning in an order. The sound of a vacuum cleaner can be a cue for redecorating urges. The metallic taste of a worn out silver-plated fork may suggest a need to purchase silver. In shops it is always tempting to feel the fabric in a garment—a fatal touch for an overspender.

Gambling

Lottery advertisements and programs on TV that depict gambling may give impetus to your urge to gamble. The feel of the dice and plastic chips in your daughter's board games may remind you of your favorite casino. The mingled smells of tobacco and liquor may be strong cues for gambling. Even the taste of peanuts can bring up a picture of the bar where you play poker on Thursday nights. The sight of your checkbook balance may remind you to bet on Saturday's horse race.

Compulsive Stealing

The sight of previously stolen objects hidden in a drawer can be a powerful cue to steal again. Handling small items as you stroll through stores irresistibly invites you to slip one into your pocket. Chewing gum may remind you of the racks by checkout counters where you have often taken some gum or mints. Listening to the late news and hearing about someone arrested for shoplifting may create uneasiness as you think of your own experiences.

Lying

Hearing others tell of their achievements may stir you to create a story equal to theirs. For Barbara, sitting at the piano was a strong cue, reminding her of lies about her musical accomplishments. The locker room smell of sweat and disinfectant can make you think of stories told there, arousing fantasies of incredible athletic feats.

Fire-Setting

If you carry matches in your pocket you will feel them whenever you reach for change. When you take them out, you can hardly resist lighting one, and the sound of the matchhead drawn across the emery, the smell of sulphur, and the beauty of the flame are powerful cues to fire-setting. Seeing and hearing about forest fires on the evening news may remind you of your last fire and make you think of setting another. The sound of a fire truck's siren may create an urge to seek the source.

Hair-Pulling

Playing with your hair and feeling its softness is a sure invitation to pull some out. When you look in the mirror it is tempting to put your hands in your hair. The pillow, where you have slept, may retain the fragrance of your hair, and draw your thoughts to hair-pulling. Sometimes when you are reading or watching TV you may chew on a strand of hair, and that will lead to pulling. Your bathroom is loaded with cues...hair spray, shampoo, conditioner, clips, and scissors. Your wig reminds you that you will be able to cover up bald spots. Even as strange an object as a pair of pliers may make you think of a more efficient way to pull hair.

Explosive Temper

The sight of your wife lying on the couch reading may be a strong cue for losing your temper, especially if she has not met your expectations about household tasks. When you hear a child crying, your muscles tense, ready to strike out. The feel of cracker crumbs crunching underfoot or the taste of burned toast may arouse rage. Getting stuck in traffic can make you impatient to the point of fury. Television provides daily examples that can justify violence.

Misuse of Prescription Drugs

The people you live with may be cues to your taking drugs inappropriately because pain and anxiety have human interactional components. The way a person looks at you or speaks to you may be a cue to seek escape. The medicine chest, with its particular odors, can stimulate a desire for relief. Maybe you keep your drugs in the kitchen. In that case the cues might be the sound of running water or the quiet bubbling of a stew. It can even be the click of a cupboard door. The feeling of lying down on your bed may remind you of time spent waiting for drugs to take effect. Any medicine bottle rattling around in your briefcase or desk drawer will draw your thoughts toward taking pills.

Irresponsible Sex

A fleeting whiff of perfume or after-shave can be enough to make you think of sex. Provocative pictures in magazines may remind you of past experiences. Television supplies plenty of examples of people engaged in sexual activity. Every time you go to a restroom you may be reminded of past encounters. The sights and smells in a bar and the taste of beer may bring similar reminders.

Overuse of TV and Video Games

The very presence of a TV set in your home is a tremendously powerful cue to watch something—anything. Hearing others talk about programs they liked or games they have played can cause you to yearn to see and do for yourself. Hearing a vacuum cleaner may remind you of the pleasant escape awaiting you at the push of a button. The smell and taste of popcorn and chips is very often associated with hours at the tube.

Teeth-Grinding

The blessing and the bane of 20th-century technology, the telephone, can be a powerful cue for grinding your teeth. The sound of it, the sight of it, and the very act of picking the thing up may trigger this habit. The smell of something burning in the kitchen may create considerable tension, particularly if you are expecting company. In the workplace, uncovering the typewriter and touching the keys may remind you of deadlines, and there you are...grinding away.

Smoking

The smell of coffee, the taste of wine, and the sight of cherry chocolate torte may create desire for a smoke. As you approach the doorway to a party the sound of laughter and happy talk can make your fingers itch to hold a cigarette. Sitting down at your desk to go over accounts may turn you into a robot, automatically reaching for the cigarette pack.

Identifying Your External Cues

You have external cues all around you. Identifying them is a key factor in overcoming your habit. Hopefully, you are still keeping track of things in your Self-Talk Record, so you already know some of the people and places that serve as cues for your habit. You circled some of them in black. Now you need to extend this record. In the space where you record where your habit happened ("at"), also begin to record objects that were present at that time.

For example, besides being a miracle of communication, the telephone is an almost universal cue for people with habit control problems. Some people dread initiating a call, and that tension leads them to doing their habit. Others experience discomfort whenever the phone rings, and just the sound will trigger a habit. Tension is produced by having to disclose information, receive information, and make decisions about that information. That can be challenging and fun, or it can be frightening and distasteful. And for people with habit control problems, the telephone has often become a bearer of bad news, such as:

"Your account is overdrawn again."

"I hate to bring this up, but after you were here the other day my son's tape player was missing."

"This is Dr. Jones. Your HIV test came back positive."

The dread of bad messages often overshadows other, more joyous messages, such as "Guess what Mom...I'm on the Dean's list!"

Certain pieces of furniture, a hair dryer, perfume, food, music, and a thousand other things can also be cues. As you find yourself carrying out your habit, take note of the objects you are using, even just those that are in your line of vision. It can be something as small as the pen on your desk or the keys in your pocket.

The next step is to invest a small amount of money in some adhesive red dots and stickers with pictures or messages. These can be found in stationery and office supply stores. Place one red dot in an easily visible place on each object you have noted. You will probably identify more objects as your awareness increases. These dots will become your cues for alternate thoughts and behaviors.

As you know from your record, people may be cues as well. It would be a little difficult to put red dots on people, but there are other methods, which will be discussed later. The following examples suggest ways dots and stickers can be used to help you break your particular habit.

Overeating

Placing a dot on your son's batting helmet can remind you to substitute visions of a fresh, juicy orange instead of the root beer float. Dots on the cake mixes in your cupboard or the pastry section in your cookbooks, will fortify you against urges to bake.

Compulsive Spending

Put a dot on the mailbox to remind you to throw catalogs away. Other important places for dots are your credit cards, the check register of your checkbook, and on your purse or billfold. Putting one on the dash in the car will help you remember to shop sensibly, rather than randomly.

Gambling

The first place to put your dot is on your checkbook. If your child's board games trigger thoughts of gambling, put dots on those. Don't overlook the TV and the dashboard of your car. Another important place to have a reminder would be the drawer or box in which you keep the household accounts. Also put one on each month's page in the account book. When you see the dot perhaps you will remember that gambling does not solve money problems. If you keep a cash box, use a sticker that says "STOP."

Compulsive Stealing

Dots on the mirrors of vehicles that transport you to shopping malls will help you resist thoughts of stealing. Even better, for you, would be a rubber stamp—imprint yourself before you go out. You can put it on the back of your hand if you don't mind other people seeing it, or on the inside of your wrist, where it is less obvious. Another place, which works especially well for women, is your thigh, where you will see it when you use the bathroom. These stamps are available at teacher's supply stores and come with a variety of messages such as, "Getting Better," "Big Improvement," "Keep Trying," and so forth.

Lying

Having examined your records carefully, you know what things get you into a lying mode. Maybe it's something at your workplace, such as a computer, or the desk, and certainly the telephone. The telephone really ought to have a self-affirming sticker. Maybe a sticker that says "You're OK." Put a dot on your right shoe so that you will see it every time you get dressed. Another one could go on the bathroom mirror. When you see it, you can say to yourself, "I love and respect myself and others."

Fire-Setting

There aren't many good reasons for carrying matches in your pocket, but if for some reason it is necessary for you to do so, then it is imperative for you to place a bright red dot on every book or box of matches. Those are your stop signs. It is also very important to put dots or stickers on the things that make you tense. As is true for nearly everyone, the telephone ought to have a sticker with a message to let you know that you can handle trouble. Put a sticker on the gasoline can and leave the can in the garage. Put a dot by the fuel gauge in your car to remind you to keep the tank full. Then there will be no need to carry a can in your car. Use your records to find all the things in your home and work environment that need dots.

Hair-Pulling

In addition to dots, buy or make a pillowcase of a striking pattern or unusual color. Neon-colored fabric would be perfect. It will never let you forget that there is a better way to handle tension than pulling hair. Use the dots for the telephone, TV, refrigerator door, and, above all, the bathroom mirror. Get little sparkly fingernail stickers, one for each finger, and secure them firmly with a couple of coats of colorless nail polish.

Explosive Temper

Place a dot on the TV immediately. Put it where you can't fail to see it when you watch a program and also put one on the remote control. Another should go on the TV log. These dots tell you to choose nonviolent programs.

You have probably seen some recurring patterns or places on your record—situations in which you have exploded more often than in others. Put dots on the light switches, the furniture, and other objects in the places where those situations occur. Have one on the center of your car's steering wheel, on the rearview mirror, and on the dash. These dots say "Calm down...breath deeply...you're OK."

Misuse of Prescription Drugs

Your dots need to go on the lids of pill bottles and on the cupboards where they are kept. Don't keep your drugs on the bedside table anymore. Place a dot in the center of your clock, and a tiny one on your watch. Be sure to put dots on the pill containers you carry around with you. A dot on the phone and on the front door at eye level will remind you that you can handle any crisis. A dot positioned on the ceiling where you can see it when lying down will cue you to practice relaxation instead of popping pills.

Irresponsible Sex

Start with the TV screen and the remote control. Then put a dot on the TV log. These dots serve to remind you to watch programs that are not highly sex oriented. Movies from the 40s and 50s are good bets, as are family-oriented channels. Place a dot on the dashboard of your car, and another on the glove compartment. A dot on your bathroom mirror will remind you of your worth. Dots on shaving cream, perfume bottles, and in your underwear drawer will help you tune in to hidden agendas. Ask yourself, "Why do I want to be smooth shaven, smell good, or wear my sexiest underwear?" Also put dots or stickers on stress producers such as the phone or computer.

Overuse of TV and Video Games

You probably know where the dots have to go first: on the TV, and on the Nintendo and game cartridges. You will also need to put dots on the things that make you want to escape, such as the telephone. Use your records to identify what things were present when you decided to turn on the TV or game.

Teeth-Grinding

You could put a dot on every front tooth so that when you smile the expression on other people's faces will remind you not to grind. You probably don't want to do that, but a dot or a sticker on the phone might save your teeth. If you work at a typewriter or computer, how about a sticker that says "Well done!" Maybe you are a musician and your guitar case needs a dot or sticker. You get the idea. Check your record and think of all those things that cause you to tense up. Driving in rush-hour traffic makes almost everyone grind their teeth. A dot on the steering wheel, on the dash, or on the mirror will remind you to relax.

Smoking

Where have you always kept cigarettes? Those are the places to put dots. People keep them in some amazing places, such as the tool chest, first aid kit, empty suitcases, and of course, purses, briefcases, drawers, and glove compartments. Other places to put dots or stickers would be on your desk, if that is where you habitually light up, the TV remote control, and the coffee pot.

Avoiding or Eliminating Cues

People are sometimes leery of using avoidance to overcome a problem. Although it is true that it makes impossible the confrontation needed to resolve fears and conflicts, in the early stages of habit control, avoidance is a legitimate strategy. Avoidance can be used for both objects and people.

By definition, elimination means to get rid of something, to do away with it, and entirely keep it out of your life. Elimination is the technique you will use for some places and objects that are serving as external cues for your habit. Obviously you can't eliminate your workplace or home, but you can identify objects and places you are better off without.

Once again, your records will be the source of information about cues that can be eliminated. As you go over your records, circle people and necessary objects in pink, and places and objects that can be eliminated in purple. That makes it easier to see what things it is possible to eliminate, and which can be avoided.

Overeating

When you are out walking, which I hope you will be, plan your route so that you don't go past bakeries, delicatessens, and so on. It is under your control to eliminate these cues. Even crossing to the other side of the street will help. When you are cooking, plan meals that don't require you to hover over the stove. If your friend Karl always stops at the donut shop on the way home from work, don't ride with him. If Sybil always wants a Big Mac or a chocolate fudge sundae after a movie, suggest another activity—one without a built-in temptation. If these people are good friends they will understand and maybe even change their own habits in time.

Compulsive Spending

You can eliminate the catalogs. Please don't rationalize that catalog shopping is convenient. It is better for you to have to make an effort in order to spend money. Unless you are 90 years old with arthritis and congestive heart failure, you don't need to shop by catalog. Go to the post office and sign a form that will stop delivery on catalogs and unsolicited junk mail.

Obviously you can't eliminate going to stores, but you can avoid shops where you have no need to be. When you go shopping, take a list, walk briskly, and avoid any sections of the store that are not on your list. If your chart shows that you overspend most often when alone, then take a sensible friend. If you usually spend more when with a friend, then you will have to go alone.

Gambling

You will probably need to avoid board games. Your daughter can play them with her friends when you're not around. Explain it to her. Children love to help their parents with habits. By staying out of bars and restaurant lounges, you will cut down considerably on your urge to gamble. Then there is the matter of those poker buddies. If that's all they are to you, they have to be cut out of your life. They won't really mind. Someone else will soon take your place.

Compulsive Stealing

Eliminate all stolen items from your drawers and cupboards. If you know where they came from, mail them back. If you don't remember, donate them to a thrift shop. Get rid of them. In stores choose short check-out lines so you can avoid standing by those racks of gum, candy, and small items. Never go into a store unless there are specific items there that you had planned in advance to purchase. When you are visiting in people's homes, stay with the group. If you have to use the bathroom, don't linger.

Lying

On your chart you will have circled things, places, and people that cue your habit. Avoid the people with whom you feel so competitive that you are forced to lie. There may be social situations that create a climate for lying. Eliminate these affairs until later, when you have more control over your environment in general. Eliminate restaurants and shops where you have lied before. Being there almost demands that you perpetuate your lies.

Fire-Setting

The first thing to eliminate is the book of matches you carry in your pocket. Put all your matches in a tightly covered container and place it on a high shelf. If your really need a match for the fireplace or barbecue, ask someone also to get the matches. Avoid TV news spots about fires. Leave the room, and occupy yourself elsewhere.

Don't keep your gas can in the car anymore. You already have the dot by the fuel gauge to remind you to keep the tank filled. The dot can remind others in the family, too, so that they will have no need for the gas can. The ideal thing is to put all flammable liquids in a locked cupboard and give someone else the key. He or she will be happy to help you. When those things are needed, make sure someone is with you...your spouse, a friend, or one of the kids. Always return the key to the other person. When you hear a siren, avoid the streets the truck is traveling. Go out of your way to detour the fire area.

Hair-Pulling

Avoid watching TV, reading, or talking on the phone unless you have something to do with your hands that would prohibit hair-pulling. When reading, for example, you can play with a "worry stone" or a couple of marbles. From your records you know there are certain times when you are most susceptible to temptation. Those times will have to be changed, eliminated, or filled with something new. You can't avoid the bathroom, but you can eliminate from it many of the cues, such as hair spray, clips, and scissors. By the time your hair has grown in, these cues will no longer bother you. Give the pliers away. If something needs to be fixed you can ask someone else to do it. This next one is hard, but you can do it, I know, because others have. Get rid of the wig. This means facing the world just the way you are. Believe me, the way you are is fine. Say out loud right now: "I am fine the way I am."

Explosive Temper

Avoid all violent movies, videos, and TV programs. This is essential. Watch documentaries and G-rated films. For now, until you learn new skills, you need to avoid confrontations. When there is discord with another family member, go for a walk. Explain this to your family in advance. They don't like your violence and will be glad to do whatever it takes to help you overcome your habit.

As you have examined your records for cues, you have seen that there are certain things in the house and your workplace that trigger your temper. If it is dirty dishes in the sink when you come home at night, don't go near the kitchen for a while until you know you can walk in there and accept the situation without anger.

Sometimes it happens that one child in the family, by nature of his or her personality, incites violence in a parent no matter what the child does. If this is true in your family, you have two options: removing yourself from the home or arranging for that child to have a nice long visit with grandparents. In either case you need to get family counseling. If the stress of dealing with other drivers on the road is your cue, you will have to devise alternate routes where there is less traffic. Be diligent in searching your record for cues you can eliminate or avoid.

Misuse of Prescription Drugs

The drugs have to be eliminated, but you can't do that without a doctor's help. *Do not* just throw them away without consulting your physician. This means more than a telephone call. Make an appointment to go in and discuss your desire to control your habit. Show your doctor this book and get his or her help in withdrawing from the drugs. If the doctor doesn't seem to support your desire to get control of your drug use, just say "Thank you," and try another doctor.

Irresponsible Sex

Study your records thoroughly. Have you circled the cues in pink and purple? Begin with cues you can avoid. Avoid bars and cocktail parties. You are also going to have to avoid certain people—including ones with whom you have formerly had sex and people you know to be promiscuous.

If you are a woman, avoid going to men's apartments unless many other people are there. Plan to leave a party with another woman. Never have men in your apartment without other people. Change your perfume to an innocent flower scent or wear none at all. Avoid provocative clothing—it's just as stimulating to you as it is invitational to others.

Overuse of TV and Video Games

Take a break from TV and video games. Put the whole works on a high shelf behind the Christmas decorations. Your children will object, but explain to them why you are doing it and use the TV time to do other activities with them. Get them interested in other types of games, reading, and outdoor activities. Build a tree house. You know from your charts what things make you want to escape. Avoid those things as much as possible. Eat popcorn only at a movie theater or when visiting with friends. If it is housework you desperately want to escape, you may be able to hire some help for a while. When you work with someone else you eliminate the need for diversion.

Teeth-Grinding

It is probably not reasonable to avoid or eliminate the phone entirely. You can, however, write letters instead of phoning on many issues that cause you stress. Often you can successfully avoid the people who cause you stress.

Your records are your guide to finding the cues that can be eliminated or avoided. If the sound of childish squabbling sets your teeth on edge, you can remove yourself from the scene. When left alone children usually solve their differences, and rarely ever maim one another. If traffic stalls are cues, avoid them by taking the long way around. It doesn't take any more time than it does to sit in a carbon monoxide fog for 30 minutes, and you may find the drive relaxing.

Smoking

There are many cues for a smoker, as you well know. Go over your charts carefully to find the ones you can avoid or eliminate. For most smokers, coffee and alcohol are cues, and must be eliminated. Get rid of all cigarettes, pipes, cigars, and paraphernalia that remind you of alcohol. You will learn more later about how to handle withdrawal. Your social life has to change because you will need to avoid places where people are smoking. Begin to surround yourself with friends who don't smoke. It sounds drastic, I know, but it is essential.

Changing Cues

Some things in your life cannot be eliminated or avoided. You can't stash the boss in the warehouse, nor can you get your co-workers fired. You have to eat on a regular basis. Housework is never ending, and your son needs his batting helmet to play baseball. But some cues can be changed. You can buy your son a batting helmet of a different color. You can keep fresh fruits and vegetables prepared and easy to get at for snacks. "For every problem there is a solution" goes the old rhyme, so let's see how inventive you can be. The following are some suggestions to get you started.

Overeating

Have a special place for eating snacks—a pleasant place where you can relax for a few minutes and really enjoy the taste of those big strawberries.

Compulsive Spending

Instead of using a checkbook or credit card for purchases, go to the bank and get only enough cash for the items you have on your list. Then leave the checkbook and credit card at home.

Gambling

Get a red checkbook cover and make all entries in the check register with red pen.

Compulsive Stealing

When you see a small item you are tempted to pick up, say to yourself, "I'm happy to leave this here for someone who really needs it."

Lying

When tempted to lie, say to yourself, "The truth is more interesting than fiction."

Fire-Starting

When you hear a siren, take it as a signal to go the opposite direction.

Hair-Pulling

Let the mirror be a cue to appreciate the beauty of your eyes.

Explosive Temper

When you come home and find a loved one relaxing, join that person. Give him or her a hug and ask how the day has gone.

Misuse of Prescription Drugs

Put all drugs, prescription and over-the-counter, in one place where they are not easy to reach. The exception would be an emergency drug such as nitroglycerin. Let the sight of a prescription bottle be a cue for reaching for a relaxation tape.

Irresponsible Sex

Keep a book of poems, scriptures, or cartoons by the TV. When an unexpected sex scene begins, pick up the book and read.

Overuse of TV and Video Games

If you have to keep the TV out and available, which I hope you won't have to do, buy educational videotapes on speed reading or home mechanics, for example, and watch one of those when you have trouble resisting the urge to sink into a marathon session.

Teeth-Grinding

Turn your desk around so you don't have to face your unpleasant co-worker. If you can't do that, picture the person dressed as a clown.

Smoking

Keep sugarless candy canes in your cigarette box.

One Piece of the Puzzle

These tactics of changing cues and weaning yourself from accustomed responses give you practice in manipulating your environment. However, by themselves they will not give you control over your habit. They are pieces in the puzzle of control. By using these techniques you are gradually learning to change your behavior.

Using Old Cues for Behavior Change

So far we've discussed avoiding, eliminating, and changing cues. When none of these things can be done, you still have another option. Remember, "For every problem there is a solution." You can change the meaning of the cue. The old cue can now trigger a different behavior.

What can you do instead of pulling out your hair, losing your temper, or whatever your habit is? The following is a starter list of activities some people have learned to do in place of their habits:

- Recite affirmations.

- Draw or doodle on a small pad of paper or do needlework.

- Give yourself a manicure.

- Wash and wax the car.

- Throw darts (at a dartboard, of course).

- Make bread.

- Paint something.

- Mow the lawn.

- Play the piano or another instrument.

- Walk, jog, run, or work out some other way.

- Clench your fists and hold them that way until the desire to act is gone.

- Whistle or sing.

- Mentally recite the words to a poem, scripture, or song.

- Carry a picture of someone special in your wallet to look at until the tension passes.

- Carry a marble in your pocket to roll between your fingers.

Here's some space for you to add ideas of your own:

Experiment with some of these things. See what works for you. Above all, don't get discouraged. Your habit is strong. You have to find a strong antidote. Now let's look at how some of these things have worked out for others.

Overeating

Randy decided to use the cue of food smells to trigger a new habit. As he walked home from the bus stop and approached the pizza place, he crossed the street and went into a market where he purchased fruit. He carried his purchases home and sat down at the table to slowly savor every bite. He enjoyed this for about a week, and then one evening, after a particularly stressful day at work, he walked toward the pizza place, hesitated, and said to himself, "I need a break." He then purchased a 16-inch pizza with four toppings. He didn't even take it home, just wolfed it down right there.

Having eaten too fast he was uncomfortable as he walked home. "I shouldn't have done that," he said, "I'm such a failure." He started to feel depressed and discouraged, wondering if a nice chocolate donut wouldn't make him feel better. Then he realized what kinds of messages he was giving himself. He took an affirmation card from his wallet and said it to himself all the way home. As he entered the house he said, "It's OK. Everyone has setbacks. I'll get right back to my new habit."

The following week Randy felt stronger and once again enjoyed stopping for the fruit. Toward the end of the week he began to feel stressed and yearn for pizza, donuts, or ice cream. "OK," he said, "on Friday I'll buy one slice of pizza, take it home, and eat it slowly. All the other days I'll have fruit." Randy was able to do this, and felt good about his progress. As the weeks went on, he sometimes found that he didn't even crave pizza anymore, but when he did, one slice was plenty.

Compulsive Spending

June had her new habit of carrying only enough cash for planned purchases fairly well established. She was enjoying the freedom it gave her to shop without guilt and to enjoy what she did buy. Ned was supportive and encouraging, and all seemed to be well. Then one day, after seeing a sale ad for summer clothes priced 50 to 75 percent off, June wavered. Wasn't this too good an opportunity to pass up? She even discussed it with Ned, who said, "Sure. Plan what clothes you need to buy now for next summer, and take enough cash for those." June felt irked. "He's treating me like a child," she said to herself, "I'm an adult. I can make decisions." She got the cash at the bank but then at the last minute tucked the checkbook into her purse. "I may not have estimated correctly," she said, "I probably won't need this."

You can guess what happened when she got to the store. She spent too much money and had more clothes that she needed. Ned was upset, but he did point out that she had not totally decimated the account as she had in the past. "You're still doing better, June," he said. June suffered the remorse and guilt as always, but this time she said to herself, "I slipped, but not all the way. This is distressing, but not dangerous." The next time she needed to shop she said to Ned, "I am an adult, but sometimes I act in childlike ways, so I'd like you to carry the checkbook and my credit card today." When she left for her shopping trip she felt in control. She had made the decision, not Ned. After that it was easier, and each time she made a decision she felt stronger.

Gambling

It was comforting to look at the red checkbook, and the neat red figures, Greg thought. He hadn't gambled at all for two months, and he felt good. The bank balance was looking a little more healthy, and he was thinking about a vacation for his family. "We haven't gone anywhere together for a long time," Greg said, "I'd like to do something really special." At noon he went to lunch with two of his co-workers—new friends he had made since he stopped gambling. He admired these men. They dressed well, and always seemed to have plenty of money. He thought about the reasons for their financial well-being and realized that he could be headed in that direction, too. He mentioned his vacation plans to his friends, and one of them said, "Say, we had a great time last year at a guest ranch in Colorado. The kids rode horses and helped stack hay. It was in the mountains, and there were great hiking trails. We came home so relaxed. Best vacation we ever had."

Greg thought that sounded just right for his family, so he asked for the name of the ranch. Later, when Greg called the ranch, he was dismayed at the cost of a four-day stay. He began to think that this was the only vacation that would do, and he became desperate to get enough money to go there. On Thursday he called home to say he had to work late. At the poker game, which was of course where he went, he wound up the evening with $4, having lost $200. He couldn't go home. He walked the streets for hours, agonizing about what he had done. When he finally got into the car to go home he saw the affirmation on the dash: "I can succeed, even when I feel like I'm failing." Greg recognized the truth in that statement. "I can succeed," he said, "I have succeeded for two months. We'll have that vacation next year, because I'm signing up for payroll savings deduction tomorrow."

Compulsive Stealing

James had completed his probationary period. College authorities were well pleased with his progress and attitude. James's friends, who had been supportive but cautious, were beginning to loosen up and trust him again. "I've won," James told himself, "I'll never steal again." He relaxed. He didn't recite affirmations. When he saw a cue, he just smiled, and thought about how he had licked the problem. On Friday evening he went to a basketball game with Karen. "I'll be back on the team next season," he gloated confidently. But at the game James and Karen had a disagreement that escalated into a shouting match. She stalked off to find another ride home, and James went to the after-game party by himself. At the party he wandered into the kitchen and saw a Swiss army knife lying on the counter. In a flash his hand flicked out and deposited the knife in his pocket. There was a momentary exultation, but then James said, "What are you doing? Are you crazy? You had it made and now you've blown it—all because of a foolish argument. You stupid..."

James felt a shock when he heard himself saying those words. "Wait a minute, old boy. Let's not get carried away. You're not stupid. You dropped the ball but that doesn't mean you're out of the game. Come on get up and try again." Slowly, James hand went into his pocket and drew forth the knife. At that moment his roommate walked in. "Hi, Don," James said, "I just had a close call. I almost took this knife. Is it yours?" "Yes," said Don, with a big grin, "I was looking for it." He held out his hand, "You've come a long way, haven't you Jim?" At that moment James felt like he'd climbed a high mountain. "I have, Don, and now I know I can keep climbing."

Lying

It had been six months since Barbara had told one of her fantastic stories. She could tell that people still thought twice about things she told them, but she felt good about her progress. It had been hard. She had to work every day at building her self-esteem by reciting affirmations and using relaxation techniques. She was actually beginning to believe, at least part of the time, that she was an OK person just the way she was. Two weeks before Labor Day weekend, in the bank where she worked as a loan officer, the subject of a departmental retreat came up. This was to be a three-day affair at which a guest presenter would work with them on interactional skills. Barbara knew that sometimes these encounters involved self-disclosure and confrontation. She was afraid of what might come out about her lying habit. She worried that this kind of emotional stress would just set her back and felt uncomfortable with the idea of revealing anything about herself to the people she worked with. With a different group of people she knew it could be a healing experience.

When they started making room arrangements, they turned to Barbara, "Do you have someone you want to room with, Barbara?" Barbara's mouth grew dry, her chest constricted, and she said, "I won't be able to go. My family is having a reunion in Bermuda over Labor Day weekend. We haven't been together for years, and I really need to be there." This statement stimulated an excited conversation. They wanted to know all about the trip. Barbara supplied details as well as she could, considering she knew next to nothing about Bermuda. It was fun for a few minutes to talk about this fantasy trip and was a relief not having to go on the retreat.

Then depression set in: "Why did I say that? Why couldn't I just tell the truth? These are nice people, they would understand." Barbara didn't sleep very well that night. Toward morning she began to think of her cue, "The truth is more interesting than fiction." She got up, showered, read the affirmations on her mirror, and had breakfast. On the way to work she said to herself, "I'm going to set this right. I'm not going to cover up with more lies. If they don't understand, that's a problem for them, but I know what's best for me. I am my own therapist, and I'm overcoming my habit."

She went in to see her supervisor first thing. "I'm sorry," she said to her, "I'm not going to Bermuda. I never was. I'm not comfortable with this retreat right now. I prefer to have business relationships be just that, friendly, but confined to business. That is not to say that I may not feel differently the next time, but this time I don't feel it is wise for me to participate." Barbara waited, relieved and frightened at the same time. Would she be fired? It didn't matter. She knew her decision was right, and she felt strong in her resolve. Her supervisor nodded and smiled. "Thank you for your candor, Barbara," she said, "I sensed yesterday that you were worried about the retreat." Then she paused, her eyes twinkling, "I didn't believe your Bermuda story for a minute." The supervisor laughed, and patted Barbara's hand. "Retreats are voluntary. You needn't go." Barbara closed her eyes and took a deep breath. Telling the truth was wonderful.

Fire-Setting

The sound of the siren had started in the distance and was now drawing closer. Bart pulled over to the curb. He didn't follow fire trucks anymore. He looked at the affirmation on his rearview mirror: "Every day in every way I'm getting better and better." Then a tiny little voice crept in, interrupting Bart's thought. "Wonder where the fire is. Hmm, two trucks, must be a big one." Bart pulled out and started after the trucks. It was a big one, all right—a house and garage well engulfed in flames by the time they got there. Bart looked at a tiny shed way at the back of the lot. "Wouldn't take much to set that one ablaze, too," he said to himself. Bart thought about edging his way past the crew to the shed. "No one would notice," he thought, excitement rising.

He had his hand on the door, ready to get out when he saw the fire chief watching him. Shame swept over him. "This can't be happening," he said, "I can't be getting back into that." Bart closed his eyes and groped frantically for an affirmation. Suddenly he heard his fifth grade Sunday school teacher's voice in his head, "The Lord helps those who help themselves, son." She said that when he got caught setting fire to a brush pile behind the church. Bart gunned the motor, spun around, and drove away as fast as he dared. He didn't know where he was going, but he had to get away.

After a while he came to a park. He stopped there, rolled down the window, and let the cool autumn air caress his face. Then he smiled. "Hey, I just did it. I helped myself…I drove away. OK, Lord, I helped myself, now you help too, please." Bart thought of the expression, "trial by fire." "I've had my trial by fire," he said, "so now I'm stronger. Now I'll make it." As he drove home he had the idea that maybe he could be a volunteer fireman. There was nothing wrong with being interested in fires. The thing was to work on stopping them instead of starting them. Before he went to bed he looked up the number and wrote it down. "I'll call in the morning," he said, drifting peacefully off to sleep.

Hair-Pulling

Catherine discarded her wig. Her short blonde hair was soft and curly even though only about an inch long. She was pleased that there were no bald spots, and her sons were proud of the way their mother looked. As final exam time rolled around, Catherine knew this would be a stressful time. She was well prepared for marathon study sessions with gum, marbles to fondle, and dots on everything that had ever served as cues for hair-pulling. The day of her hardest exam, the one she dreaded most, Ethics, she woke up feeling very tense. Catherine had no qualms about any of the math, physics, chemistry, or lab exams, but ethics had been her least favorite class. She simply disliked it, and had not spent much time in preparation. It was too ambiguous. She entered the exam room with a black feeling. "I don't think I can do this," she said to herself, "It never makes sense, and I guess I'm just too dense to understand."

At the end of the exam she turned in her blue book and went straight to the car without talking to anyone. "That was terrible…I'm sure I failed. If I don't get a B, I'm doomed." In this mood Catherine drove home with one hand in her hair, yanking and pulling. Some hair came out and then more. As she stopped in the carport, she looked at the clumps of soft hair in her hand. She buried her head in her arms on the steering wheel and began to cry. "How could I do that?" she mourned.

Eventually she became aware of a tapping sound. She lifted her head to stare into the eyes of the boys, who were tapping on the window. "Open the door, Mom. What's the matter?" Catherine opened the door and gathered the boys into her arms. "I'm having a tough day, guys," she said, "How about if I wash my face and we'll go out for pizza?" They voiced no objection to such a plan, so Catherine hurried into the house.

As she looked in the mirror she saw an affirmation that she hadn't noticed for a while. "It's OK to fail on your way to success." Catherine thought about it as she washed her face. "That's right," she said, "anyone can make a mistake. The important thing is to never give up. What happened to me today was just negative self-talk getting me down. I don't need to do that. I'll be ok."

"OK, guys," she called as she headed for the car, "I want double cheese and black olives. How about you?"

Explosive Temper

Life had been very pleasant in Cal's home for several weeks. The children were losing their fear, and his wife had stopped threatening to leave. There had been several long discussions about her job, and how tired she was after coming home to face laundry, housework, and childcare. Cal was beginning to understand why she was often lying down when he came home. It was almost automatic now to give her a hug and a kiss when he came home, no matter what she was doing.

But one day at work Cal was served with notice of a $500,000 lawsuit. He was stunned. Things had been going so well he had almost forgotten the man with the broken leg. A malpractice suit could be the end of his career. All through the day he felt increasingly tense. He snarled at the bookkeeper for no reason. "I've been a dedicated, careful practitioner for 12 years," he said to himself, "and now one mistake is going to ruin me. Who the hell do they think they are, playing God with people's lives? That man is just fine now. I made sure he got the best treatment. Why is he doing this to me now?"

By the time he arrived home in the evening, he was trembling with rage. As he opened the door he could hear the kids fighting. Their shrill voices clanged against his already vibrating nervous system. Then he saw his wife, reclining on the couch, reading a book. Savagely, he turned to the children. "You kids get!" he yelled, making them scurry for the door in terror. He lunged toward the couch and crouched over his wife. She stared back, wide-eyed with fear. "Cal, please," she said. Cal raised his fist, furious at this indolent creature. Then he saw the tiny gold star they had placed on her glasses many weeks ago. "Give her a kiss," the voice in his head said. "Hell, no," he answered back. "Come on, Cal," the voice said, "You're stronger than this. Breathe deeply, relax." Slowly he lowered his arm and then sank to his knees beside the couch. "I'm sorry," he said, "I'm in control now."

"I know you are, Cal," his wife said, "You didn't hit anyone. You stopped yourself." The tension was gone—all that was left was sadness. "Something happened," he said, hugging his wife, "but we'll work it out."

Misuse of Prescription Drugs

Larry had become skilled at relaxation. He had several tapes of affirmative messages, and he was able to reach for those instead of the pills. His pain had a cycle that seemed to be related to activity, weather, and stress. Sometimes it was hard to find the balance between no activity and the right amount. He was gradually withdrawing from drugs with the help of his doctor. With the Fourth of July coming up, the family was begging for an outing. "We could go to the lake," they said, "and you can just sit in the shade, Dad." Larry didn't want to say no. It felt good to be able to enjoy the children now. But he worried about the boat and whether they could handle it without him. His wife, Jean, assured him she could take care of it.

When they arrived at the lake, there were several other sailboats going out, and Larry felt reassured that others could help his family if they got into trouble. He settled himself in the shade, ready to watch them sail. As he saw them trying to maneuver the boat away from the ramp, he felt a twinge of guilt. "What kind of father am I," he thought, "sitting here like a lazy slob while they struggle?"

Then he noticed that they were laughing and obviously enjoying their struggles. He began to pity himself. He wanted to be out there with them. He loved sailing with a passion. "Why did this happen to me?" he asked, "All the things I like have been taken from me." His back was throbbing. It got worse. He fidgeted and tried to relax. He got up and walked around. It didn't help. The pain worsened. "I give up," he said," and reached for his pack. Inside were three pain pills, the total number allowed for the day. "I'll have to take at least two right now," he said, "this is no ordinary pain." He took out the two tablets and held them in his hand. Then he opened a can of soda.

Half an hour later his family returned, laughing and soaking wet, to find Larry deeply asleep. They stopped laughing. They knew that kind of sleep was from drugs. "Well, we'll just have to let him sleep it off," his wife said, disappointed. The family withdrew to a picnic table nearby and tried to enjoy their lunch. Larry didn't wake up until midafternoon. He struggled up out of the drug haze to see his children tossing a ball, and his wife sitting on a rock watching him.

"I blew it," he said.

"I know," Jean answered.

Everyone was quiet as they loaded the boat and started for home. "You really did it," Larry scolded himself. "Ruined the first family picnic we've had in a year."

Silence. Then, "Dad," a young voice spoke from the backseat, "at least you came with us." Another voice, "Yeah, Dad, at least you were there."

Jean reached for his hand. "That's true, Larry. We've gone on a lot of picnics without you."

"OK, listen to them," Larry said to himself, "you did come, and yes, you did slip up, but you did come."

He turned to the children. "Listen, gang, I'm glad I was there—at least my body was. Next time we go, I'm leaving those blankety blank pills at home."

And as he said it, he knew that he would. That night he made a new self-talk tape. The messages affirmed for him that his mere presence was appreciated. He could talk and he could listen, even if he couldn't always do.

Irresponsible Sex

Polly had managed to avoid most of her old friends who were sexually promiscuous. She stayed away from singles bars entirely and avoided being alone with anyone. The hardest part was that she still had the reputation. She had become wary of meeting new men since they were often acquainted with her old friends. About six weeks after her last sexual encounter she was invited to a party by a woman she had met at work. Discrete questioning had reassured her that it was not a drinking party and that it was not just couples. At the party she was introduced to a man who had recently moved from Chicago. He was attractive and interesting. Polly began to feel some of the old feelings returning.

They went into the family room, where another couple was going through videotapes, and joined them in the search for a good movie. When they had all agreed on one they settled themselves on a long couch with the popcorn bowl close at hand. The movie was not rated, but Polly thought it looked fairly innocent. But it wasn't long before it became clear what *unrated* meant. The other couple were huddled in an embrace at one end of the couch. Richard made his move; Polly resisted. The scenes on the screen became more torrid. Richard became more insistent, and Polly felt her resolve dissolving.

"Don't do this," she said to herself. And then, "Oh, just this once."

"Come on, honey, relax," Richard murmured, "I know you want it."

The word *relax* reverberated in Polly's head. It reminded her of a relaxation exercise in which she affirmed for herself that she was whole, pure, and lovely all by herself.

"Hold it!" she said, sitting up so abruptly that Richard nearly fell over. "I don't want it. I'm sorry I gave you that impression. It was a weak moment for me and very unfair to you. Please excuse me." Without waiting to listen to Richard's protestations, Polly hurried from the room, ran out of the house, and drove home feeling frightened at how close she had come to failure, but at the same time pleased with her strength.

Overuse of TV and Video Games

Robert's family had been supportive of his decision to overcome his TV habit. Although his children had been reluctant to give up the video games, they had agreed that they were spending too much time with them. So the TV and the games had been on a shelf for several months. The children were spending more time outside in imaginative play, and the whole family had enjoyed evenings of working together or reading aloud. A presidential election was coming up in the fall and the children needed to watch the conventions for their social studies classes. Robert had seen some new games that were designed to help children understand the two-party system. The family agreed they were ready to enjoy these things in moderation.

During the summer Robert's job had kept him working longer hours than usual. He was tired when he came home. After dinner it was a relief to just sink into his lounger and watch the conventions. He stayed there, mesmerized, even after the evening sessions were over and the family had all gone to bed.

The next Saturday he felt too tired to work on the children's tree house, so he rented a couple of tapes and they spent the entire morning in a darkened living room watching science fiction movies. In the afternoon the children went off to soccer practice, and Robert lay down on the couch. Idly his hand reached for the remote control. He noticed the fluorescent orange dot he had placed there months ago. "Uh-oh," he said, out loud. "What am I doing?" He lay back and thought a while. He realized that his intention when lying down was to rest. He was worn out from working 12-hour days. "OK," he said, "I am tired, that's real. But I know better ways to cope with fatigue." He thought of the wasted morning, and made a new decision.

That evening he called a family meeting. "Listen, gang," he said to them, "we got a little carried away with the TV today. We need to make a plan for how we are going to use television."

With a certain amount of moaning and groaning the family was able to come up with a schedule that allowed a reasonable amount of time for watching carefully selected shows. They also made rules about video games: to play the games only after chores, homework, and practicing were done and to consider other options before deciding to play.

"So now let's go for a walk and see if we can catch a firefly," Robert said, taking his wife's hand. Nella smiled. She had worried all day about Robert's relapse.

Teeth-Grinding

Sam had learned over the past month that his main cues for grinding his teeth were his cello and the concertmaster, who was in his direct line of vision. The concertmaster was a tall, stout woman who grimaced a great deal while playing. She had an arrogant attitude that literally set Sam's teeth on edge. He had also learned to keep his mouth closed with his teeth apart while playing, and felt he had that under control. He had managed to avoid looking at the concertmaster most of the time. He felt he was doing well.

On Friday morning Sam went to the last rehearsal before that evening's concert. The cello section had a difficult, exposed passage, which had not sounded well in any rehearsal so far. During that rehearsal it seemed they could do nothing right. The conductor stopped the rehearsal and glared at the cello section. "That is abominable," he said. Sam glanced up and saw the concertmaster looking at him, laughing. Her mouth was open, her large teeth exposed. Sam was filled with rage. Tension mounted until Sam felt a sharp pain in the left side of his jaw. He realized his teeth were grating, forward and back, with a vengeance. "That witch," he said to himself, "Why doesn't she shut her big trap." Then he thought about how the section really sounded. "It's not her fault," he said to himself. "I missed that high note three times in a row, just scooped up there like..." A smile began to grow on Sam's face. The conductor pointed his stick at Sam. "I see nothing humorous about so-called professional musicians being unable to play an ordinary passage after an entire week of rehearsal," he said, his face red. Sam looked at her and said, "I don't either, maestro. I was just thinking that we sound like cats in heat." Everyone laughed. The concertmaster's mouth was wide open, showing the large teeth as she laughed heartily. "She looks like a clown," Sam thought, "poor thing." The conductor allowed himself a smile. "Very well, gentlemen, and ladies...let us tame this kitty."

The tension was gone, the passage flowed beautifully on the next try. People were smiling at Sam. "From now on," Sam said to himself, "I'm going to see Bertha as she really is, and not assume that she's thinking badly of me. In fact, I'm going to try to get to know her better. She's a good violinist. Why should I be jealous? The rehearsal continued. Sam sat, lips together, teeth apart, occasionally smiling at Bertha.

Smoking

The first three days after giving up cigarettes had been hard, but Ida survived that, and had not smoked for three weeks. She was somewhat worried about a reception for the Democratic congressman the next weekend. Ida had been working on his campaign and didn't feel there was any way to avoid the reception. There would be smoking there, she knew. After avoiding places where people smoked for these past weeks, she wasn't sure she was secure enough to spend three hours in a room with smokers.

At first it wasn't too bad. The room was well-ventilated and Ida stayed near the open windows. As the evening wore on and the room became more crowded, the smoke haze increased. Another campaign worker wanted to talk with her, so they sat on a sofa near the window. The other woman lifted the lid of a box on the table and took out a cigarette. "Smoke?" she said to Ida. "No thanks," Ida said, "I've recently quit smoking."

"Really?" the woman said, in disbelief, "Well, good luck. I've quit a hundred times." And so saying, she exhaled a stream of smoke in Ida's direction. Ida looked at the box. Her hand itched to reach for a cigarette. Her lungs pleaded for a smoke.

"Oh go ahead, have one," the woman said, offering the box, "you can quit again tomorrow."

Ida took a cigarette, held it in her fingers, relishing the comforting roundness of it.

"Light?" said the woman, holding out her lighter.

Ida lit up. She breathed in deeply, looking fondly at the box. A picture flashed into her mind of her own cigarette box, which now contained sugarless candy. "What are you doing, stupid?" she thought. "All your hard work gone down the drain. You are such a jerk." Ida laid the cigarette in an ash tray.

"Snuff it out, dummy," she thought. "I don't want to," she talked back, "I can never quit, anyway, it's too much a part of me." Her hand reached for the cigarette. "Now you hold on," she continued, "you haven't failed. Think. What's in your purse?" Ida remembered the hard candy she had tucked in for situations like this. Quickly she stubbed out the cigarette, opened her purse and unwrapped a candy. "You're OK, Ida," she told herself, "you're a winner." Then to the other woman, who had been speaking volubly the whole time, "What did you mean when you said this campaign is a lost cause unless Mark quits waffling on the abortion issue?"

When Other People Cue Your Habit

As you have probably noticed in your records, people as well as objects can cue your habit. Naturally, you can't go around putting red dots on the people in your life. People as cues present interesting challenges. It is sometimes not practical or desirable to avoid people. The man who works at the desk next to yours is going to be there unless one of you changes jobs or quits. Your teenage son is going to be around for quite some time, too. You probably don't even know why the person is a cue, but somehow, when you are around him or her you find yourself getting tense and then doing your habit.

There are essential two approaches to the people problem. If you dislike the person, then you might consider that when you let your hostile feelings lead you to a destructive habit, you are giving that person power over you—which is probably the last thing you want. When you view another as an enemy, what you want is power over that person—not the other way around. From now on, whenever you think of or see that person, say something like this to yourself:

> This person is not powerful enough to make me do something I
> don't want to do. I don't need to feel angry and resentful—he/she
> is not that important. I choose not to give him/her that power.

Now take this a step further. How can you use this person as a cue to give yourself a positive affirmation? One way would be to say to yourself,

> When I look at this person I realize that I have the power to make a
> decision about how I feel and what I do. I am a strong person.

Reinforce this by thinking about the people in your life who are really important and special to you. If you're in a down mood you may wonder if there are any special people who care about you. I assure you, everyone has someone, somewhere, past or present, who does care. Think about that person.

If it turns out your cue person is someone you like and admire, then the challenge is a bit different. This, too, is a matter of power, but in reverse. When you like someone very much you want that person to notice you. It is normal to need to be special and important. Sometimes, very early in life, people decide they are inadequate in some way, and when the habit develops, that makes them different. People notice. Being noticed is a way of having power. Even negative attention is better than no attention at all.

Next time you are with this person try getting his or her attention in a new way. Be interested in his or her life, things the person is interested in and likes to do. Ask about his or her family or work. Try to learn something from the person. Say to yourself

> I am an interesting person myself. I have the power to control
> myself in all situations. I want to know more about this person, and
> I want her [him] to know more about me. I will not use my habit as
> a distraction.

Do this also when you are not in the person's presence. Think about the things the two of you have in common. Think about the good and unique things about yourself.

At this point let me emphasize that people do not have habits *just* to get attention. A habit is more complex than that. Habits start for a variety of reasons—sometimes simply by accident. Nevertheless, once you have a habit, it does attract attention in numerous ways. Anytime we get attention for something, we tend to repeat it. A habit is not deliberately and consciously done to get attention, but it can be reinforced and maintained by that attention.

What you have learned thus far is how to evaluate your habit, label it, and target it with actions you can take to control it. Your next bit of work will be to train yourself in the treatment of your habit, beginning with goals.

5

Goal Setting

Up until now you've just been in the emergency room, taking the vital first steps to staunch the flow of your habit. You have been transfused with awareness of the cues that set your habit in motion, so that what you once thought was automatic behavior you now see as being the result of your thoughts and how those thoughts are verbalized. You know that certain things or people can push the button for your habit, and you know that you can stop. But as with any problem, whether medical, emotional, or social, emergency treatment is not enough. You must learn to pull back and look at the larger picture.

Living Systems

This chapter is designed to help you set goals by thinking of yourself in terms of *ecology*, the interrelationship of organisms and their environment. You yourself are an ecological system made up of the parts of your body and your emotions, beliefs, and behaviors. You are also part of the larger ecologies of society on many different levels, from nuclear family to world family.

To see how this works, think of yourself as a bus in a city's public transit system. You have a motor and various electrical parts that keep you running. You also have a driver (your brain) who thinks and makes decisions. You carry passengers who depend on you, your driver, and on each other. You belong to a group of other buses, and if you don't function well, other buses have to do your work. If you don't work well, it concerns a lot of people: school children, office workers, older people .

But it also works the other way around. If your passengers are noisy and ill behaved, the driver gets tense and may not be able to use good judgment in driving you.

If your driver gets upset enough, she may forget to give you oil and your motor will seize up. You'll have to be towed to the shop and stay until you're fixed.

Your driver might also get in an accident. This, of course, upsets your passengers. Not only that, but you are obstructing traffic and keeping still more people from doing their jobs. You are a system, and anything that goes wrong in one part of the system affects all the other parts, as well as other systems in your environment.

These interrelated networks are called *living systems*. Living systems as a field of study was pioneered by James Miller, a behavioral and biological scientist. He defined living systems this way: "General systems theory is a set of related definitions, assumptions, and propositions which deal with reality as an integrated hierarchy of organizations of matter and energy. General living systems theory is concerned with a special subset of all systems, the living ones."

Psychiatrist and surgeon Fred Kolouch was influenced by Miller's living systems theory when he was devising a method to help his patients deal with chronic pain. His approach is holistic. It considers the person in the context of his or her environment—as part of a total ecology.

For our purposes here, using living systems will enable you find solutions by evaluating your personal and social assets and liabilities. Using that information, you then can identify resources that will help you to set realistic goals. In this way you have a chance to make positive changes—not only in controlling your habit, but also in improving the quality of your life in general.

Taking Inventory

Assessing yourself within the context of your environment is like taking inventory or making an end-of-year balance sheet. In order to make things balance, you have to know what your assets and liabilities are. Sometimes it turns out that you have too many liabilities and you need to look for resources to help even things up. Sometimes you are surprised to see that you have more assets than you imagined.

At the end of the chapter are the Life Systems worksheets. Those pages will function as your emotional and social balance sheet. But first you need to consider how your habit fits into your ecology.

Consider the Consequences

A chain of events is set in motion when you carry out your habit. Not only does it affect you personally, physically, and emotionally, it also affects your family and friends and your job or school situation. You, and others around you, experience many consequences. In the spaces below, write down the consequences you are aware of when you do your habit.

What physical symptoms do you experience (rapid heart rate, shaky feeling, muscle aches, tension, headache, nausea, and so on)?

How do you feel about yourself?

What are the reactions of your family and friends?

Has it affected your job performance or grades in school?

What has it done to your social life?

What financial problems have you encountered that are directly related to your habit?

Are any other areas of your life affected?

Now you have an opportunity to expand your treatment with deeper understanding. In my experience, focusing solely on behavior is not enough. Putting your behavior in the context of your constellation of systems, however, enables you to make lasting change. Up until now you've been working on a symptom—your habit—now it's time to work on the cure.

The Life Systems worksheets are designed to help you do that. They are divided into the following categories: assets, liabilities, resources, action plan, and long-range goals. We will examine each one in turn.

Assets

Assets are the things and people in your life that are good and helpful, including your own personality traits, skills, and beliefs that serve you well. How you look and how you feel physically are important areas to consider. Having perfect vision is a wonderful asset. A nice smile and good posture are definite assets. Sometimes when I ask people to tell me about their assets they begin to list negative things. You must be stern with yourself and think only about the positive things about yourself. You undoubtedly have more skills and talents than you give yourself credit for. Just focus on yourself first.

Next, turn your attention to members of your family, those who are close and those who are far away. Think about positive things about your parents, sisters, brothers, grandparents, children, and so on. List the ways in which each one is an asset in your life. Don't worry about the negatives—we'll get to that. Even if it turns out that there is only one positive thing about a person, list it.

Next, consider neighbors and friends, ministers, teachers, and professional helpers. Be specific—name names and write down how each person is an asset to you.

It may be somewhat harder to identify the ways you are affected by the larger systems of organizations, community, city, state, nation, and the universe. Think about the police and fire departments, laws, ordinances, and judicial proceedings that affect you. Take plenty of time to really think about it. The stop sign on your corner makes it easier to go downtown and safer for your children. A leash law makes going for walks or riding your bike more pleasant. Zoning laws keep noisy businesses from disturbing the quiet of your neighborhood. The list goes on and on.

At the state and national levels, there are social programs: Medicaid, Medicare, Social Security, schools, emergency assistance. There are agencies to help the poor, elderly, and disabled. How do these things affect you? Are they assets, even potentially? Are you affected by labor unions? The armed forces? Anti-nuclear demonstrations? Abortion rallies—pro and con?

The world offers a diversity of experience and culture. Do you travel, or would you like to? Do you simply like going out for Chinese food? Our planet is a beautiful, miraculous place; what about it do you most value?

The universe is the level of your beliefs. What do you believe? What are your values, your ethics? What is life all about? What beliefs motivate you to do your best?

Thoroughly evaluating the assets at all systems levels is not a superficial task. It will take time and thought. It's important not to rush through it, though. Give yourself the time the task requires.

Ida's Experience

After Ida got through the emergency room phase of learning to control her smoking habit, she was excited at the prospect of goal setting. But as she began to contemplate her assets she encountered a stumbling block. At first she would think of an asset and then counter it with a "Yes, but" that turned it into a liability. She had to be quite strict with herself in order to keep her mind focused on assets. After a few tentative starts, however, she found that she could think of many more assets than she had expected to find. Sometimes, when she was unsure, she checked it out with another person.

"Would you agree that my homemaking skills are assets?" she asked a friend.

"I'll say they are, " the friend replied, "A lot of people envy you that ability."

In this way she was able to assemble her Assets list. Take a look at Ida's assets. Then spend some time making your own list.

Life Systems Worksheet

Assets

Self *Ida Smythe*

   Intellectual: *Intelligent, read a lot, interested in current events. Religious, have faith.*

   Emotional: *Care about others. Perfectionist, good homemaker.*

   Physical: *Physically strong, reasonably attractive.*

Family *Mac, Jamie, and Tom. Aunt Sal. Mother and sisters are alive and healthy. Father left me some money when he died.*

Friends and Neighbors *Susie and Caleb are good friends. I can count on them. Neighbors speak to one another.*

Organizations *Church, Garden Club, medical system, League of Women Voters, Community Center, Fire and Police departments.*

Community *Nice people, mostly older.*

City *It's home. Good community spirit.*

State *Beautiful. Good climate.*

Nation *Freedom.*

World *Fascinatingly diverse. Beautiful.*

Universe *Strong belief in God.*

Liabilities

Try not to get the cart before the horse. Assets come first, and only when you have thoroughly evaluated them is it appropriate to go back over and define liabilities. Start again with yourself, listing habits, personality traits, and so on, that are not useful and do not make you feel good about yourself. If you haven't had a physical exam in the last year, get one. It is important to know where you stand with regard to your health. For example, high blood pressure is a liability, but often isn't something you know about yourself. (Don't depend on a drugstore machine—they aren't all accurate.) The good thing about a physical exam is that you also confirm what your assets are. But the main point is that you need to have complete information and knowledge about yourself. Knowledge ends confusion and allows self-control.

On subsequent levels, you may be surprised to find that nearly every person for whom you found assets will also provide you with liabilities. Does it seem shocking to think that your darling little red-haired daughter could be anything but an asset? Children are always both asset and liability. They cost money, they get sick, they have problems. That doesn't mean you don't love your little girl, or that there is something wrong with her or with you. It is simply a fact of life that nothing and no one is either total asset or total liability. You, for example, are both asset and liability to your parents, your friends, and your spouse.

Some of the things in the larger system levels that you considered as assets are also liabilities. Parks, libraries, clean air and water, shelters for the homeless are all paid for with taxes of one kind or another. Jury duty can be a major inconvenience and voting a minor one. Virtually every asset has its cost.

Even at the level of the universe, you may find that not all of your beliefs are assets. Perhaps you need to question whether your beliefs serve you well. Are you happy with what your beliefs have produced in your life? How do your beliefs affect others? Belief in giving yourself what you want right now may seem pretty good while you are engaging in the fun, but it may short circuit long-range goals. A belief in putting others before yourself may cause you to be taken advantage of at times.

Sometimes people hesitate to examine or challenge their beliefs for fear of losing them or finding out something upsetting. However, it is usually the case that a belief that is truly an asset is strengthened by the challenge. Often in this process, people find that their beliefs were not clearly defined. At some time in life it becomes necessary to know what you believe, and now is a good time to find that out.

When you have completed your inventory of assets and liabilities, go over it again. Each time you do this, you will find things to add or to delete. This evaluation is an ongoing process, just like life. The most predictable thing about life is that it will change. Your assets and liabilities will also shift, but by knowing where they are, you have control.

If you study Ida's Liabilities page, you will see that some of her assets are also liabilities. Her children, for example, are listed as assets. But under liabilities, you find that Jamie is rebellious and Tom messy. She lists her husband as an asset, and then you find that he ignores her. Her beliefs are an important asset, but sometimes the high expectations she places on herself cause her to become tense. It will be interesting and very enlightening for you to see how your assets and liabilities have similarities.

Life Systems Worksheet
Liabilities

Self   *Ida Smythe*

    Intellectual: *Not educated. Haven't been to church in a long time.*

    Emotional: *Overprotective of children. Work on house too much, nag and scold. Have had bad habit of smoking. No will power. Lonely.*

    Physical: *Too thin. Hate my hair, too brittle. Chronic sore throat. Cholesterol count 280. Early chronic obstructive pulmonary disease. Early osteoporosis. Gum problems.*

Family   *Jamie is rebellious. Tom is messy. Mac does his own thing, ignores me. Mother and sisters mad at me. Father died, I miss him.*

Friends and Neighbors   *Some neighbors can't keep their property looking good. A few don't care. They keep to themselves. I rarely get to see Susie and Caleb.*

Organizations   *Garden Club is time consuming. Dr. isn't always responsive. Haven't been going to church, feel like a stranger there.*

Community   *Beginning to look run down. Some vandalism recently.*

City   *City Council too easily swayed by dominant, moneyed people. State taxes too high.*

Nation   *Jerry died in Vietnam, useless war.*

World   *Intolerance. Wars and famine.*

Universe   *Sometimes I feel I can't live up to expectations.*

Resources

Although you've made a good start, knowing your assets and liabilities is not enough. What we all strive to do in life is get rid of our liabilities. When your financial balance sheet has too many liabilities, you begin to search for resources to get you out of the hole. You'll never entirely eliminate your liabilities, but you can keep them within reasonable limits.

As an example, suppose Ida's son, Tom, likes to skateboard. But in Centerville, where he lives, skateboarding on streets and sidewalks is prohibited. If he gets in trouble for skateboarding in violation of the law, his parents will be his resource for that. However, if he wants to have a sanctioned place to ride his skateboard, he's going to have to look further afield. One resource for that might be the city's parks and recreation department. He could propose to them that a skateboarding arena be built. If he's turned down there, he might approach businesspeople to see if they would like to invest in that kind of recreational facility.

An interesting point to observe here is that Tom's best resource is himself. He is the one who has the ideas, makes the decisions, and goes out to act upon them. On your worksheet, opposite "Self" on the Resources page at the end of this chapter write your own name.

Life Systems Worksheet
Resources

Self *Ida Smythe*

Intellectual: *My mind. State college. Bishop.*

Emotional: *Myself. Affirmations. Book on habit control.*

Physical: *My body. Hairdresser. Dr. Stanley. Nutritionists. Diet book. American Lung Assoc. Cancer Society. Women's clinic. Dr. Worley.*

Family *My attitude and strength. Mental Health Alliance. Church.*

Friends and Neighbors *Garden Club. Susie and Caleb.*

Organizations *Conversations with myself. President of church women's group. Dr. Stanley.*

Community *Police dept. Garden Club. Community Center.*

City *City Council meetings. Public Records dept. League of Women Voters.*

State *League of Women Voters.*

Nation *Veterans Administration. Books. Vietnam Wall.*

World *Amnesty International. United Nations. Oxfam. Unicef.*

Universe *Church. Scriptures. Prayer. Minister. Myself.*

For each liability on your worksheet, try to find a resource. If you have high blood pressure, you also have a medical helper who is a resource. The library is also a resource for information about the causes and treatment of hypertension. Armed with information, you become your own resource in understanding how to change your lifestyle, diet, and exercise and work habits. Take a look at the resources Ida came up with.

Some liabilities have several identifiable resources, while others may be more difficult. If nothing else, perhaps there is a person, or agency, who can help you identify resources. Some resource agencies you might approach are listed in Appendix A

Such resources are available just about everywhere. If no organization is listed that directly applies to your problem, try one of the agencies with a similar area of concern. They will probably be able to refer you to a more appropriate resource. Spend some time with local publications, including the phone directory.

For each of your liabilities, remember to include yourself as a resource. Your brain is still the driver of the bus and can take you to the right stop.

Action Plan

Now that you have resources, you can make your Action Plan. As you look over your list of liabilities, some seem more compelling than others. In your Action Plan those are the ones you will choose to work on. Your habit is one of the liabilities, of course, although by this time it is beginning to come under control. How have you found your habit to be an asset? Does it seem to be linked to other liabilities? The following example shows how such a pairing works and how it can be handled in your Action Plan.

Debby's Plan

Debby had always been fascinated with fire. She enjoyed seeing flames and liked the fear and excitement when the fire trucks came. She had had the habit of fire-setting. When she did her living systems inventory, she saw that she had another liability that seemed to be connected with her habit. That liability was her father.

Debby's father was a cold, distant man and rarely made any contact with his daughter, who had been setting fires since childhood. In thinking about her habit and her father, Debby remembered when she was small, remembered her father reading and smoking his pipe. Always reading—she could never get his attention. Her father never took an interest in her activities. The only time there was a moment of communion between the two was when her father's pipe went out, and Debby was called to fetch the matches. In fact, she was invited to light the match and hold it while her father sucked air to light the tobacco.

Debby hadn't thought about that for a long time. Maybe there was a connection. She thought about her father. He lived in a distant city, never called, never visited. Debby only saw him when she made the effort to visit him. Over the years her father hadn't changed much. He was still quiet, remote, emotionally removed. Debby began to realize that her father might be lonely, but had no experience in how to reach others.

Debby wrote into her Action Plan a weekly letter and a monthly phone call to her father. She didn't expect him to respond, she just knew she had to reach out. She decided to work first on her relationship with her father, while at the same time continuing to work on her habit. She had other liabilities, but they could wait.

It wasn't easy to write the letters to her father, but she had recently joined a singles group at her church (one of her resources), and the group members were helpful in suggesting that she just write about what she was doing. Debby decided not to write about her feelings at first, because she was really angry at her father, and what she wanted was to establish some rapport. Angry feelings wouldn't help. So Debby wrote a short letter every week, telling her father about her work, her boyfriend, and the group she was in. After a few months she told her father a little about her fire-setting impulse, and the progress she was making. She wrote about her red dots and the statements she made to herself, and she tried to do this with humor. Once she told her father that she was thinking of putting a red dot on her supervisor's nose, but thought better of it, and simply said to herself, "This guy has no power to make me do foolish things."

Over the course of about a year and a half, Debby found that she didn't feel angry at her father anymore. She was thinking about him in a more tolerant and kindly way. Her father had become more real to her, more of a person, more of a father, even though he didn't reply for the first nine months. Something else was happening to Debby, as well. Even though she had a couple of setbacks with her habit, she thought about fire-setting less and less. She began to feel she was in control of her habit.

Then Debby and her boyfriend decided to get married. About a week after she wrote her father about the upcoming wedding, Debby received a letter from him. It wasn't a long letter. Her father simply stated that he was pleased his daughter had become a successful and responsible person, and wished her well in the marriage. At the end, he said, "Your courage has inspired me to quit smoking." It was the beginning of the relationship Debby had yearned for all her life. Even now, three years later, Debby has no desire to set fires. She continues to monitor her stresses, using the techniques she learned for controlling herself and her environment. She now has a family of her own.

Keeping the Balance

Remember that when something goes wrong in one part of the system, all the other parts, as well as other systems, are affected. Debby will need to continue to work on her liabilities in order to maintain a state of physical, emotional, and social health.

Living systems are constantly striving for balance. Have you ever made a mobile—one of those dangly things that seems to float and dance in air currents? It's hard to do. Each piece has to be properly weighed and all the parts must balance. Otherwise it just sags all on one side, looking pathetic. As with the mobile, you have to balance the assets, liabilities, and resources in your life. Your Action Plan will help you achieve and maintain that balance.

Obviously, you can only work on one or two items on your Action Plan at a time. Debby had already begun working on her habit, so it was possible for her to begin to address another problem. Since she felt a connection between her habit and her relationship with her father, it was appropriate to address that problem as well. You have also been working on your habit as you have worked your way through this book. Now is the time to select another liability, create a plan to deal with it, use your resources, and get to work. One will help the other. Take a look at Ida's Action Plan on the following page to get some ideas. But bear in mind that it wouldn't be realistic to actually do all those things at once—neither Ida nor you is a superhero or saint.

The Action Plan is where you will make decisions about things you are going to do immediately. Long-Range Goals, is where you set goals and make your dreams of health and peaceful living come true.

Long-Range Goals

Your long-range goals are the distillation of your picture of your ideal self—in realistic terms of course. Most people do well if they have at least one goal in each of four basic categories:

- Physical

- Emotional

- Intellectual

- Spiritual

Let's look at each of these in detail.

Physical

What do you have planned for yourself with regard to your physical health and appearance? Do you have some ideas about what kind of exercise would be good for you? Remember that exercise needs to be something that doesn't require a lot of prepara-

Life Systems Worksheet
Action Plan

Self   *Ida Smythe*

Intellectual: Sign up for class at State. Go to church Sunday.

Emotional: Continue with habit book. Use affirmations every day. Family or individual counseling, call therapist now.

Physical: Let perm grow out and use oil treatment. Low cholesterol diet, start today. Stay out of places where people smoke. Join Lung Assoc. COPD water exercise program. Begin calcium. Join walking group Monday. Brush and floss 3 times daily.

Family   *Find out about therapist for family counseling and grief (short term). See if Mac will go to couples class at church.*

Friends and Neighbors   *Arrange Garden Club class at Community Center. Tell neighbors about it. Talk about a co-op lawn service. Call Susie just to talk.*

Organizations   *Say no to some Garden Club activities. Say affirmations. Talk to president of women's group, tell her how I feel. Take list to Dr.'s office.*

Community   *Organize neighborhood watch program.*

City   *Attend open Council meetings and express my concerns.*

State   *Take League's pre-election class.*

Nation   *Visit the Wall. Get books on Vietnam and read.*

World   *Join Amnesty and letter-writing campaign. Contribute to Unicef.*

Universe   *Begin attending church meetings this week.*

tion or too much time. If you make it too complicated, you will wind up procrastinating and then just not doing it at all. How about diet, smoking, drinking? Is your blood pressure too high? How about your cholesterol? Are there changes you want to make in the way you dress or wear your hair? Where it says "Physical" on the goals page, write your physical well-being goal. At first just write general thoughts. Then become very specific about what you are going to do, in behavioral terms. For example, I knew one person with a very high cholesterol level who decided to read labels on packaged foods for fat content. He also decided to stop eating ice cream at bedtime and to limit his consumption of red meat.

Emotional

Emotional goals have to do with happiness, satisfaction, feelings of self-worth, and accomplishment. They are usually closely tied to relationships. Do you want to strengthen family ties or friendships? By now I think you have some ideas about the kinds of activities that give you a sense of emotional well-being. Write down your thoughts and then figure out specific goals. It may be as simple as giving yourself some private time without distractions. Or it may involve trying to phone or visit a family member who lives far away. The key is to be specific. Vague, generalized goals are not very useful.

Intellectual

What do you like to do to stimulate your thinking and stretch your brain? What excites your imagination? How have you been inspired at other times in your life to improve your knowledge? Perhaps you have dreamed of being a newspaper reporter. How can you get into the field? Will you need to take classes? What is your goal for improving your mind? Write it down.

Spiritual

Everyone believes in something. If you say you believe in nothing, that too is a belief. How do you define a spiritual person? Everyone has their own idea about this. What is the state of your spiritual being right now? In what way do you want to add to your spiritual growth? How will you accomplish it? Some people find a return to their childhood church beneficial. Or perhaps you need to investigate other churches and find one that is right for you. Many people, on the other hand, feel that spirituality is not necessarily connected with a church. Perhaps you want to set aside more time to study and read. Write out what you believe and then get specific about the actions you will to take to achieve your spiritual goal.

Formulating Your Goals

Ida used the questions listed here to help clarify her goals. As you can see from her worksheet, she wrote out where she wanted to go over the next few years in the four goal areas. At first she wrote in a rambling way, expressing feelings, hopes, fears, and dreams. Then she began to look at how to state her goals briefly, in terms of behavior. For Ida, and for you, this helps to keep goals within reasonable, attainable bounds. She realized that in this way she would be able to actually see the progress she was making toward her goals.

Life Systems Worksheet
Long-Range Goals

Physical
1. *Reduce cholesterol to 180*
   a. *Low fat, high fiber diet*
   b. *Walk 3-4 times a week*
2. *Improve lung function*
   a. *COPD pool group*
   b. *Walking*
   c. *Avoid contaminated air*
3. *Increase bone density*
   a. *Diet*
   b. *Weight-bearing exercise*
   c. *Calcium supplements*

Emotional
1. *Develop positive attitude*
   a. *Affirmations*
   b. *Get to know neighbors and help them*
2. *Improve family relationships*
   a. *Family counseling, 6-12 sessions*
   b. *Write to Mother and sisters, whether they write back or not*
   c. *Hold family evenings*
   d. *Couples class at church with Mac*
   e. *Give Mac positive feedback when he does things for me or with me*

Intellectual
1. *Work toward Journalism B.A.*
   a. *Take 1 class each semester first year*
   b. *2 classes each semester second year*
   c. *Full load after Tom and Jamie both start college*
   d. *Read 1 book per week outside assignments*

Spiritual
1. *Become spiritually in tune with myself, God, universe*
   a. *Read scriptures 10 min. every day*
   b. *Pray and meditate daily*
   c. *Attend church meetings*
   d. *Accept church assignments to teach, etc.*

Ida already knew the who, what, and where of her habit. She knew her assets and liabilities, and she had identified the resources available to her. What she had to do was look at one liability at a time, examine the resources, and come up with a behavioral goal in the four areas discussed above. This is not as difficult as you may think. By now you have collected a lot of information about yourself. You know what you're capable of, where your strengths and weaknesses lie, and what interests you. Using that information, you now need to come up with a concrete, step-by-step method for achieving your goals—as long as those goals are reasonable and achievable. Say "I want to learn about physics," not "I want to win the Nobel Prize in physics."

Most people who have destructive habits struggle with low self-esteem. Positive self-talk helps to improve feelings of worth, but more is needed to ensure continued progress. How are you feeling about yourself now? You probably feel better than you did when you had no control over your habit. Nevertheless, continuing to work on building self-esteem is insurance against setbacks. Working toward and achieving goals is an important way of maintaining your feelings of self-worth. Here's an example of how Ida's goals worked to improve her life.

Ida's Goals

Ida decided to work on liabilities at the physical level first. She thought some of the liabilities at other levels would be easier to change after she felt more in charge of her body. The congestion in her lungs was of great concern. She was short of breath after minimal exertion, and she coughed constantly. First she consulted her doctor and told him of her plan. He was surprised and pleased that she had quit smoking. He said that alone was going to improve her pulmonary function and cholesterol count a great deal. After examination he told Ida that she did have some obstructive disease in her airways, commonly known as chronic obstructive pulmonary disease, or COPD. He approved of her plan to join the American Lung Association's pool program and wrote the necessary letter. He also gave her the American Cancer Society's diet book.

Ida left the doctor's office feeling good about her decision. Her resolve to follow through on her goals had been strengthened by the doctor's approval and cooperation. For the first time in a long time Ida really felt that she was in charge. On the way home she stopped at the grocery store and stocked up on fruits, vegetables, and high-fiber cereals. In the meat department she chose fish and chicken. She also bought low-fat yogurt and skim milk.

While Ida was putting the food away, her son, Tom, came in. "What'd you buy, Mom," he asked, peering into the refrigerator. "Hey...no hamburger?" Ida looked at him thoughtfully.

"Sit down and have a cookie and a glass of milk, Tom," Ida said, "I want to talk to you."

Watching Tom stow away a dozen cookies, Ida ask him what he thought of her not smoking.

"Gee, Mom, you know I think that's great," he said, stuffing in another cookie.

"Well then," she said, "I hope you'll think it's great that I'm going to take care of myself, and all of you, in other ways, too."

Then she told him about the problem with her lungs and the high cholesterol level. She explained her plan, then waited.

"I know about cholesterol," Tom said, studying his cookie, "Coach talks about it all the time. He's a nut on diet. Actually, your diet'll be good for me, too." He looked at his mother and grinned. "But we can have hamburger once in a while, can't we?"

Ida expected resistance from Jamie. She was so rebellious lately, objecting to things before she even knew what was wanted. Consequently it came as a big surprise when she was accepting of Ida's plan. "Mom," she said, "I feel terrible about how heavy I am. I know I shouldn't eat junk, but I just do. If you are only buying good food, then it will be easier for me."

Jamie also suggested they talk about it on their family home evening so they could all agree on what kind of food they would have. "Dad may not like it," she predicted.

Indeed, it turned out that Mac was the only dissenter. He still had his smoking habit and his favorite meal was prime rib, mashed potatoes with lots of gravy, and a big piece of chocolate cream pie for dessert. He usually didn't have much to say on family home evening, but he said plenty the next Monday night.

"I don't have to eat that pig food," he said, referring to the drawer full of vegetables in the refrigerator. "A man needs a hearty meal…meat and potatoes. You can't expect me to work on carrots."

Tom, who was the apple of his father's eye, began to explain to Mac all the things he had learned from his coach about cholesterol. "I wish you'd quit smoking, too, Dad," he said, "I don't want you to die."

Jamie came to her brother's support. "Dad, you won't starve just because you don't have beef every night. Anyway," she added, "you're important to me. Please take care of yourself. Give Mom a chance."

Mac threw up his hands. "OK, OK! But don't expect me to give up pie."

Ida smiled, "You'll still have your pie, dear."

Dietary changes are not easy to make, but over time the family got used to this new way of eating. Tom said his running time had improved. Jamie was tickled about her weight loss. And Ida was feeling great. Dad still grumbled, but not as much.

Every Tuesday and Thursday evenings Ida went to the COPD group at the pool. She was breathing better and coughing less. The exercise made her feel stronger and more energetic, too. She had little desire for a cigarette and was finding her husband's smoking difficult to tolerate. As the time for his yearly physical approached, she suggested to him that he get his cholesterol checked. "Just for fun," she said. She thought he would resist the idea, but he shrugged, and said, "OK."

When he came home from the doctor's office he glared at Ida. "Did you set me up?" he asked.

"What do you mean?"

"Well, when Dr. Stanley listened to my chest he said I should go with you to that damn pool group."

"Really?" said Ida. "I didn't have anything to do with that, but I would dearly love to have you go with me."

"Well, I'll go once," he said, "but don't count on it as a regular thing."

Once Mac got started he went faithfully twice a week. He said he did it for Ida, but it was apparent to the family that he was feeling better. He began to make friends with others in the group. He listened to them talk about how they quit smoking. Ida never said a word. He and Ida began to occasionally participate in social activities with some of the couples in the group. One evening in the home of one of these couples Mac declared his intention to stop smoking, and they agreed to help.

The next day Ida was looking over her Living Systems Worksheet. "My goodness," she said to herself, "by working on this one goal, several things have changed." She realized that she was no longer lonely. Mac spent time with her now, and she had friends. The diet was a success. Her latest cholesterol count was 230 as opposed to the original 280, and she knew it would come down more. Mac was quitting smoking. Jamie was so pleased with her improved appearance that she was a much more pleasant person to be around. Tom's standing on the team was secure because of his improvement in endurance and timing. Ida's liability list was shrinking. "I guess we don't need family counseling after all," she said. "I'll think of a new goal for that one."

During this time she had also been working on emotional, intellectual, and spiritual goals. As her negative self-talk was replaced with positive affirmations, she found she was becoming a calmer, more peaceful person. Her journalism class had made her look in depth at local events and had given her a way of seeing the larger picture and beginning to understand the problems of unemployment, homelessness, and governmental corruption. This led to her becoming involved with a county feasibility committee to study options for unemployed and homeless people. As a result she no longer obsessed about the cleanliness of her home. If it was clean and neat by ordinary standards, she could forget the minutiae that had driven her to scold and nag.

This left the problems with her mother and sisters. Ida resisted therapy for a number of reasons: money, time, and a fear of having painful experiences exposed. Her spiritual goal called for her to meditate and study scriptures every day. As she read about forgiveness and thought about the causes of the rift with her family, she began to feel a need to discuss these things with someone. The question was, how would she find the right kind of person? After consulting her bishop, who was one of her resources, she was referred to a therapist who was of her faith.

The therapist was an older woman with years of experience. Ida felt comfortable with her right away. Because Ida had developed a positive attitude, and because she was mentally prepared for the experience, it took only six sessions to discover the source of the problems and learn a way to deal with it. Ida's biggest asset in therapy was that she was willing to follow through on all assignments and worked with the therapist openly. The end of therapy was the beginning of building relationships with her mother and sisters.

Goals and Change

Every change Ida made had an impact on the people around her. Her living systems work had opened doors to new opportunities and better family relationships. Ida periodically reviewed her Live Systems worksheets, adding assets, deleting liabilities, and expanding her resources. More and more she realized that her two biggest assets were herself and her faith in God. At times of crisis there were sometimes new liabilities to add, but now Ida knew how to change them. Sometimes the change was a change in her attitude toward liabilities over which she had no control. The only thing certain about this life is that things change, with or without your help. You have control over your reaction to events. And you have some control over the direction and degree of change. You also have the ability to accept things which cannot be changed.

Over time Ida found that she needed to make new goals. When her lungs were better and the diet was automatic, she made a new physical goal. She joined a walking club for the dual purpose of improving fitness and strengthening her bones. She also changed or added to other goals in the other three areas from time to time. Evaluating goals became a part of the everyday fabric of her life.

As you work toward your goals you will also be able to go on to learning new techniques for handling stress and solving problems. One of these, relaxation, is discussed in the next chapter.

Further Reading

Kolouch, Fred. "Hypnosis in Living Systems Theory." *American Journal of Clinical Hypnosis* 13 (1970): 1-22.

Miller, James G. *Living Systems*. New York: McGraw-Hill, 1978.

Life Systems Worksheet
Assets

Self

    Intellectual:

    Emotional:

    Physical:

Family

Friends and Neighbors

Organizations

Community

City

State

Nation

World

Universe

Instructions: Feel free to make copies of this worksheet as necessary or to adapt it to another format. You might want to tape the individual pages together to get an overall picture, or you might need more space. The worksheet is intended to get you started; what you do with it is up to you. Use this page to list your assets.

Life Systems Worksheet
Liabilities

Self

   Intellectual:

   Emotional:

   Physical:

Family

Friends and Neighbors

Organizations

Community

City

State

Nation

World

Universe

Instructions: Use this page for listing your liabilities. Don't worry if some of your liabilities are also listed as assets. Most things in life have both good and bad aspects.

Life Systems Worksheet
Resources

Self

    Intellectual:

    Emotional:

    Physical:

Family

Friends and Neighbors

Organizations

Community

City

State

Nation

World

Universe

Instructions: List your resources on this page. Remember that your first and best resource is yourself. If there are liabilities on your list you can't think of resources to help you with, do some research. Go to the library, look through local magazines and newpapers, check the phone directory, ask friends and medical and service providers.

Life Systems Worksheet
Action Plan

Self

　　Intellectual:

　　Emotional:

　　Physical:

Family

Friends and Neighbors

Organizations

Community

City

State

Nation

World

Universe

Instructions: This page can be used in two ways. One is to use it to brainstorm ways of dealing with all of your liabilities. You will probably find, however, whether you do that or not, that some liabilities feel more urgent to you. The second use is, once you have singled out a particular liability, use this page to come up with ways to work on that liability in a variety of areas. Not all areas will be appropriate for every liability, but each area should be considered.

Life Systems Worksheet
Long-Range Goals

Physical

Emotional

Intellectual

Spiritual

Instructions: On this sheet, first list the long-range goals you want to accomplish over the next year or so. If you can start but not finish them in a year, that's OK. Remember to be realistic. Think of things you want to *do*—not what you want to *become*. The second part of this task is break down your goal into achievable steps. How will you go about it? What are the concrete actions you will take toward your goal? It is virtually impossible to be too detailed or to make your steps too small, so take as much time and space as you need.

6

Relaxation

Fight or Flight

"It's a jungle out there," the harried middle school teacher exclaimed as the last horde of restless students rushed out of the building.

The principal looked at him with concern. "You'd better relax, Tom," she said, "Don't let the savages get under your skin."

Of course, in actuality there are few similarities between a jungle and a school: no dense foliage, no wild animals, no savages with poison darts. But schools and city streets, even workplaces and homes, *feel* to millions of us as if they are hostile, dangerous environments. And our bodies respond accordingly.

The constant threat of danger, whether in a South American jungle, a city street, or alone in your room with anxious thoughts, produces a profound physiologic response. Hans Selye, a pioneer in stress research, called it the *fight-or-flight* response. In hostile territory there are two choices when your life is threatened. You can stand and fight, or you can run away as fast as you can.

In order to run or to fight you need a sudden surge of energy and strength. Adrenaline is poured into the bloodstream, making your heart work fast to get a good supply of oxygen-bearing blood cells to the muscles. The immune system is signaled to provide extra lymphocytes, which may be needed in the event of injury. You are alert, tense, and watchful. The fight-or-flight response should be of short duration. It is supposed to end when you are out of danger. For our ancestors, hunting or in a battle, that was exactly the way it worked. Stresses were sporadic and short term. As society became more civilized, however, the stresses changed. Worries about crop failure, crowding, or loss of employment created an extended fight-or-flight response we call *anxiety*.

Along with other 20th-century wars, the Vietnam War provides dramatic examples of prolonged stress response (also known as everything from "shell shock" to "post-traumatic stress disorder"). In that war men and women knew that their lives were constantly, unpredictably threatened. They had to be alert every minute, waking or sleeping, fearing that the next step on the path would be mined. A sniper could be waiting around the bend. They were dangers that could not be fought or conquered, or run away from. Thousands tried escaping into drugs or liquor. But these things didn't remove the danger. Consequently, their bodies were in a constant state of preparedness. Those who survived are often still paying dearly for the effects of that perpetual state of biochemical arousal. Today, all it takes is a thought, a dream, or a momentary mental image to re-create what they felt then—physically and emotionally.

This chronic excitation of the fight-or-flight reaction is also what your tension is about—albeit on a smaller scale. Feelings of chronic anxiety are the constant companions of people with negative habits. Your habit came about accidentally sometime in the past when it relieved your state of tension. As with the stresses in Vietnam, you can't run away from bills or taxes or congested traffic. You can't fight and conquer an arrogant co-worker. You feel trapped by myriad circumstances that seemingly cannot be escaped. The tension mounts and becomes intolerable. Your whole system demands that action be taken. That is when you do your habit. By doing something the tension is relieved. In fact, it works so well that you began to use the habit again and again as a tension reliever.

Changing Your Response

The good news is that the entire fight-or-flight response is controlled by your brain—as we have discussed before. You have already seen how you can change this response by what you say to yourself and by how you use environmental cues. This chapter will teach you alternate ways to release tension: relaxing your muscles, slowing and deepening your breathing, and visualizing calming scenes. You will also learn about self-hypnosis and relaxing activities that will take the place of indulging in your habit.

The first two techniques—progressive relaxation and deep breathing—are basic physical skills that everyone should learn. Master these first. They will quickly relax your body and can be done easily just about anywhere. I know people who do them on the ski lift before a difficult run. After mastering these skills, experiment with the other techniques to see what works best for you to deepen and prolong your relaxed state.

Perhaps you are still wondering about drugs. You probably have tried some of the muscle relaxants and anti-anxiety drugs. These drugs were developed for the purpose of blocking or lessening anxiety. Although well-intended, they are not the answer. There is no magic pill for the kind of tension you have. Drugs carry with them the risk of toxicity and dependence. And, when used for a long time, they may rob you of the initiative to work on controlling your habit by your own means. The best drug for anxiety lies within you.

Progressive Muscle Relaxation

Most hospitals and clinics offer classes of one kind or another in relaxation. Many psychotherapists include it in their repertoire of treatment techniques. There are also hundreds of books about it, but you can teach it to yourself. The method presented here is a composite of the work of many people. I have used it for many years. If you are interested in further study, one excellent resource is *The Relaxation and Stress Reduction Workbook,* by Martha Davis, Elizabeth Robbins Eshelman, and Matthew McKay.

The concept of progressive relaxation, which was originated by Edmund Jacobson in 1929, is the basic preparatory step to learning other relaxation techniques. Jacobson believed relaxation could be learned, if the person first understood the feeling of tension. How often do you wind up at the end of the day with a stiff neck and aching shoulders? You have held those muscles tense for hours without being aware of the tension. Your muscles became tense in response to anxiety-provoking thoughts and events. This physiological tension invites more anxious thoughts, thus creating a vicious cycle of tension...anxiety...tension, and so on. In the past, when these feelings became intolerable, doing your habit relieved the tension. Jacobson believed that deep muscle relaxation, by reducing physiological tension, interrupted this cycle.

Jacobson's method of flexing a muscle group and then relaxing will help you to quickly learn the difference between muscular tension and relaxation. This technique is also used as a part of other relaxation methods such as visualization and self-hypnosis. Relaxation, visualization, and self-hypnosis are first presented separately in this chapter. In later sections they are combined—after you have become skilled in the primary streps.

Record the following instructions in your own voice. It is better to do this than to use a purchased tape. You are your own therapist; you need to hear your own voice giving instructions. As you read be sure to pause for a slow count of three for each ellipsis (...).

Make yourself comfortable in a chair, bed, or on the floor. Take time to adjust your arms and legs so that you do not feel strain on any part of your body. If you need a pillow under your knees or arms, do that now. Close your eyes, if you wish, to shut out distractions.

Now clench your right fist, making it tighter and tighter. Be aware of the tension you feel in your hand and forearm...Now relax, let go, feel how limp your hand and arm are now...Let your arm be warm, soft, and limp, like a sleeping baby's arm...Now tense your fist again...focus on the feeling of tension...Now relax, let go, and enjoy the soft, warm limpness of your hand and arm. Take a moment to enjoy the loose feeling...how different it is from the tension you experienced a few moments ago.

Now clench your left fist, clench it tight, tighter...feel the tension, and let go...Feel the relief of letting go...Now clench your fist again...wait...let go...Enjoy the soft, warm limpness of your hand and arm...Clench both fists hard and tight...let go...relax...soft, warm, limp...

Bend your elbows and tense the muscles in your upper arm, the way weight lifters do...Hold it and experience the feeling of tension...let go...let your arm flop down, limp and soft...feel the difference...Now once again...bend....hold...let go, just let all the tension melt away...See how warm and limp your arms are now.

Focus on your face... wrinkle your forehead...tight, strained... now let go...feel your forehead smoothing out...soft and smooth, like a baby's face...Frown, hard and tight...hold...and relax... smoothing out all the wrinkles...close your jaw...hold it tight...feel how painful that tension becomes...relax and let go...your teeth are apart, your jaw slack...how much better that feels now...Press your tongue against the roof of your mouth...where do you feel discomfort?...Let go, relax your tongue, jaw, and face...smooth and serene...Now purse your lips up tight, like an angry old woman... hold...and relax...enjoy having your face, jaw, lips, and forehead loose, smooth, at ease.

Now tighten the muscles in your neck...when you do that you can feel your stomach tighten, too...hold...and let go...feel your shoulders drop...feels like they go down six inches...feel the comfort and warmth in your shoulders and neck...enjoy this feeling of limp warmth...just breathe deeply...feel how much more deeply you can breathe in this relaxed state.

Now tighten your stomach and abdomen...pull those muscles tight, as if you were trying to make them flat...hold...feel the tension...and let go...let everything sag...loose and comfortable.

Now tighten your back muscles by very slightly arching your back, not too much, just enough to feel a little tension in the lower back...let go and relax...take a moment to enjoy feeling limp and relaxed.

Now tighten your buttocks and thighs, pressing your heels into the floor...hold...and relax...Stretch your toes like a ballerina, pointing them...feel the muscles in your calves tensing...hold...relax.

Draw your toes upward...hold...feel what happens along your shins...relax...let go...breathe slowly, deeply...enjoy the heavy warmth and comfort of relaxation...feel how your body sinks heavily into the chair or bed...totally supported...There is no need to make an effort to support any part of your body.

Rest and enjoy...When you are ready to get up and be active, open your eyes...stretch...yawn...and get up slowly...You will have more energy as a result of being relaxed.

Using the Tape

Before using the tape you've made, you will need to make certain preparations.

1. You need a comfortable chair or bed, or you can lie on the floor. Some people find that a pillow under the knees is need in order to avoid back strain.

2. Eliminate interruptions. Choose a time when you are alone, or when other people in the house are occupied. Discuss your exercises with your family, and enlist their cooperation in not disturbing you. It may help to hang a sign on the door of the room you use to help them remember to leave you alone.

As you look at the following exercises, they may appear terribly long. When you actually do them, however, very little time is needed. The first time you will need about 15 minutes—just because you are new at it. After that, 5 minutes will suffice. When you get to the Quick-Fix method, you will need only about 30 seconds.

Deep Breathing

This second basic part of the relaxation process is something you need to become so familiar with that you will automatically use it in any stressful situation. If you can use it when the prehabit tension is building, you will be saved from many setbacks.

Most of us tend to breathe shallowly, using only the top quarter of the lungs. This unhealthful practice allows stale air to stack up in your lungs, inhibiting the oxygen-carbon dioxide exchange upon which red blood cells depend to nourish all the tissues in your body. Your brain cannot function without oxygen. You become tired, depressed, and have poor coordination. Also anxiety is created when you have too much carbon dioxide in your blood. Nothing in your system will work as well as it should without properly oxygenated blood. The following exercises are good ways to learn how to breathe deeply. Try them both and choose the one that seems to work best for you. After you have mastered one of these exercises, you will be ready to learn the Quick-Fix method, for everyday use.

Exercise 1

1. Lie flat on the floor. Rest your left hand across your chest, right hand on your abdomen.

2. Inhale so deeply through your nose that your abdomen pushes your right hand up. Your left hand should rise very little.

3. Breathe out slowly, pursing your lips as if you were about to whistle. Blow out all of the air.

4. Repeat this exercise six times.

Exercise 2

1. Lie flat on the floor. Rest your left hand on your chest, your right hand on your abdomen.

2. Bend your knees, keeping your feet flat on the floor.

3. Inhale through your nose so that your abdomen pushes your right hand up.

4. Breathe out slowly through pursed lips, as if you were whistling, while pressing your hand gently in and upward on your abdomen. Breathe out until all the air is gone.

5. Repeat six times.

You will know when you are successful in getting all the stale air out of your lungs because your breathing will feel easier and you will feel energized.

Now try getting up and walking around while breathing in this new way. Walk around the house or down the block. Now that you know what deep breathing feels like, you won't need to put your hand on your abdomen. As you walk, breathe in through your nose, feeling the air go clear down to the bottom of your lungs. Your abdomen and rib cage will automatically expand when you do this. Hold your breath for two steps and then begin to breathe slowly out through pursed lips. This will take several steps. Continue breathing in this way as you walk. Imagine that your lungs are limp balloons. As air is blown into a balloon, it fills slowly from the opening to the bottom. That is the way you want your lungs to fill with air. It is impossible to inflate the bottom of a balloon without filling the rest.

Do this walking and breathing exercise every day until you know that you can breathe deeply and slowly and you can empty and fill your lungs completely. Then you can stop pursing your lips. Then when you walk you can breathe deeply and no one will wonder why you do that funny thing with your mouth.

Quick-Fix Method

When you get into stressful situations you tend to breathe shallowly. We all do. Now you need a cue for breathing deeply in moments of acute stress or anxiety—when you feel tension building. Since we've already talked about a balloon, use a mental picture of a balloon in your favorite color as your cue. Picture it floating upward, signaling you to breathe. You already have other cues to remind you to relax or use positive affirmations, so those same cues can also tell you to breathe. You can say to yourself when you see these cues, "Breathe." Eventually it will become automatic.

Breathing and Relaxation Exercise

You will find it restful and healing to practice a combination of breathing and relaxation. Make it a part of your plan to do this every day. You can write out your own talk and tape it, or you can use the one given below. The time will come when you won't need a tape because you will discover that your brain is an excellent tape recorder all by itself—your thoughts will direct you.

> Make yourself comfortable in your chair or bed. Be sure that you are comfortable. Take time to adjust your position so that you do not feel muscle strain anywhere in your body. Now pay attention to your breathing, being aware that when you breathe in, you create energy, and when you breathe out, you experience relaxation. This is a wonderful thing about the way our bodies are made. We could not bear to have a perpetual state of energy and tension. Therefore, breathing out allows us to relax.
>
> Take your time. Breathe in deeply through your nose, filling your lungs completely. Now slowly breathe out, letting all the air be emptied from your lungs. Take another deep breath, and when your lungs are full hold your breath...then let it slowly out...Once more, a bigger breath than before...a deep, deep breath, all the way to the bottom of your lungs...hold it...hold it...hold it...and slowly let it

all out...all out...empty.

Now continue to breathe slowly and deeply, but focus more and more on the feeling of letting everything go when you breathe out...In...Out...In...Out.

Now think about your toes. Be aware of how the little muscles in your toes and feet will let go when you tell them to...Your feet become very heavy, limp, warm...As you breathe out, tell the muscles in your calves to let go...relax...feel them become limp, warm, and heavy...Your legs are completely relaxed, just like those of a sleeping baby...Now the muscles around your knees...letting go...your thighs and hips letting go...becoming limp, warm, heavy...Tell all the muscles in your lower back and abdomen to just let go... No need to hold your stomach in...just let it go...The muscles in your upper back and shoulders...just letting go.

Your body is well supported...you have no need to keep any part tense...If you feel any tension, breathe full deep breaths and let that feeling go...let those muscles relax...All the muscles in your neck and up across your head can let go now, too...Your forehead smooths out...the muscles around your mouth relax...As you relax more and more, your body...your head...your arms...and your legs will feel very heavy, as if you cannot lift them.

Just lie there and rest...breathing slowly...deeply...evenly...enjoying this state of relaxation. [This is where you will insert a visualization later on.]

Stay there as long as you need to...and then...when you are ready to get up...gently and slowly stretch one arm...then the other...slowly and gently...Now stretch your legs very slowly... turn your head very slowly from side to side...enjoying the relaxed feeling of soft muscles...As you come to a sitting position, take your time...breathe...just sit for several minutes before standing.

As you now go about your tasks you will feel more calm, relaxed, and content. If you begin to feel tense, remind yourself to breathe and relax. Your body will learn to respond to this request as you practice your relaxation every day. Practice twice a day for the first two weeks.

Relaxation, deep breathing, and similar techniques are just skills, like tying shoelaces or reading. Throughout your life you have learned many skills. Think about all the skills you have. They all required a certain amount of practice before you got to your present level, right? What was the hardest skill you ever learned? In the space at the top of the next page, write about that skill, and all that you had to do to perfect it.

You can see that you have the ability to learn a skill. Therefore you can also become an expert at relaxation and deep breathing.

Visualization

Visualization is the creative act of using your imagination to be somewhere you would like to be or to do something in your life that you have not yet done. Your body responds to these mental images as if you were really there. For example, when I go to the dentist, I don't use an anesthetic. No painful shots in my mouth. Instead, I visualize myself going cross-country skiing. It is wonderful to be out there with a friend enjoying the crackling mountain air and the whispery crunch of the skis gliding along. I often see rare birds and interesting animals. This is my creation, so I can see whatever I like. When the session is over and the crown securely fixed to my tooth, I feel rested and relaxed. I've actually had quite a good time. Even though in real life I was not a very good skier, in my visualization I never fall down!

Evan, whose habit was sexual promiscuity, needed to learn that being by himself was not something to be avoided by impulsively hopping into bed with just anyone he happened to meet. He developed the following visualization, which you may use, if you like—if it fills a need for you. More than likely you will create one of your own. Repeat your previous breathing and relaxation talk on a new tape, inserting your visualization where indicated. Read slowly, taking a three-count for each ellipsis. This allows time for you to carry out instructions and experience the feelings and images.

> In your comfortable, relaxed state, I want you to take a trip with me. We are going to walk through a lovely forest, where we can hear birds chirping and smell the piney fragrance...There is just a small breeze, hardly more than a suggestion of air moving, but it is enough to make the aspen leaves shiver in a soothing way...After a while we come out of the forest and find ourselves standing at the

edge of a cliff, overlooking a wide river...There are steps cut into the side of the cliff, and so we walk down them. The steps are broad and safe. We go down slowly, counting the steps as we go... There are 10. 1...2...3...4...5...6...7...8...9...10...

As we approach the river we see a large raft moored there...It seems to be a strong, safe raft...so you get in and push away from the bank...It is a soft, comfortable, secure, raft...As you drift out into the river you find there is a lot of white water...you begin to travel very fast...Then you get caught up in a whirlpool and the raft begins to swing around and around...faster...faster...until you think you cannot stand it...Then, just when it becomes intolerable, you feel yourself slowing down...The river is slowing...becoming broader...You can relax into the softness of the raft...realizing that you are safe...

The canyon walls are leveling out, and the river becomes slower...broader...slower...broader...You see that you are drifting out onto a large, calm lake...The water is deep and clear and cold... there is no one else there...It is completely still...and peaceful...As you drift, you put your hand into the cold water...it soothes you... Put some of the water on your forehead...see how refreshed you feel...It is a warm, sunny day...not too hot, just pleasantly warm... You drift toward the bank and find yourself coming to rest under the shade of a large tree...You feel calm...peaceful...tranquil...

This is your lake...You can come here whenever you need to feel calm...peaceful...tranquil...And you can always stay as long as you wish...When you feel secure in your calmness...and you are ready to go back to your daily tasks...you realize that you can do this and still keep the feeling of being calm...peaceful...and tranquil...

Now open your eyes...and stretch slowly...Take your time about sitting up...Stretch your arms and legs gently and slowly...Look around you at your everyday surroundings...and when you feel ready, you can go about your life feeling calm, peaceful, and tranquil.

You might try this one first, just to get the idea of what a visualization does, and then write one of your own. You know better than anyone else what you need to experience in order to relieve anxiety and be in control of your response to stress. Write several visualizations and tape them so that you will not be distracted by trying to read and picture them at the same time. You'll know when you have the best one because you will feel tranquil and relaxed. The effect of that will be a decrease in the urgency you feel to do your habit. Many people have been able to stop doing their habits entirely by becoming masters of this technique.

Self-Hypnosis

All hypnosis is really self-hypnosis, because you are the one in control of your mind. Like relaxation, it is an altered state of consciousness, often referred to as the *Alpha state*. This state occurs in relaxation, too, but it is more profound in hypnosis. You already know how to do it. You've been doing it all your life, but you probably called it *absent-mindedness* or *spaceyness*. Have you ever been sitting in a meeting or class and suddenly found that for the past few minutes you haven't heard what was said? You may not have any idea of where you went, but part of you definitely left the room. We all take ourselves away like that. Children are especially adept at this—much to parents' and teachers' disapproval at times. It's a useful skill, however, one you can learn to use creatively to help yourself solve problems.

There are many ways to induce hypnotic trance; probably as many ways as there are people. The method I will discuss here is one you can use to give yourself suggestions about making some small change in your behavior. If it works well, after a couple of weeks you could give yourself another suggestion to expand what you did the first time. If you like it, and you want to do more than just give these behavioral suggestions, you could consult a therapist who is skilled in hypnotherapy. The best way to find a qualified therapist is through the department of psychiatry and counseling at the nearest university or medical center. A therapist who is properly trained will be licensed by the state in which you live, so another way to find one would be to call the licensing agencies for social workers, psychologists, and psychiatrists.

As with relaxation and visualization, the following induction should be read onto a tape, and played back when you can relax and not be interrupted. The nice thing about doing your own induction is that you can time your suggestion to your own breathing. When a therapist does it, he or she has to watch your breathing carefully and try to pace the flow of words at about the same pace as your respirations. For example, when counting down, each number should be said at the end of an exhalation. Ellipses and commas are indicators to pause and breathe before continuing.

> Make yourself comfortable, so that no part of your body has to be
> tense in order to support you. It is best if you place your hand limp-
> ly on your thighs, rather than having them folded in front of you...
> Now find something that is in your line of sight...that you can see
> without straining. It may be a picture, a crack in the wall, a light fix-

ture, or a door hinge. It doesn't matter what it is...Focus your gaze on that object and look at it constantly...never allow your eyes to stray away...As you are looking steadily at this object, you will find interesting things beginning to happen. The object may seem to fade away and return or become lighter or darker. It may change in various ways...This is because the eye tires very quickly when forced to look undeviatingly at one place...The complex mechanism for sending visual signals to the brain weakens.

As your eyes become more and more tired, you will find it difficult to keep them open...your eyelids want to droop...your eyes want to close...Just allow this to happen as it will, in its own way and time...Although it doesn't matter whether your eyes are open or closed, you are probably feeling that it would be a relief to let them close...Just let whatever happens, happen, and if your eyes are tired and want to close, just let them do it...That is good...

Now I want you to take a very deep breath, filling your lungs completely...Then slowly blow all the air out of your lungs, until they are completely empty...Now a second deep, deep breath, filling every tiny space inside your lungs...Very slowly now blow it all out...all out...Now a third breath, deeper than you have ever breathed before...When your lungs are full, hold your breath, and hold it...and hold it...and hold it...and now slowly let all the air out. As you do this you will find yourself feeling incredibly relaxed, and yet light...floating...you may even have some tingling in your hands or elsewhere in your body...this just part of the trance...it is good...

Now as you breathe normally, every breath will carry you deeper and deeper into trance...Your deeper mind will be aware at all times of the sound of my voice...other sounds, such as telephones or traffic noises will not disturb you...you are concentrating totally on my voice...Now you are going to slowly drift downward to an even more comfortable place...Every breath out will take you down...and down...and down...10...9...8...7...6...5...4...3...2...1... Deeply and completely relaxed...deeper and deeper...

In this state you will be able to make some decision about your habit...let your mind drift back through time to the last time you did your habit...See yourself going through every bit of that experience...Just let yourself feel again how you felt before you did it... Take your time...there is no hurry...Just let yourself see and feel... and hear...everything that went on during that experience...Now allow yourself to fully experience what happened after you did your habit and later...How are you feeling about your behavior?

Now it will be interesting for you to see what will happen when you ask yourself a question...As you ask this question, which I will give you in a moment, you will see before you a yardstick standing on end, with 36 on the floor and 1 at the top. As you ask yourself, "How willing am I to give up this habit?" one of the numbers on the yardstick will stand out darker and bolder than all the rest. Say that number out loud. If the number has not been clear, it is all right...

As you repeat this process again and again in the days to come, a number will become clear to you. It may come at some unexpected time, when you are doing something else. That is good, too. Having a number, no matter what it is, confirms your willingness to give up your habit...If you have the number now, just say it again, and see how it feels to know that you will be giving up your habit sometime in the near future...

Now just rest and relax...Feel the comfort of being rested...Your body has received as much rest from this state of trance as if you had had a 20-minute nap. When you wake up from a nap you do it slowly, luxuriating in the calm and rested feeling that comes from sound sleep. To help yourself become awake and alert without losing the pleasant effects of the trance, you may count from 1 to 5 in the way I will do in a moment. On each count you will feel a little more awake and alert, feeling confidence in your ability to lose your habit.

I am going to start counting now...1, beginning to wake up, feeling rested and refreshed...2, waking a little more, feeling confident that you can have control over your body and your behavior...3, a little more awake...feeling content and happy...4, almost awake, and feeling fine...and 5, wide awake!

When you have completed this exercise, take your time about getting up. Let your body adjust to its surroundings again. Look around, realize who you are and where you are. Then go about the task of living.

In future sessions you can give yourself suggestions about specific behaviors involved in the process of doing your behavior. Give only one suggestion in each session.

Mary Ann

Mary Ann had a habit of explosive temper. As she was preparing for her second hypnosis session, she tried to think of a small behavior that usually occurred at the beginning of an outburst. She realized that once her temper was in full swing, the physical actions would be hard to stop. Often her young children were the victims of this temper, and she knew that the outburst gained momentum with the words she said. Ashamed as she was of it, she could admit that she called the children names before she hit them or threw things at them. In a hypnotic trance she was able to decide to substitute other words when she was angry. What came into her mind while in the trance state was the phrase, "You little darlings." She said these words aloud several times while in trance. When she was fully awake she wondered if it would really work. Nothing had worked very well before. She wasn't at all sure she would remember to say "You little darlings" instead of "You stupid little turkeys" when her temper was boiling over. She felt that when she was beginning to get out of control she would not be able to behave rationally.

Inevitably, in the course of daily life, the children's squabbles triggered her temper. She threw the book she was reading into the air and jumped to her feet. To her very great astonishment, what came out of her mouth was "You little darlings!" It was like stopping a film in mid-action. She stood motionless, open mouthed. The children stopped their flight into the hall and turned to stare. Then she sat down and began to cry, the anger draining away.

It would be nice to say that she never had another temper outburst, but of course that is not true. She had to continue to add to her hypnotic suggestions. That episode, however, was the beginning of control. Mary Ann does have her temper habit under control at the present time, but she is ever watchful for cues that have the potential for setting her off. One of the bonuses from this is that she has been able to teach her children about self-control so that they will not grow up to be abusive parents.

Some people enjoy self-hypnosis, while others do not find it useful. This is not a matter of concern. Self-hypnosis is just one way to help yourself. Other methods work as well. As you try these things, you will find one way that is best for you.

Using Art for Relaxation

Painting

As prime minister of Britain, Winston Churchill naturally had a great deal of anxiety and stress during his career. In his little-known book, *Painting As A Pastime*, he talks about many remedies for worry, such as exercise, travel, rest, and retreat. He believed that the common element in these activities is change. He said that change is like a master key. When the mind gets worn out from constantly processing worries, it can be rested by using other parts of the brain. He wrote these things in 1965, so he probably did not have much knowledge of the right and left brain theories, which makes what he says all the more interesting.

Churchill recognized the difficulty in just telling the mind to rest, to leave the worries alone. He said, "The mind keeps busy just the same. If it has been weighing and measuring, it goes on weighing and measuring...it is only when new cells are called into activity that relief, repose, and refreshment are afforded."

Churchill painted. He began this at about age 40, with no training. He said that plunging into this new and intense activity, with its paints, palettes, and canvases, was an astonishing and exhilarating experience. He advises us to not be too ambitious or aspire to masterpieces, because then anxiety would arise about the quality of the painting. He says to just content ourselves with a "joyride in a paint box."

He tells a story about being outside with his new paints and a canvas, hesitantly regarding the sky. Rather timidly, he took a small brush and dipped into the blue paint. Then he made a tiny mark on the canvas. About that time, a friend, Sir John Lavery, came along and stopped to observe what Churchill was doing. Reportedly, he said, "Painting! But what are you hesitating about? Let me have a brush...the big one." With that, Sir John proceeded to wallop onto the canvas a bold slash of blue color. Churchill then saw that his own timidity would never let him anywhere and his "sickly inhibitions" rolled away. After that he was able to attack the canvas with gusto. You might enjoy reading his book for yourself.

Kara's Paintings

Kara was a young client of mine who had severe pain in her jaw from grinding her teeth. She accepted the challenge to try painting, and eventually she presented me with four paintings. One was done with a sponge, using black and red paints on a white background—big splotches of color. She named that one *Controlled Rage*. The next was *Uncontrolled Rage*, in which red, black, and yellow paints had been thickly applied with a palette knife. Embedded in the thick paint were a knife and a razor blade. The third painting was bright red and green slashed on in a wild geometric design. She said that represented dissonance. The last painting was lavender and shades of pink blending into each other. It looked somewhat like a pink ballerina ascending diagonally up the canvas, but she said she did not intentionally do that. She had simply taken a square of glass, covered it with paint and pressed it against the canvas. This nondesign spoke of peace and tranquility as eloquently as any poetry.

Kara said that while working on these paintings she did not grind her teeth at all, which gave her some pain-free time. She has continued to paint as a way to relieve anxiety and relax her jaw. She found, as Churchill did, that painting was a complete distraction. He said, "I know of nothing which, without exhausting the body, more entirely absorbs the mind."

More Than a Distraction

Some fascinating research being done by David Hubel, a neurobiologist at Walter Reed Hospital, is helping scientists understand how the primary visual cortex at the back of the brain processes information registered by the eyes. Working with Torsten Wiesel, Hubel found that the cells in the primary visual cortex are arranged in orderly columns that correspond to precise tasks. When you look at television, for example, a very complex process is called into action. Some cells in the visual cortex extract form, others color, while still others are concerned with movement, distance, or texture, all within one image registered by the eyes. Putting all of that information together takes only the tiniest fraction of a second.

When you create a picture of any kind, from real life or from imagined images, you are using a part of your brain completely separate from the part that takes care of worrying. In addition, you are immersed in a project that is distinct from the rest of your life. Like daydreaming, it is a way of taking a brief mental vacation.

You don't need a lot of expensive equipment to begin painting. You could use crayons and a tablet of newsprint. Just five tubes of paint, the primary colors, plus black and white, will afford you with almost endless combinations of color. Books for beginners, which are low in cost, can be found in art supply stores. Other visual arts such as drawing, photography, and sculpture offer similar pleasures. Adult schools and junior colleges often offer low-cost classes if you feel you need a "jump start."

Music

Music and painting have much in common from the standpoint of creative process and mental absorption. Both can also develop problem-solving skills. Making music, whether by singing or playing an instrument, can also develop neuromuscular coordination and can stimulate the release of endorphins.

You already own one instrument—your voice. Unfortunately, not everyone has the best anatomical equipment for developing a fine voice. If you like to sing, though, this may be the instrument for you. Singing allows you to express yourself in a beautiful and artistic way. You could join a choral group or sign up for lessons. Many vocal teachers now have group lessons for adults, which may be a little easier for the timid beginner.

Manufactured instruments, such as horns, drums, keyboards, and stringed instruments can be learned by nearly anyone. Some people are physically better suited to one than to another. Some people do not have the right mouth or dental structure to play brass instruments. But there are many other instruments to choose from. Playing an instrument can cost very little, or it can become quite expensive. If you don't have a yen for a particular instrument, you might want to start with a recorder. It is not difficult to learn. You can even teach yourself from a book you buy at a music store.

Gabe's Violin

Gabe had never thought about playing an instrument, but as he walked around a music store, trying out the idea in his mind, his eye was taken by a violin. On that day he just looked at it lying in its case behind the glass, but he didn't handle it. He knew if he touched it he would buy it.

Gabe had a compulsive spending habit of many years duration. His habit had been to stop at a shopping mall on the way home from work, where he browsed through the stores, unwinding from a stressful workday. The problem was that he had trouble resisting the urge to buy. His credit cards were charged to the max, and he often could not pay his bills because of his spending habit. One of his goals was to stay out of clothing and sporting goods stores, except when he had made a plan for what he would buy.

Gabe went back to see the violin several times. When he held it in his hands, feeling the warmth of the golden brown wood, he became even more interested. The salesman played a little tune for him and assured him he would be able to learn. But Gabe didn't buy the violin that day, either. He had learned enough about habit control to know that he could go home and think about it, maybe talk to some people. His neighbor gave him the phone number of her daughter's violin teacher, so he gave the teacher a call. The teacher turned out to be surprisingly supportive and said that yes, adults do learn to play the violin. She said it wasn't an easy instrument, but it was challenging and rewarding. Challenging. Gabe thought that was just about what he needed, but instead of buying a violin, he rented one, and then arranged for lessons with his new teacher.

At the first lesson he could see that this would require training his muscles in a way they had never been used before. It certainly was a challenge. Getting his fingers to go in the right place while at the same time trying to move the bow firmly and steadily across the string required intense concentration. This is like rubbing your head and patting your tummy, he thought, but when he heard improved sounds following the stroke of his bow, he felt an urge to keep trying that was nearly as strong as his urge to spend.

Gabe began to lose interest in going to the mall. After work he wanted to hurry home to practice. Gabe's teacher had a group of adult students who played together a couple of times a month, so he began to develop a new circle of friends. These friends were not very much interested in shopping. Gabe liked the kinship he felt with them. He also liked the feeling of growing strength in his arms and hands and was stimulated by the precise coordination required to produce a good tone. Eventually, when Gabe had to go to the mall to buy something, he was usually in too big a hurry to spend much time there.

What happened to Gabe was that he was using a part of his brain that had not been used very much before. As with visual arts, this process was not compatible with processing anxiety. In addition he was learning new social skills, which had more to do with the pursuit of a goal than just satisfying an impulse. Best of all, he was accepted by the teacher and his new friends just for himself.

Other Creative and Physical Pursuits

The act of manipulating tools and materials to make something is a time-honored way of making yourself feel good—like you're really worth something. Even if you never thought of yourself as creative, trust me, you can create. People have preferences for different kinds of materials. What do you like? Do you admire fine wood, the look of it, the feel? Or perhaps you are more of a fiber person. Do you delight in the sensuous feel of velvet or satin? Or perhaps the simplicity of cotton is more to your liking. Some people are fascinated by leather, while others find paper more interesting. What about glass? Or bread dough? The list of possibilities can go on and on. Many thousands of books have been written about what can be done with various materials. I have shelves of them myself. There is something in the world for you to make, and there are classes to teach you how to do it.

Creativity is power. My husband likes to make wooden toys, and gives him threefold pleasure: first when he feels the satisfaction of turning bits of wood into boats or puzzles, second when I admire what he has done, and third when the grandchildren exclaim in wonder at Grandpa's cleverness. Look around, take a risk, try something.

Dancing is good for some. There are all kinds of dance classes and books about dancing. Square dance groups can be found in nearly any town, and may provide just the right combination of lively physical activity, upbeat music, and new friends. There are classical and modern ballet classes for all ages and all levels of skill. Tap and interpretive dance are favorites with many. Maybe you want movement, but not dance. Tai Chi is a Chinese exercise form that resembles slow, quiet dance. Classes in Tai Chi are often listed at colleges or community recreation facilities, or you can do it by yourself if that's what you prefer. Jazzercise and other aerobic dance classes can be found in abundance. Similar exercise programs are shown on TV and are available on videotape. There are also books. Yoga is an excellent discipline; it can be done in a group or alone.

Perhaps you thought you might like to write. The way to start is to sit down with a notepad or at your typewriter and put words on paper. It doesn't matter what they are, just write, and pretty soon ideas will begin to flow, and lo and behold…you're writing! It doesn't need to be the great American novel. Writing a personal journal every day is a wonderful way to see your growth over time. It's fascinating reading for you, and for the generations who come after you. There are books in the library about how to write anything.

The essence of all of this is that doing any creative, distracting, pleasant activity in which you can become totally involved is an unbeatable tension-reliever and a great alternative to your habit. Returning to your Life Systems worksheets, you might want to add to your list of resources some of the places you have discovered where you can get materials and instruction for doing creative activities.

Now is the time for you to take some risks in trying things you have not done before. Make this a time for experimentation. Find the anxiety-relieving methods that work best for you. This is a big step toward permanent control of your habit. Go to music and art stores and ask some questions. Look at course listings. Visit libraries, art centers, and museums. Ask more questions. Follow up on the answers and get even more information. You have already come a long way. Doing this will help you maintain the gains you have already made and grow even closer to the person you want to be.

Further Reading

Churchill, Winston. *Painting As A Pastime.* New York: Cornerstone Library, 1965.

Davis, Martha; Eshelman, Elizabeth Robbins; McKay, Matthew. *The Relaxation and Stress Reduction Workbook.* Oakland, Calif.: New Harbinger Publications, Inc., 1988.

Fanning, Patrick. *Visualization for Change.* Oakland, Calif.: New Harbinger Publications, Inc., 1988.

Green, Morris; Osterweis, Marian; Solomon, Fredric; eds. *Bereavement: Reactions, Consequences, and Care.* Institute of Medicine, Washington, D.C.: National Academy Press, 1984.

Petty, Thomas and Louise Nett. *Save Your Breath!* Ridgefield, Conn.: Boehringer Ingelheim Ltd., 1980.

Selye, Hans. *Stress: A Treatise Based on the Concepts of the General-Adaptation-Syndrome and the Diseases of Adaptation.* Montreal: ACTA, Inc. Medical Publishers, 1950.

Stewart, Doug. "Interview with David Hubel." *Omni,* February 1990, p. 74.

7

Dealing with Other People

You have many relationships in your life. You have, or once had, parents. Perhaps you are married. You may have children. You undoubtedly have at least one friend. Your habit has affected these other people, as you well know. Now that your habit is controlled, you will probably be faced with doubt and disbelief from the other people in your life.

Coping with Skepticism

My husband and I have been good friends with Mick and Terry for over 20 years. When we first met, Mick was a drinker and a smoker. One night a week he played poker with his buddies, and Terry had to endure a kitchen filled with evil smelling clouds of cigar smoke and the odor of stale beer. These habits were very offensive to Terry, who didn't smoke or drink at all and would have preferred a different Friday night activity. All of their friends were concerned about what Mick's habit was doing to his health.

Not long after we met, an interesting thing happened to Mick. He "got religion," as they say. Suddenly one day Mick was claiming that he had kicked his habit for good. He had tried quite a few times over the years, but always fell back. Naturally, given his history, it was a little hard for people to believe that this was a permanent change. He kept telling his friends that he was a changed man, and they wanted it to be true, but when he said that, you could see the reservations in their eyes. They were no doubt saying to themselves, "Sure, we'll see."

One night, many weeks later, the four of us went to a restaurant where Mick had been many times with his business friends. The waitress asked if we wanted cocktails. Then she gave Mick's shoulder a friendly nudge and said, "Want your usual, Mick?"

"No, no," he protested, "I don't drink at all anymore...not a drop." The waitress laughed. "Sure," she said, "and I just won a million dollars." Mick had to spend several more minutes trying to convince her that he did not want an drink.

You may have had some similar experiences. It is a very frustrating experience to know in your heart that you are different and then find that not everyone believes you. The reason this happens, of course, is that it is human nature to take a few steps forward and then slide back one. Everyone has had personal experience with trying to change a habit and then having a setback. That's what those temporary lapses are called...*setbacks*. Other people call them failures.

When other people are skeptical about your change, remember, the surest route to failure is trying to please everyone. Why did you want to overcome your habit in the first place? Wasn't it because you felt terrible? You maintain your success to please yourself. In this way, you will have the strength to continue your new style of living without feeling upset because someone doubts you. If you have faith in yourself, others will sense that, and gradually their faith in you will be strengthened. Ralph Waldo Emerson expressed it something like this: Believe in yourself, and what others think won't matter.

My husband and I never had any doubt that Mick's change was permanent, because he simply exuded confidence. He knew with certainty that he would never drink or smoke again, and so we knew it, too. His attitude was one of "This is the way I am now. I'm happier and healthier this way, and I like it."

You probably want to know if Mick maintained his change. It is now 23 years since that night in the restaurant, and he has not smoked once nor taken one drink in all that time. At other times in his life when he tried to quit to please Terry, he always slid back. But now his change appears to be permanent. I believe that it is.

Sounds too easy, doesn't it? It is simple—but not necessarily easy. The way to make it easy is to have a plan for how you will handle the doubt and skepticism of others. As you have done in the past, you have to make a plan and then stick to it by *role playing*—rehearsing your responses in advance.

Acknowledge the Skepticism

Take it as a given that some of your family and friends will not believe you. The repertoire of skeptical remarks might include, "Same song, second verse," or "Haven't I heard this before?" and even, "Who are you trying to kid?" This is a normal human response. The most dramatic example of doubt I can think of is the origin of the expression "Doubting Thomas." After his resurrection, Jesus Christ stood before his disciples, in the flesh. But Thomas demanded to see and feel the wounds before he would believe the man was who he said he was. Like Thomas, your friends are going to want to see for themselves that you are different.

State Your Intention to Change

Think about how you are going to let people know that you no longer do your habit. Mick is by nature loquacious. He told everyone about his decision to stop smoking and drinking. James, on the other hand, was more reticent and found it easier to reassure people who knew of his habit in a quiet, confidential way. To his neighbor, from whom he had stolen on numerous occasions, he said, "I'm not proud of my behavior in the past, but I want to assure you that I have overcome my habit of stealing."

In anticipation of facing others with a declaration of change, use the space below to write out statements you might make. First write them. Then say them aloud to yourself and then to someone who understands what you are trying to do. When the time comes to use them you will feel comfortable about taking your stand. Then you can handle skeptical responses.

Ask for Cooperation and Support

Sometimes, not only will you get skeptical retorts, some people will continue to goad and tempt you, even to the point of trying to trick you into doing your habit. It sounds mean spirited, but it can happen. If it does happen, you need to be able to ask those people for help. For example, Mick might have said to the waitress, "I realize I've said I'm quitting before, so I don't blame you for not believing me this time. But I really am through drinking, and if you want to help me, stop offering me drinks." Said in a calm and respectful manner, this kind of statement allows the other person an opportunity to assume a different role in your relationship.

Transactional analysis therapists, the "I'm OK, You're OK" people, teach that when you can speak to someone in a logical, adult mode, he or she will respond in the same way. When someone says to you, "Aw, come on, one drink (or one smoke, or one porn film) won't hurt," that person is speaking as a child to a playmate, "Aw come on, your mom won't know we took the cookies." Resist the temptation to respond defensively in the same mode. Logical statements and questions will switch the person into adult mode where he or she can understand and cooperate in helping you. When a person tempts you in this way, you could say, "Why are you asking me to do this?" or, "I don't care to engage in a tug-of-war over whether I'm going to smoke or not." Practice this kind of conversation in advance with yourself in the mirror, or enlist someone to role play with you. Rehearsal will assure success in confrontation with disbelievers.

Cal

Cal's children had learned the hard way to disbelieve their Dad when he said, "I'm not going to lose control like that anymore." They had been hit so many times, had cowered too often in fear of their father's explosions at Mom, that they had lost trust. When Cal knew he had control and was in the process of real change, he took his children out for burgers. He watched their faces as they sopped up the last of the catsup with fries. They hadn't talked a lot during the meal. They responded to his questions about soccer and school cautiously. Finally, as they were sucking up the invisible remains of chocolate shakes, he cleared his throat.

"Adam," he said, his voice hoarse, "Carrie, and Tim" you haven't had it easy. I've hurt you in a lot of ways and I'm real sorry about that. I don't know if you can forgive me right now, but I want to ask for your help." The three looked up, eyes wide.

"I've been working hard on getting control of my bad temper habit. Maybe you've noticed." Adam and Carrie nodded; Tim just watched, wary.

"I know it's hard for you to believe me when I say I will never explode and strike out at you again, but I'd like you to know that I really am changing. These are not just words, Tim," he continued, looking at Tim, who had muttered "Oh, sure," under his breath. "It's not your fault when I lose my temper. I'm responsible for that. There is one thing that really bothers me, though, and that's coming home from work to a big mess. It would help me if you could pick up your stuff before I get home. Even if you forget to pick things up, I promise you, I will not strike out, I'll just have to leave the house for a while. It would just be easier on all of us if you could help. That way we'll have time to throw a few balls before supper."

"Sure, Dad," said Carrie, "No problem. Say, can we stop in the park and swing?"

Tim looked at his Dad for a moment, then grinned. "Yeah, Dad, let's go to the park."

That conversation changed their relationship from adversaries to that of partners.

Saying No to Temptation

Suppose you are going to bake a cake. The first step is to preheat the oven. Then you will need to follow the recipe or instructions. If you do those two things you will probably have a perfect cake. These are also the two keys to resisting temptation. You "preheat" by making a decision in advance that you will not yield to temptation, and then you follow the "recipe" (rules) for assertive behavior.

Assertion means that you are responsible for your own behavior. No one else decides how you will behave. What you think, what you feel, and what you do, are the products of your own thinking, not someone else's. That also means that you are not responsible for anyone else's thoughts, feelings, and behaviors.

Assertion means that you can stand up for your personal rights without violating another person's rights. You can say what you think and feel directly and honestly, without denying another the right to say what he or she thinks and feels. The two of you may not agree, but you can express yourselves without belittling or degrading each other. Assertiveness enhances friendships because it builds mutual respect.

You have legitimate rights and needs, and it's OK to ask for them to be respected as long as you are calm, logical, and respectful of other's rights and needs. If that sounds kind of like the Golden Rule, I think it is.

What all this means is that when someone tempts you to do something that is not good for you, you can say no directly, honestly, and firmly. You are responsible for taking care of yourself. You are not responsible for pacifying or appeasing someone else by doing things you don't want to do.

Some habits are so private that another person may not be around when you do them. It would be unusual for a hair-puller to be in a situation where someone else would be egging him or her on, saying, "Come on, one more pull. Do it for me, kid." On the other hand, other habits almost always involve another person. Let's talk about some of these habits and how assertive thinking and behaving will help you to resist temptation.

Overeating

Going to dinner at a friend's house may be a situation fraught with danger. If your friend has spent all afternoon baking creme puffs and whipping up other high-fat dishes, the temptation will be great. My friend Maryann had an experience like that recently. The wonderful fragrance of roast beef could be detected as soon as Maryann opened her car door. She knew she was in for a tough time. She sat in the car a moment, taking time to make a decision and mentally rehearse some statements she had prepared.

Ted answered the door wearing a big smile and an apron that said, "Kiss The Cook." The smells inside the house were even more heavenly than those outside. Once at the table, Maryann said, "Ted, everything looks and smells marvelous. I'm sure I could gobble it all up in a minute. I hope you won't be offended when I only eat a little of some things. It won't be because it isn't good. It's just that I've been working on overcoming an eating habit, and I'm not going to lose control."

"Hey, now," Ted protested, "I worked all day on this, Maryann. Eat up! You can be good tomorrow."

"No, Ted," Maryann answered, smiling at Ted, "I'm taking good care of my body now, and that's important to me. Please don't urge me to eat more than I know is good for me. I need your help."

Ted accepted that, although Maryann could see him struggling with his need to have his culinary arts appreciated. Throughout the meal Maryann praised him lavishly for the excellence of the meal. She let him know that she respected his skill and the caring shown by his preparations.

Compulsive Spending

If your habit has been to spend compulsively when in the company of another, then you will need to learn to deal with your friend assertively. When Candace called to ask Betty to go shopping, Betty knew she would have to rehearse how she would handle her friend's invitations to spend. The expected happened. When they entered an exclusive dress shop Candace immediately began to exclaim about a certain dress that would look "perfect" on Betty.

"Candace," Betty began, "I'm not even going to try that on. In fact, I'm not planning to buy anything today, except socks for Jim." Candace looked shocked. "What do you mean, you're not going to buy anything? That's no fun, Betty."

"It may not be fun," Betty replied, "But this is a decision I've made because I have a spending habit that got completely out of control. I'm in control, now, and I'm going to stay that way. I think it will be more fun if you buy what you need without feeling you have to urge me to buy, too."

Candace not only accepted Betty's decision, but admitted that her own spending was getting out of control. As it turned out, they were able to help each other with habit control.

Gambling

Except for buying lottery tickets, you don't gamble by yourself. Someone else is always involved. Let's suppose that you are worried about what to say on Friday when your friends start hassling you about joining the weekly poker game. Think of an assertive statement, perhaps something like this: "I know this is something we've enjoyed doing together for a long time, and I appreciate your friendship. But at this point in my life it's important to me to overcome my gambling habit. It's upsetting my marriage—and my credit rating. I'd appreciate it if you wouldn't invite me anymore."

Now, shut yourself in the bathroom and practice saying your statement to yourself in the mirror. Say it different ways, using different words and changing the inflections in your voice. Practice it smiling, and not smiling. Then you can check out the effectiveness of your statement by asking another person to role play the Friday scenario with you. By the time you have to face your gambling buddies you will be comfortable saying no.

Misuse of Prescription Drugs

Although you use your prescription drugs in private, you can't get them without an exchange with the doctor and pharmacist. Doctors are trained to relieve suffering. Even when they are aware of the possibility of addiction, it is hard for them to see someone in pain and do nothing. The tools most of them have are drugs. It is your responsibility to say no to their offers of relief, but you don't want to alienate the doctor, either. Also, at times, if others see you suffering, they may invite you to take drugs when it is not appropriate.

Connie found that even after her doctor was aware of her progress in controlling pain without drugs he would still offer them. On one occasion, when Connie had a viral illness causing muscle aches, her doctor said he would give her a prescription for an analgesic containing codeine. Connie had anticipated this possibility and was ready with an assertive statement. "Thanks, Dr. Smith, but no thanks," she said. "I prefer to handle this discomfort without drugs."

Dr. Smith was surprised and also pleased by Connie's strength. This honest and earnest expression of Connie's feelings enhanced her relationship with the doctor.

Irresponsible Sex

The inner and outer pressures to have sex are enormous, even for people who don't have an irresponsible habit. The kind of assertive approach required is called *escalating assertion*. In order to avoid negative consequences that could come from refusal, such as an unpleasant scene in a public place or inviting violent behavior on the part of the other person, you can make what psychologists D.C. Rimm and J.C. Masters call a "minimal" assertive response. This kind of response does not involve expressed negative emotion. If your minimal statement is not effective, you then escalate to another, firmer statement, and continue escalating if you do not get the proper response. It works like this:

> Pretend that you are at an outdoor concert with a friend. An attractive man sits down beside you, close enough that you catch the fragrance of aftershave.
> "How about if I buy you a drink?" the man asks.

Your reply might be, "It's very nice of you to offer, but I don't care for anything."

When the man persists, and perhaps moves closer, you could say, "No, thank you. I'm here with a friend."

"I'll buy her a drink, too," he insists.

At this point look him in the eye and say, "This is the last time I'm going to tell you that we are not interested. Please go and sit somewhere else."

It is unlikely the man will persist beyond this point, but if he does, you might say matter of factly, "I've asked you to leave us alone. Now our only choice is to go to the security guard and tell him you are annoying us."

Now you've given him notice of possible consequences if he does not respect your request.

The same technique pertains whatever the situation and participants.

Smoking

The bane of the reformed smoker's life is the repeated invitations to have a cigarette, cigar, or what have you. The social climate for not smoking is improving, but there are still those who just can't stand to see you abstaining. Maybe it's simply a case of it appeasing their guilt when they can get you to light up. In any event, you need a repertoire of statements that will fit any occasion.

A simple, "No thanks, I don't smoke," may be all that is needed. If you feel your statement should contain some understanding of the other person's needs, you might say, "You may not realize it, but I have a strong conviction that smoking is not good for me. Please don't offer me cigarettes anymore."

About Role Playing

Again, role playing and talking to yourself in the mirror are valuable tools to help you say no. You can usually anticipate certain situations that might set you up for doing your habit. Suppose you have been invited to a party with all the managers in your firm. You find yourself worrying about your appearance, what to say, how to act. In the past, in such circumstances you have pulled your hair or relied on chain smoking to get your through the tension.

Explain the coming event to a friend and ask him or her to play the part of someone at the party. Describe what you plan to wear and discuss other aspects of your appearance. Practice saying assertive statements with your friend taking the role of tempter. Then reverse roles and find out what it feels like to be the one doing the tempting. When your friend makes an assertive refusal, how does it feel? Work on that until you have effective, nonemotional, honest statements.

Making Amends

Alcoholics Anonymous is an organization that has served as a model for many other groups of people who are trying to change their lives. It uses a 12-step program. The first step is what Mick decided on his own: he admitted he was powerless to control his drinking and smoking habits. He recognized that his life had become unmanageable. The next step was his decision to turn his will and his life over to a higher power as he understood it. For Mick, this was God. He admitted to himself and to God, as well as to other people, the exact nature of his problem. He was ready to have God's help in overcoming his habits. Those things are taken straight out of AA's 12 steps, although I don't think Mick knew that. Another step, which is important for anyone overcoming a habit, is to make a list of those people who were most affected by your habit. Even if you would be unable to contact these people because of death or separation, include them in the list. Make the list in the space below.

Now, starting with the first name on your list, analyze what you need to do to set things right between the two of you. Ask yourself these questions:

- In what way was this person hurt?

- What do I need to do (apologize, explain, express concern)?

- How will I do this (letter, phone call, face-to-face meeting)?

- What is my goal in taking this step? What do I want to have happen?

- Is there something that needs to be repaired or replaced such as money or objects?

The importance of this process is frequently overlooked. In order for you to be comfortable in your system, you have to pay attention to every part of the system. Remember the city bus? When the bus malfunctions, there are people who need to be taken care of. Children need to get home to their parents. The driver has to have help getting the bus to the shop. Even though you made this big change for yourself, you know that you were not alone. Success is not complete until every part of the system is seen to.

Letters

Writing letters is a good way to make amends. These letters should not be self-punishing or self-degrading. There are four parts to a letter of this kind:

1. Statement of the fact that certain things happened, such as stealing, gambling, and so on.

2. Recognition that the other person may have been adversely affected by your behavior.

3. Brief, matter-of-fact statement of your concern, apology, and desire to make amends.

4. Closing statement about what the future holds for you.

Then forget about it. If the letter is to a living person, you may get a reply, or you may not. It doesn't matter. You have done what you needed to do. Whatever happens after that can be dealt with as it comes. Strange as it may sound, it is also quite appropriate to write letters to people who aren't around anymore. The writing of the letter resolves your own cognitive dissonance. Write what is in your heart.

Phone Calls

For many people, letters are easier than phone calls. For some, talking face-to-face is most comfortable. If you have chosen to make a phone call, get together with a good friend and role play. If you are extremely uneasy about this, it would be money well spent to pay a therapist to do it. Before you make the call, role play every possibility with your friend. You probably have some idea about how the person will respond, but you need to be prepared for surprises, too.

One format of the call might be something like this:

1. Informal chit-chat about family, acquaintances, activities.

2. Statement about the problem you had, such as, "Do you remember how I used to pull my hair, and how embarrassed you were when my wig came off in the restaurant?"

3. Recognition of the other person's discomfort, injury, sorrow, and so forth.

4. Statement of apology, concern, or desire to make amends. Make it clear that you now have control over this habit and how it has changed your life to be free of it.

5. If the other person politely insists that there was no harm done, accept the statement and follow with some expression of good will toward that person.

6. If the person is accusative and angry, listen carefully. Recognize any truth in the person's statement and ignore everything else. It does no good to defend yourself or argue. Just let it go, realizing that they have probably wanted to express their feelings for a long time, and part of making amends is allowing them that opportunity.

7. Make a statement such as, "I understand how you could feel that way. I just want you to know that things are different now. The purpose of my call was to let you know that I understand the pain you have suffered, and that I am sorry to have contributed to it."

8. If the person was severely hurt, you may have to go through steps 6 and 7 a couple of times. Stick to your guns. Do not become defensive. After the third time, just say, "I hear what you are saying and I respect your right to say it. I have stated my desire to make amends, and that is all I can do." Hang up as graciously as you can. Speak calmly, even if you are beginning to feel quite upset and angry yourself. Getting into a fight won't undo the old hurts. Just let it go. You did your very best, and that's all anyone can do.

Face-to-Face Meetings

Role playing works very well in preparing for face-to-face confrontations, too. Consider every possible way the other person might react. If you are prepared for anything, you will handle it well, and then, when it's over, it's over. Don't waste a lot of time and energy doing postmortems on everything you said, and he said, and you said.

The people whom you have hurt may forgive you, or they may not. If they are not forgiving, that is their problem, not yours. You can't make someone have a forgiving spirit. Assume that they have some inner tension of their own to work out, and they will do that in their own way and time. You made the effort and that is all you can do. Even if you have to pay back money over a period of time, that is what you do. Forgiveness is the other person's responsibility.

Getting Support

We all need a cheerleading section when we're striving toward a goal. You need people who are accepting of you, who will be for you in the down times, and who will encourage you onward in the good times. Of course there are groups, such as AA, Overeaters Anonymous, and therapy groups for people with various kinds of problems. Often these are listed in classified ads, or information can be obtained through community mental health clinics and resource centers.

Sometimes, however, these groups focus so much on the down side of having a habit control problem, that it is hard to remain positive and talk to yourself in the right way. Because of this, they may be better suited to the earlier stage of habit control than they are to maintenance. One group that is better for maintenance than most is Recovery. You've learned some of the Recovery principles already in this book.

But even Recovery should not go on for too long. You have come far enough now that it would be better to think about support from your friends, peers, and relatives— everyday, ordinary people whom you know and like, and who certainly have their measure of problems in life, but are not intent upon spending an entire evening talking about them. This means the people you bowl with, members of the hiking club you belong to, or friends you have at church or school. If they are friends they accept you, and they accept your past. They anticipate a future with you. If they are friends you can tell them when you are a little down, or a lot anxious, and you can ask them to help you stay positive. Friends are realistic and genuine in their support. They don't gloss over the trouble your habit may cause you, but they don't go on and on about how terrible it is either.

Here's an example—a conversation Peggy had with her neighbor, Lil, recently. They were both out on a Saturday afternoon raking some leaves. Lil put down her rake and came over to chat.

"How're you doing, Peggy?"

"Well, I'm OK, I guess."

"You seem kind of down. What's happening?"

Peggy hesitated before answering, but she really did feel this woman was a friend. "Well, you remember my bad habit...I had a setback the other night, and I just feel disappointed in myself."

"I'm sorry," Lil said, "I'm sure that's disappointing."

"Well, yes," Peggy said, dropping the rake and facing her friend directly. "I really thought I had this under control for good. Sometimes I get tired of trying."

"I'll bet you do. You've done really well with it though, and I don't think a setback means you've lost everything you've gained. I think you'll go a lot longer without a setback each time. I admire your courage so much. You're a good example to me."

That's the kind of support you need now. I think the time for therapy groups is long past. Think about your friends. Are they genuine in their conversations with you? Do they occasionally confide some difficulty in their lives to you? How do you respond? Can you count on them for friendship and support—no matter what?

Being Part of a Group

There are other ways to receive support, too, although it may not be directly related to your habit. Being engaged in a group activity where your success will be noted is another way to have support and encouragement. Even though you are being congratulated on progress in an area other than your habit, it is still support, and the feeling of being recognized for success tends to extend to other parts of your life. If you play on a volleyball team and have a particularly good game one night, it feels good to be a part of a winning team effort. The success is shared equally among the members. Somewhere in your innermost being you know that if you can succeed in one thing, you can succeed in others. People don't have to be talking about your habit all the time to give you support. They may *never* talk about it if they are busy talking about how great you are at volleyball.

I play in the second violin section of a symphony orchestra. The goal is for us to play as if we were one big violin. This is hard to do. The violinists don't know much about each other's private lives, so we rarely talk about the concerns of an individual. When we play a good concert and our section does indeed sound like one big violin, it is everyone's success, and we tell each other about it. We feel good. I feel good, and I go home better able to cope with the rest of my life. Never forget the city bus. Whatever happens in one part of that bus system—driver, passengers, and other people—affects every other part. Many times children who have gotten a rough start in life have become successful in school because of success in a music lesson or the swimming pool.

Asking for Support

Now, while you are helping yourself to overcome a habit you may need to ask some other people to support you. The hard work you are doing is not always obvious to others. Your friends may not know that you did not gamble your entire paycheck at the races last Saturday. If you are a hair-puller and you wear a wig, most people will not know about the progress you are making. Select two or three people whom you admire and respect and with whom you feel fairly secure. Talk to them about your habit. Explain that you are working on overcoming it, and you need their help. Be specific in identifying the ways in which they can reinforce you.

One way of doing this is a support agreement—a kind of contract with the person you are asking for help. This agreement can be signed by both of you if you feel good about that, or you could simply make a list of ways in which they could offer support and hand it to them. Keep the list short so your friends won't feel overwhelmed by your requests. Here is an example of a formal agreement:

Support Agreement

I, _____ , agree to help you, _____ , in your habit control program. To the best of my ability I will:

Compliment you on your determination.

Accept you just the way you are.

Comment approvingly on progress that I see.

Notice and comment when you look better.

Remind you of your goals when you are discouraged.

Console you during setbacks.

Keep my doubts to myself.

Reinforcements of this kind apply to all habits. You may want to be more specific about something that would help with your particular habit. Spend some time remodeling this list for your needs.

When Catherine's hair began to grow over the bald spots a little, she was able to go to a hairdresser. He encouraged her to throw away the wig. He also taught her how to care for her hair, and helped with an attractive short hairstyle. The people who knew about Catherine's habit were able to reinforce her with compliments about her new look. In addition, Catherine was able to ask people for other kinds of reinforcement. In her work she felt that her performance was often unnoticed and unappreciated. Catherine talked to one of her employers and simply asked for an expression of thanks when she did something well. Her employers were able to do this, and that was one more little building block for overcoming the habit. She was also able to ask family members to provide her with verbal reinforcement.

Helping Others

Every person in the world needs help at one time or another. There are people whose need is obvious, such as those who cannot walk, or read, or see. And there are many more whose need may be more hidden. Help can be given person-to-person, or, in a more structured way, through an agency. During a low point in my life I was ill, couldn't work, had no money, and felt that I was of about as much worth as a piece of chewing gum on the bottom of someone's shoe. I needed pool therapy in order to become strong enough to walk again, but I couldn't afford it. Then I heard that volunteers at the rehab hospital were allowed to use the pool free. I went there in a spirit of selfish desperation to see what volunteer job I could do. There wasn't a lot I could do because I was weak, but they found something for me. I was invited to write articles about various hospital patients and staff for their newsletter. Something happened to me there that was much more profound than pool therapy, although I had that, too.

As I interviewed people about their injuries and disabling illnesses, I began to want to help them. Since I was trained in a helping profession, it was a short step to actually being in a helping role. I began to feel better about myself. I wasn't a piece of chewing gum anymore. I was a person with a problem helping other people with problems. After a while I regained my confidence, as well as my strength, and affirmed for myself once again that there are no worthless human beings, and that included me.

Volunteer Programs

Since that time I have always recommended helping as a means to bettering self-esteem. It seems to never fail. Read the newspaper; there are always pleas for volunteers to help people with some kind of problem. Teach an adult to read, for example. Talk to people at the library, hospitals, and nursing homes. You could even read books on tape for blind people. One terribly depressed woman I knew finally agreed to be a "grandma" in the intensive care nursery. She went there for an hour every day and rocked tiny babies who were struggling to survive. Watching her change was like seeing a beautiful butterfly coming out of a chrysalis.

Helping someone else achieve success will also reinforce your own success. If you like kids, there are thousands in your area who need a helping hand. Some people like to coach soccer or little league ball. Others like to help learning disabled children learn to read. A lot of students need help with math. Children today need a lot of help. There may be a Partners program or Big Brother/Big Sister program in your area. There you will find an opportunity to help kids of all ages—especially troubled teens. You could teach a 4-H class, or lead Girl or Boy Scouts. Some of these young people have problems with habit control, too. You may have an opportunity to be a support and an example to them. Who could do it better than you?

Maybe you like old people. Volunteers are desperately needed to help run programs for the elderly. Old people need lots of words of encouragement and support. They have problems that are sometimes virtually insurmountable, but with a good cheerleader they can have a better quality of life. Old people are very appreciative of your help, and they encourage you to come back.

How about the Red Cross or programs for mentally disabled citizens? Everywhere there are people trying to overcome problems. You can help. You know the right words to say. Saying those words to someone else who is struggling will ease your own struggle.

Another way to help others is through public service. This is different from service to individuals in that what you do affects many people and sometimes even changes public policy. Campaigning for a political candidate whose ideas are important to you is one way to do this. Getting petitions signed in causes that concern you is another. Manning a Salvation Army kettle at Christmas, or joining the civic chorus or community band are other ways to help. Read the paper; be alert for news about events that concern you. You can help, and you will benefit from the effort more than anyone. The talking you do to yourself and others, and the words you receive back, are master keys to protecting the progress you have made.

Further Reading

Fanning, Patrick. *Lifetime Weight Control*. Oakland, Calif.: New Harbinger Publications, Inc., 1990.

Berne, Eric. *Transactional Analysis in Psychotherapy*. New York: Grove Press, 1961.

Lange, Arthur J., and Patricia Jakubowski. *Responsible Assertive Behavior*. Champaign, Ill.: Research Press, 1976.

Rimm, D. and J.C. Masters. *Behavior Therapy: Techniques and Empirical Findings*. New York: Academic Press, 1974.

8

Maintaining Your Gains

You now have a repertoire of skills, a medicine bag for habits. You have reached graduation day in your school of control. What you've learned is a little theory and a lot of practical techniques. Pretend, for a moment, that you are a nurse just completing four years of training. You would not remain a nurse very long if you didn't work to maintain and improve your skills. Likewise, maintaining new behavior patterns requires ongoing practice and reinforcement.

The nurse who takes a job in a hospital emergency room has daily practice in using her skills. Through this practice she learns even more about nursing techniques. For this she is tangibly rewarded with a paycheck and perhaps a complimentary report from the supervisor. Another reward for the nurse is the satisfaction of doing her work well and seeing improvement in her patients. The third way she is rewarded is by the stream of self-talk in her mind. She will be telling herself, "Mr. Jones has a better color now, oxygen was a good idea," or "I was good with that needle, Mrs. Crane didn't feel it," and many times with just simple messages: "Good job," "great," or "Now you've got it!"

You are going to learn more about these kinds of positive reinforcements. You'll also learn how to set up negative reinforcements, if you need them, to serve as deterrents against setbacks. Finally, you'll learn how good diet and exercise can act to reinforce the changes you've made in your life. It's exciting to have arrived at this point in your progress. This is the fun part.

Positive Reinforcers

Tangible Rewards

Most people like presents. The great success of mail-order companies lies not in convenience, although that is the reason most people give for using them, but in a basic human desire to receive gifts, to be surprised. Even when you ordered the article yourself and paid the money, the pleasure of opening a package and seeing this "gift" for the first time is immensely rewarding.

Tangible rewards are things you can touch, see, and feel—like a paycheck, a new dress, or a merit award. The tricky thing for the person with a habit is to determine what kind of reward will be sufficiently reinforcing to encourage him or her to permanently relinquish the habit. It is not a reward if it is something you would buy or do anyway. Let's look at some possible rewards for overcoming certain habits.

Overeating

Sarah hated her fat clothes. She had been looking in shop windows at dresses in a style she thought suited her and decided to strengthen her commitment to habit control with a reward. She put an expensive dress of a smaller size on layaway. She would only be able to take it home if she maintained her diet and exercise plan for six months. When she finally was able to wear the dress, she felt secure in her belief that she had her habit under control. Sarah had also learned the principle of delayed gratification. That is, she did not have to give in to every impulsive desire.

Compulsive Spending

My friend Maria rewards herself for sticking to a budget by putting quarters in a huge piggybank, one quarter for every day she doesn't overspend. She makes a plan for something she would like to have, something not necessary, just one of those extravagant "wants." When the bank is full she gets all dressed up and spends half a day finding just the right thing. After that, whenever she uses her new possession she is again rewarded for not overspending. This has become a continuous method of reinforcement that strengthens her commitment. A quarter a day requires planning, and sometimes sacrifice, which are valuable skills for daily living.

Gambling

The reward Greg wanted more than any other was to have his debts completely paid off so that the family could plan a special vacation. His first step was to sit down with the calculator and figure out how much money he needed to earn in order to pay the debts off in one year. The amount he needed each month was considerably more than his present salary could accommodate. The family had a conference and agreed that they could handle having Dad work two jobs for the next year. It meant that they all had to be responsible for themselves and for each other in more ways than ever before, but they wanted the reward as much as Greg did. Greg didn't want his wife to work more in order to help with his debt. He felt strongly that he needed to be the one to make that effort and he wanted her at home to keep things together while he was absent. Greg was able to get an extra job four nights a week, and another on Saturdays, which more than doubled his income. It was a long, hard year, but the reward was worth it.

Compulsive Stealing

Melissa was a lonely girl. Former friends avoided her, teachers viewed her with suspicion, and her own family always looked at Melissa when something was missing. She filled her lonely hours by writing. She filled many notebooks with ideas, events, and then stories. Melissa wanted a computer. She visited a computer center and talked to the manager about a job. She told him she would like to clean their building after school and on Saturdays. She said, "When you give me a paycheck, I will give it right back to you to apply toward a computer." The manager thought this a rather unusual job application, but agreed to try it for two pay periods. He thought she might give up when she realized that she was doing hard work without anything immediate to show for it. What the manager didn't know was that Melissa had contracted with herself that she would stick with this as long as she didn't steal. If she slipped up, she would have to start all over, thereby forfeiting the money she had thus far earned. Melissa did get the computer, and she also received another reward—new friends who had no reason to distrust her.

Lying

From childhood Barbara had yearned for a grand piano. Not a big grand, just a small one that would fit into the corner of her living room. Many times she had looked at pianos. Some were of about the same worth as her house. Others cost about the amount of half a year's wages. Perhaps a used one, she thought. After extensive searching, she realized that she could probably get an older piano that she liked for half the cost of the lower-priced new ones. Barbara made a plan. At the end of each week, if she had told no lies, she would put a certain amount of money in a savings account. In this way she would be able to get a piano in about nine months. Whenever there was a lie gathering on the tip of her tongue, she thought of the piano. Once she had the piano, the pleasure of playing it served to reinforce her habit control.

Fire-Setting

Bart was a football fan. He was particularly fond of the Denver Broncos. To attend a Bronco game in Denver meant a long trip and an overnight stay, plus the cost of a ticket. When the schedule came out in the fall, Bart selected a game toward the end of the season and began to plan how to achieve this reward. A Bronco game, he thought, is as exciting as a fire, and much safer. First he had to buy the ticket, which he then gave to his probation counselor to hold. "If I do OK by the time this game rolls around," he said, "you give me the ticket. If I mess up, you go to the game." Next, Bart had to save money for the trip. He did this through a payroll savings deduction. Every time Bart watched a game on TV he was encouraged to practice his habit control skills. The day finally came. The counselor handed over the ticket with a big grin and a handshake, and Bart was off. While at the game, he purchased a small Bronco pendant, which he attached to the sun visor in his car. It was a daily reminder of his achievement.

Hair-Pulling

When Catherine's bald spots were pretty well filled in and the hair about an inch long, she decided it was time to set up a maintenance reward. Catherine liked sophisticated clothes—clothes that were beyond her means. She particularly wanted a tailored black suit she had seen in a shop window. One lapel was inset with a geometric red and white pattern. The skirt fit snugly over the hips with tiny rows of tucks, flaring out to mid-calf in a swirl of fine cloth. The suit was $280. Catherine put it on a six-month layaway, paying for it in weekly installments. By the time she picked up the suit, her hair had grown and thickened so that she could have a chic style appropriate for the new suit. Catherine used this reward system on a regular basis as insurance against setbacks.

Explosive Temper

As a boy, Cal had greatly enjoyed a toboggan the neighbors had. They would often invite him along when they headed for the snowy hills. He knew his children would like one, and it would be something different they could do as a family. He decided this was the best reward he could give himself. He solicited help from the family in monitoring his behavior. They agreed that occasional cross words might be acceptable, but name calling, abusive language, hitting, throwing, or shaking were out of bounds. At the end of each peaceful day, he put a dollar in the "toboggan can." Sometimes it was hard to be sure he had a dollar left over at the end of the day, but he never failed to do it. It was a proud day for the whole family the day they went to buy the toboggan. Even in the summer, when it hung idle on the garage wall, Cal saw it every day and was reminded of how he had changed.

Misuse of Prescription Drugs

Larry's activities were still somewhat restricted by his back injury, but he no longer used drugs for pain. He had that under control with exercise, diet, and self-hypnosis. He wanted a reward that would make him a part of the family. He couldn't play ball or other active games, but he loved to watch them. One day, as he was watching his oldest son in soccer practice, he said to his wife, "Man, I wish I had a movie of that." They looked at each other and laughed. "There's your reward," she said. Larry decided he would have to find a way to get a video recorder.

He had recently started an at-home business, repairing small appliances, and he had an idea that he could trade services for goods. As he went around to the camera shops examining and pricing equipment, he would talk to the managers about his own work. Finally, in one small shop where he felt on friendly terms with the owner, he was able to express his desire. The man was interested in his proposal. Having seven children and not enough money, there were always broken toasters, irons, and clocks in his home. He and Larry came to an agreement that Larry would do a specified number of repairs in exchange for the equipment of his choice at half price. The interesting outcome was that Larry became so interested in photographic equipment that he took a training course and was eventually hired as a salesman and technical assistant at one of the large shops. This job, in addition to making videos for his family, is an ongoing reward.

Irresponsible Sex

Polly loved turquoise jewelry. Whenever she passed a jewelry store she stopped to see what they had. She used her vacation days to haunt shops specializing in Indian jewelry, but rarely could afford to buy. She decided that her reward for sexually responsible behavior would be a ring she had been admiring for some time. As she began to save for this ring by working overtime, she would visit the ring, always fearful that someone else would buy it. The fact that she could not put it on layaway added to her determination in earning enough money. The day came when she was able to walk out of the store with the ring on her finger, walking with a lighter step, savoring the significance of the reward. The ring, in fact, was endlessly rewarding—a symbol of change.

Overuse of TV and Video Games

Robert knew his reward had to be something that would keep him actively engaged in a project of some sort. He thought about new camping gear, but that seemed like more of an obligation than a reward. Then when he went to back-to-school night, he noticed a magazine in the woodworking shop that was full of home workshop projects. As he leafed through the magazine, his eye fell upon a picture of a Victorian dollhouse. He noted that a kit was available at a reasonable price, so he jotted down the address. That night he lay awake for a while thinking of the fun of putting together something so intricate and pleasing. He thought about the little furniture and the tiny windowpanes. His mind lingered on the shiny wood squares in the parquet flooring. Yes, he thought, that would be a fine reward. The next day he sent for the kit. Two weeks after he started work on the dollhouse his wife gave birth to a baby girl. Then his excitement was increased by the thought of his little daughter someday enjoying this dollhouse. A double reward, he thought, and a perfect symbol of my success in habit control. His sons became interested in the project, too, and soon the three of them were in the workshop working on projects of their own. There was little time or desire for TV and video games.

Teeth-Grinding

As a cellist, Sam had a list of possible rewards. There were so many interesting works for cello that he had never played and innumerable cello accessories he knew he would enjoy. Sifting through these ideas he found himself returning again and again to the idea of a special kind of cello case, a hard case with two little wheels to make transport easier, and a humidifier inside to protect the instrument. His old case had taken quite a beating through the years and he yearned for a new one. The cost of a new one was high, and Sam knew he would have to give up something in order to obtain it.

For many years Sam had used caffeine-laden cola drinks to keep him going while practicing, driving, performing, and even for no reason at all, except that he was addicted to caffeine. He figured out how much money he would save by never buying these drinks and discovered that he could buy the cello case in about six months. The bonus in this plan was that he knew caffeine was not good for him, and it would be good to be free of that addiction. At first it was hard, but he began drinking water instead. After about three weeks he found that it was a better thirst quencher and he no longer needed the caffeine. When he did get the long-awaited cello case, he decided not to go back to caffeine drinks. The cello case constantly reminded him that he now had control in two areas.

Smoking

Ida had always wanted to go to a fitness farm, and now that she was no longer smoking she thought she would be able to do the activities without respiratory distress. She researched the options and found a program in a medium price range that had most of the features she was looking for. The next step was to arrange for a three-week vacation, which was all her vacation time for the year. It was a reward worth waiting for. Once there, she learned a variety of ways to improve cardiovascular function that she could continue on her own for very little money. She also received instruction in low-fat food preparation so that she could enjoy tantalizing meals without jeopardizing her health. It became a challenge for her to prepare gourmet meals that were high in fiber and low in fat and sugar. The reward she gave herself improved the quality of her life, and was beneficial for her family as well.

Finding Your Own Rewards

As you can see, the proper reward must involve planning, preparation, and sacrifice. Before we discuss it further, however, you need to brainstorm a list of things that would be really special to you—things that would require some effort and sacrifice to get. Go back to your Life Systems worksheets and reexamine your goals. Is there anything about these goals that would serve as tangible rewards? Perhaps some equipment you need in order to reach your goal? One of Ida's goals was to achieve cardiovascular fitness. When she chose to take her vacation at a fitness farm she was furthering her progress toward that goal. Review your records and use the space below to brainstorm your rewards. Write down everything that pops into your head, even if it seems fantastic or silly. The cardinal rule of brainstorming is that you don't judge any idea as to its merit or feasibility. Just write everything down.

Now that you have a number of ideas, you need to evaluate them to determine how easy or difficult it would be to get them. At the end of the chapter you'll find the Reward Rating Worksheet. Answer the questions on the worksheet for each reward you brainstormed. Eliminate the easy ones right away. Work on rewards that at first seem unobtainable. After you have rated each reward, you will be able to judge what the probability is that you will actually be able to achieve this reward. Then choose the best one for you.

We have talked about intrinsic, or internal, reinforcers (cues), as well as external reinforcers. Both are necessary. The value of the tangible reward is more than simply that of a cue. While you are striving to obtain your reward, you are developing some new skills and habits that are more useful to you than the old habit.

Picture a garden full of lovely flowers. It is a well cared for garden, but in one place there is an ugly weed, with very strong roots, which seems impossible to get rid of. Every time you pull up the weed, it grows back. If you are a wise gardener, you will not only pull up the weed, but spend time working with the earth in that spot, preparing it for something more fitting for your lovely garden. Then you plant some plants that are not only beautiful, but very hardy, and will fill up the space, crowding out the roots of the weed. That is exactly what you are doing now. As you eliminate your habit, you replace it with new habits that crowd out the old.

Tina's Reward

Tina had a habit of exploding in angry temper over little things. Sometimes she even hurt other people when she was out of control. Tina did all the things you have been learning about in this book—preparing the soil for new plants. Then she was ready to choose a reward.

Using the Reward Worksheet, she considered several possible goals—new car, better clothes, a wide-angle lens for her camera. She also listed a trip to Italy, although at the time it seemed unobtainable. As she filled out the chart, the goal that stood out as most desirable was the trip to Italy, the land her grandparents had come from. She did a lot of research and determined that the trip would cost $3500. Tina was an art teacher, so the opportunity to see great works of art was enticing.

School teachers don't make much money, so getting $3500 was quite a challenge. After more research, in the community this time, Tina learned that there was no after-school art program. She decided to run a two-hour art class for elementary school children. Seeing children in groups meant that she didn't have to charge any more than the parents would pay otherwise for after-school care. It also meant that some children who went home to empty houses would be usefully and pleasantly occupied.

The response was greater than she expected, and she found that it would take only nine months to earn the money she needed for the trip. This meant that she was able to plan on going to Italy as soon as school was out in June, provided she didn't lose her temper once during the nine-month period.

As the school year wore on, she found herself looking forward to the children coming to class. She spent more time looking at art supply catalogs and dreaming about new ways to teach rt to children. At first if someone spilled paint she would feel her anger welling up, but as time went on, she discovered she really didn't have that feeling anymore. Irritation and frustration, at times, but not angry temper. The children had taught her patience.

Tina's husband, from whom she had been separated because of her outbursts, was at first puzzled by the change. Was it an act? Was she just playing nice in order to get him back? Eventually, he began to believe the change was real. Tina had lost her angry temper. By teaching the children to express their own feelings in art, she had learned a new skill for herself. As it turned out, Tina had no angry outbursts from October to July, and she went, with her husband, to Italy in August. She continued her children's art classes that fall. She now has flowers in her garden.

Success Memories

I recently had a commonplace experience that was positive and made me feel great. My husband planted a lot of tomato plants, and since he is a good gardener, these plants inundated us with hundreds of luscious red beauties. We gave them away and ate them three times a day. One morning it became clear that canning them was imperative. I didn't really want to because it is a chore to get out the equipment and endure the mess and the heat. But it had to be done, so I did it.

As each bottle was filled and the aroma from the steamer began to seep through the house, I began to feel better. It was fun. The really great feeling, however, came when the bottles were out of the canner, lined up on the counter in shimmering crimson glory. Not only had I overcome my resistance to a necessary task, I had activated a pioneer instinct to be prepared for the unknown trials of the winter. I had won an age-old victory.

I enjoyed that feeling for several days before I put the bottles into a dark cupboard. In winter, when I make soup, I will have another opportunity to experience that rush of satisfaction.

You already have the victory of overcoming your habit. Now you need a repertoire of positive feelings to reinforce this victory. This is the time to develop *success memories* as positive reinforcers. Go back over your Life Systems worksheets. How many liabilities do you see that have already been converted into assets? You can probably find other successes in your past.

Use the following questions as triggers for a memory search. Get a pen and pad of paper and write down every positive experience you can remember, as far back as you can. Allow yourself the luxury of lingering over these memories, recapturing the feelings you had at the time. Some negative experiences are going to want to pop up as well, but this is not the time to dwell on them. Just tell them to sit on a shelf until later. There is a way of dealing with these negative memories, but you're not ready for that, yet.

What can you remember from ages 3 to 6, or even before?

Now try ages 6 to 12. You probably remember more from those years.

Don't overlook the incredible teen years, with all their confusion, extreme highs and lows, and the way you changed between 13 and 19. Focus on positive experiences.

You probably thought you were an adult at age 20. I know I did. List your positive memories from age 20 to the present. Set the negatives aside for future treatment.

Now go back over this list. Your list may be short or long. It doesn't matter. Even if you only had one positive memory, it will be enough. From your list select one or a few of the most positive, pleasurable experiences to use for reinforcement. You can learn to reexperience these memories, intensify them, and thus renew good feelings about yourself. You need to be able to nail down or anchor these feelings. In the unlikely event that you could not think of even one pleasant experience, don't give up. You can create one. Just keep reading.

Anchoring

The term *anchoring* in this context comes from a communication model called *neuro-linguistic programming*, or *NLP* for short. Psychologists Richard Bandler and John Grinder created techniques for therapeutic communication that can help you to do better what you already do, learn new skills easily, and make pervasive changes in how you live. Actually, this is just what you have already begun to do. What you are going to do now is apply one specific technique—anchoring—to reinforce all that is good and powerful within you.

The following exercise should be done when you have a little time to yourself. You may want to record the steps, as you have done with other exercises, so that you don't need to worry about having to read them.

> Make yourself comfortable in a chair or on your bed. Rest your
> hands and arms easily upon the arms of the chair, beside you on
> the bed, or across your abdomen. Your hands should not touch.
> Close your eyes and do the systematic relaxation you have already
> learned to do.
>
> Let your mind drift back through the months or years to one of
> the positive memories you selected earlier...When you get there...
> take a deep breath...and let every sensation of that other time wrap
> around you...Be aware of the sights...the sounds...the tastes...the
> smells...and the feelings...See who was there...See yourself...Hear
> what was said...and feel again the confidence and self-acceptance
> you felt then.

Let yourself get deeply...deeply...into...that...good...feeling... At the moment you feel these good feelings intensely...touch your left wrist with your right hand...Touch it firmly...in a specific spot that you will always remember...Anchor this wonderful...positive...feeling...with that firm touch on your wrist...you will be using this same anchor in this same place again later on...Repeat this process with other memories you have selected...It may be that a new...positive memory will spring up...You can anchor that, too, in the same way, by touching your left wrist in the special spot.

Tina's Anchor

Tina's trip to Italy was everything she ever hoped it would be. She said she felt more peace and self-acceptance on that trip with her husband than she had ever before experienced. When she got home she went through the experience, reliving the good feelings and anchoring them with a touch on her wrist. Now when she needs that kind of pick-me-up all she has to do is touch her wrist in that place and the good feelings surge back. Recently she had an opportunity to discover just how powerful this anchor is.

Tina and her husband, Martin, had been living together ever since the Italy trip. Things had been going well until a problem arose about all the paraphernalia Tina needed for her young artists program. There were paints and large pads of paper on top of the clothes dryer. Easels and boxes were stacked in closets. Piles of catalogs multiplied on the coffee table. Martin had suggested several times that they needed to find other places for these things, but somehow Tina had not made time to do anything about it.

One day she came home and found all these materials stuffed into boxes and piled in the garage. Hot sparks went off in Tina's brain. She stormed through the utility room, shaking with rage. Through the door she saw Martin working at the kitchen counter, chopping vegetables. She had a flash of herself yelling at him, throwing something at him. Suddenly she stopped, raised her hand, and touched the spot on her left wrist.

Calm swept away the rage. Her breathing returned to normal. "I'm not a person who does that sort of thing," she said to herself, "There isn't anything worth getting that mad about." The memory of that wonderful time in Italy filled her mind with happy pictures. Tina walked into the kitchen. "Making something good, Sweetie?" she asked. Later they were able to negotiate a more acceptable method of storing Tina's materials.

Memory Restructuring

Now you get to do something about those negative memories that wanted to intrude when you were searching for pleasant things to remember. Let your mind pull up one of those now, and write it down just the way you remember it.

Now rewrite this memory, changing it to the way you would have liked things to happen. In other words, you will write a new script for painful events of the past and anchor the new good memory in place of the old.

Julia's Memory

Julia remembered her first day at kindergarten as being terrifying because her mother took her there unprepared and left without a word. She had a storehouse of feelings of anger and diminished self-worth because she felt she'd made a fool of herself by screaming so loudly that people across the street came over to see what was going on. She rewrote her experience this way:

> Mother and I walked to school hand in hand. I had on a new red and blue dress. I was scared, but mother talked to me about when she first went to school and that helped. When we got there, some children were already there, and I noticed that their mothers were sitting in the back of the room. My mother took me right up to the front and introduced me to Miss Armstrong. Miss Armstrong knelt down and told me she was glad I was there and that if I'd like to sit down, she was going to read a story. Mother patted my shoulder and said she would stay until recess if I wanted her to. I did want that.
>
> Miss Armstrong began reading the story, and I kept looking back to see if Mother was still there. Whenever I looked at her, she would smile and wink in that special way she had. When recess time came, I had to stand in line, but mother just kept smiling and winking. When we got outside, I noticed other mothers leaving, and I was frightened.
>
> I ran over to her, and she put her arms around me and told me that she was just going home to bake cookies for me to have after school. She said she would be back to get me when I got out. I was still a little scared, but the thought of her baking cookies helped me to feel better. After that, I got interested in all the things Miss Armstrong was having us do, and I kind of forgot that I was there alone.

Julia said that as she wrote the new scenario, it became real, and she experienced the feeling of being loved and cared for, just as if it had really happened. She was able to visualize and experience this memory easily whenever she needed it after she had learned to anchor the pleasant feelings.

She had a habit of compulsive spending, and found it interesting that the feelings of tension she had before a buying spree were closely tied to the same kind of fear she had experienced when going to school that first day. After anchoring the restructured memory she was able to replace this fear and tension by touching her wrist and again experiencing that feeling of being loved and cared for. In this way she effectively averted the impulse to spend.

Although rewriting does not change history, it changes the happening in fantasy, and the better feelings are real. In fact, these better feelings are necessary to your emotional well-being. When you have good feelings about your past, you have the biochemical reaction that enhances self-esteem. The other thing rewriting does is show you that there is more than one way to handle a situation. At age 5, you didn't have the skills to exercise options. As an adult, you have acquired techniques for handling life's stresses in a variety of ways. Rewriting is a rehearsal for future successful times.

Positive Feedback

Determine now, from this moment on, to give yourself only positive feedback. No matter what happens during the course of a day, no matter how many mistakes you made or foolish things you said, you did something right. For one thing, you did the best you could for that day, and when you recognize that, you will realize that there are other things you did that you can congratulate yourself about.

Arnie

I know a wonderful young man named Arnie. Arnie grew up in a Kentucky holler. His family had every kind of problem you could imagine, and then some. If you knew all the details of incest, violence, and substance abuse that went on in his home, you would think Arnie didn't have a chance. He was born with Fetal Alcohol Syndrome because his mother was an alcoholic. That means that his brain was damaged in certain ways, and that he has had a lifetime struggle with a craving for alcohol. He also became a drug addict.

At one point, when he was about 17, Arnie felt so worthless, so totally depressed, with no self-regard at all, that he decided to die. He bought a lot of cheap liquor and went into an alley to drink himself to death. He should have died, but he didn't. A policeman found him there in a coma and took him to a hospital. He had been in hospitals before, but this time, when he woke up and found himself alive, he decided to do something about living. Over a long period of time, as he reasoned things out, he began to recognize that he was not a weakling as he had always thought. He was strong. He had survived childhood and had made decisions to not do a lot of the things he saw happening in his home. Even though given to violent outbursts of temper, he saw that he was basically a kind person. He learned to look at each day, and accept his goodness as well as his mistakes. He can now say after becoming angry, "Man, I almost hit that dude, but I didn't, and that's good." He got married recently, and now has a baby daughter. He is a good dad. He knows what his personal values are and that he is basically a good person with problems. He doesn't put himself down.

A Daily Appraisal

Every person has goodness in them. You must be a pretty strong person yourself or you would not have worked your way through this book. Arnie found a process that worked for him. You might like to try it.

Every evening, review your day and identify three things. Write down and think about

- Some things you did or said that pleased you

- Some way you could do other things differently next time

- Events over which you had no control and cannot change

Treasure what you discovered in the first task. Take time to enjoy the good feelings that go with good performance. Next, develop a plan for the second task. You may want to write out a scenario, changing the sequence of events and interactions in a way that will make you feel better. Most importantly, let go entirely of everything in the last item. It's a waste of time to worry about things you can't change.

Feeling good about yourself has to include this kind of realistic appraisal. In everyday life, everyone does some things well, makes some mistakes, and has experiences that are beyond his or her control and cannot be changed. After you have made this evaluation, say to yourself, "I did the best I could with what I knew today."

As Arnie made his end-of-the-day review, he found that as he recognized himself for having done and said some good things, he began to improve in that area. More and more he was pleased with his performance during the day. He was less inclined to become angry with people. He noticed that he was listening to others and weighing his thoughts before speaking them.

In looking at the second item on the review list, Arnie always had some interaction he knew he could have handled better. Most of us do. At first there were many that caused him to worry and berate himself. Gradually, as the good experiences increased, Arnie had fewer of the unsatisfactory encounters. He became quite skilled at what he called, "making up them little plays," and that improved his behavior also.

Probably the hardest thing for Arnie was learning to let go of things he couldn't change. He needed a visual, concrete procedure for doing this, so we covered a tissue box with wallpaper and labeled it "The Incinerator." At the end of the day he would write on a slip of paper a word or two symbolic of the situation over which he had no control.

Sometimes it was "neighbor" or "dog," and a couple of times it was "cops." As he placed the paper in The Incinerator, he said out loud, "I can't do anything about this, so burn."

This kind of daily "housecleaning" allows you to accept the fact that your life is like anyone else's, part good, part not so good, and part lousy things that you can't do anything about. In other words, you are average, and it's OK to be average. Average people excel at some things and don't do so well at others. In most areas, average people manage pretty well, with minor ups and downs.

It's OK to Be Average

Average people have faults and make mistakes. They do some things better than other things. You actually excelled at doing your habit. You were very good at it. Now you are very good at overcoming it.

Psychiatrist Abraham Lowe described three main philosophies that are current among human beings: realism, intellectualism, and romanticism. Intellectualists believe they have superior ability to reason. Romanticists focus on their capacity for vigorous feelings, interesting sensations, and strong impulses. These two groups hate to be thought of as average.

Remember your teen years? Most teens want to be exceptional. I remember my daughter spelling her name with an ! at the end. One day she expressed some feelings to me and I said, "That sounds normal."

"I don't want to be normal," she exploded, "I'm different." She has since given up intellectualism and is happier as a realist.

The realist sees people as being average—not perfect, not exceptional, but worthy people with average efficiency. Their averageness may be of good, plain, or poor quality, but essentially they are average in all areas of existence. And so is the realist himself. He is average in thought, feeling, and action. He does not expect himself or others to be exceptional in every area.

Most people believe in both exceptionalness and averageness. The truly average person balances his dreams of exceptional performance with the reality of his own limitations. If the dreams are recognized for what they are, they can be useful in inspiring you to be creative and productive. When unrealistic dreams guide your behavior, you are apt to get into trouble, as you well know.

Take a 5x8 card, and in large letters print this statement:

It Is OK To Be Average

Lowe said that average life for the most part consists of trivialities. Daily routines of meals, working, attending to children or aging parents, washing, cleaning, putting gas in the car. These are all tasks that become tedious, even boring at times. In the average life there are occasional exceptional events, such as weddings, the birth of a baby, a promotion, or some outstanding performance. The home or office routine may not give much stimulation if it is done just for it's own sake. However, these mundane tasks become more satisfying if done with an eye to its usefulness and their meaning in terms of maintaining a family or contributing to society. They take on importance, dignity, and comforting feelings of fulfilling responsibility.

Lower Your Expectations

Most often people with impulse control problems have been looking for the high of exceptionality and operate under the driving urge of romanticism. These feelings are not everyday occurrences in the average life. Therefore, the irritability produced by not having these feelings on a daily basis produces the buildup of tension preceding the acting out of a habit. However, other people are often not understanding of acting-out behavior.

In order to gain and keep the trust of the important people in your life, it is necessary to live an even, stable existence, where the highs are moderate and realistic. You will need to find pleasure in the trivia of average life. This means, also, that you will become accepting of the averageness in others and stop looking for them to be exceptional all the time. When you lower your expectations of others, you will not be disappointed.

A teacher of young violin students will have success if he enters every lesson with an open mind, not having preset ideas about what he is going to make the child do. If he is not expecting exceptional performance, he can honestly praise every attempt to play well, and can offer solutions for problems in playing. But if he expects the child to play every note in tune in the first ten minutes of the lesson, it is likely the child will never realize this expectation. The teacher will be disappointed, the child will feel defeated, and progress will become slow and painful.

It is no different with the people in your life, whether family members, friends, employers, or others. Getting rid of expectations, which generally are exceptional in one direction or another (good or bad), will free your mind so that you can learn to know the other person. Then you won't have the disappointment and annoyance that comes when someone does not meet your exceptional expectation. Even if your expectation was for the person to be exceptionally bad, you will still have a great deal of anger, which only fuels your tension.

Record the Details

One way to help yourself learn to live an average life is to keep a day planner, or a small notebook, that you carry around with you. Get one in your favorite color. This will be a place to record the daily trivia of your life. Each day make a list of things you need to do. At the end of the day go back over the list and check off the things you did. If the undone tasks are things you really want to do, forward them to the next day's list. You may find, however, that some of them are not as important as you thought and can be eliminated. Ask yourself why you did the things you did and why you want to do other things on tomorrow's list. What was the purpose? What would be different about your life if you did not do some of those things? How are others affected? Most importantly, at the bottom of the page, each day write at least one thing for which you are grateful in your average day.

Negative Reinforcers

So far we have talked about positive reinforcers. There is a place in your treatment for negative reinforcers, too. A negative reinforcer can be a look, a word, a gesture, or it can be a behavioral contract.

Making a Contract

Dan, who was a fire-setter, made an agreement with his friend Tom that he would give Tom a check for $500 made out to the campaign fund of a politician he detested. His friend agreed to hold the check for three months. If, during that time, Dan didn't start any fires, the check would be torn up. If even one fire was set, the check would be mailed. Several times during the three months Dan wanted to set a fire, but the thought of having that money used to reelect "that Bozo" was so abhorrent that he could not set the fire.

On a sheet of paper, write out some ideas you can think of for contracts. Write several, so that you can choose the one that will work best. Use the following questions as a guideline:

- What kind of contract could you make?

- With whom?

- How much money (or other cost)?

- For what period of time?

This technique is actually both positive and negative. You are getting positive support from a friend as well as the negative impact of what will happen if you do the behavior. Choose a friend you can trust—someone you know will carry out his or her part of the agreement, someone who really will mail the check.

Risking Exposure

Another technique that works well for some people is to again enlist the help of a trustworthy friend, and with that person write out an announcement for the local newspaper.

Karen had been shoplifting and stealing small trinkets from friends for about three years. She asked her friend Ann to assist her. This is what they came up with:

> This is to announce that Karen Blank took three bracelets and a pair
> of stockings from Grant's department store today. Anyone who
> wants to watch her return them may do so Friday morning at 10:00
> a.m. at the manager's office. Karen lives at 990 Trilby Court.

Karen and Ann had talked a great deal about the seriousness of her problem and the embarrassment it caused her family. Ann understood that it was going to take an extreme measure to eradicate this habit. Karen knew she could trust Ann to put the announcement in the paper.

Karen agreed to report to Ann each evening. Would Karen lie to Ann? No, because Karen desperately wanted to overcome her habit. This is truly a drastic measure, but it effectively stopped Karen's habit. Karen said that whenever she went into a store, or was tempted by a trinket in a friend's house, she was filled with dread at the thought of that notice appearing in the paper. She pictured her parents' faces when they read it. She shuddered at the thought of people watching her go to the manager's office with the stolen articles. Her impulse to steal disappeared entirely after three months. The agreement with Ann remained in effect for one year.

In the following space write out your notice, and then write a description of what it will be like for you if it appears in the paper.

Newspaper Notice:

How will I feel?

How will it affect others?

These negative reinforcers are desperate measures. All other methods should be used first and practiced well. Hopefully, you will never need these drastic techniques. You need to be aware of the risks because unless the contract is firmly adhered to by both parties this technique will not work. Ask yourself these questions to assess risks in negative reinforcement:

- What are the risks to other people?

- How will it affect my relationship with the contracting partner?

- How will it affect my self-esteem if I fail?

- How will it affect my standing in the community?

- Are there other risks? What are they?

If you understand the risks and still feel this technique is necessary, then you can probably use negative reinforcement and succeed.

Let's move on now to making positive lifestyle changes that will be totally positive and rewarding in many ways over your lifetime.

Diet

Your brain is not going to work very well if what is carried to it by the bloodstream is junk. Similarly, the brain cannot receive nutrition if the arteries are clogged and narrowed from too much fat and cholesterol and from smoke.

Remember how Wonder Bread used to advertise " 12 building blocks for healthy bodies?" While the nutritional value of bleached white flour is questionable, it is true that certain things are required by cells to maintain a state of mental and physical health. Food is the major source of the biochemicals used by the body for energy, growth, and tissue repair. Food alone can either prevent disease or create illness.

Your limbic system has a powerful effect on the body's biochemistry and consequent behavior. Messages that are received and transmitted through the limbic system are carried in the blood, and affect mental processes as well as metabolic ones. Picture your brain and limbic system sitting there waiting for the food (after it has been converted to biochemicals) to come along. If everything necessary is not there, the system cannot function well. If the food that comes along contains toxins, such as something to which the body is allergic, then the body reacts. No matter how mild the reaction is, it will in some way result in less efficient brain power. If you are going to be well—physically, emotionally, intellectually, and spiritually—you must respect the needs of your wonderful machine.

By and large, people hate diets. Hopefully, however, your commitment to emotional and physical health will allow you to consider eating in a new way. The healthiest food choices include whole grains, vegetables (green, yellow, and starchy), fruits, and legumes. These foods are low-fat and low-cholesterol and have high nutritional content as well as high fiber. Low-fat dairy products are preferable to those with a higher fat content and fish is the healthiest meat choice. Chicken and turkey, without the skin, are next best. Lean red meat is OK in limited amounts. Fast food—burgers, fries, fried chicken and fish—is high in fat and low in fiber. Also it lacks many nutritional elements.

Horton Hodsen, a biochemist who is at the forefront in nutritional research, suggests that you arrange to enjoy a wide variety of small, regular meals in a friendly atmosphere. He says, "Your digestive organs function best when (1) they are not overloaded, (2) your system is prepared for a meal, and (3) you are relaxed. Take time to chew food well before swallowing; this is an important initiator of digestive processes." He also suggests eating different foods every day to prevent developing food allergies or having a nutritional imbalance. A wide variety of foods is most balanced.

Fresh fruits and vegetables are recommended over cooked or processed foods. If you are used to eating pre-prepared fruits and vegetables (canned, dried, frozen) start increasing the proportion of raw foods in your diet. When you cook vegetables, steam them lightly or stir quickly in a wok or skillet to leave them crisp inside. Heat destroys nutrients. The limp things you are often served in restaurants have very little to offer, nutritionally or in taste.

Raw nuts and seeds are fine, if not used to excess. Sprouted grains, beans, potatoes, whole grains (wheat, rice, barley, oats), and breads made from fresh whole grain or unbleached white flour should become an important part of your diet. Avoid candy, cakes, or other treats that contain processed sugars; and butter, margarine, and other added fats and high-fat foods. Artificial flavors, food colorings and preservatives should also be avoided, as should all but small quantities of salt.

Supplements

There is a great deal of controversy about the use of nutritional supplements. Some say they are "absolutely unnecessary;" while others claim that toxicity can occur from imbalances of these supplements. Still others suggest that you can't get complete nutrition without supplements. My feeling is that, given the lifestyle most Americans lead, most people need nutritional assistance in supplement form.

The trouble is that this is a very complicated area. Unless you have had nutritionally oriented biochemical training it is hard to figure out what you really need. There is a possibility of unbalancing your own chemistry or overdoing one vitamin to the point of toxicity. The chemical balance in the body is delicate. Proper supplementation requires very small amounts of a variety of vitamins and minerals in a balance that is right for you. It is better to consult someone who can assess your individual needs and recommend supplementation that will provide optimum health. One resource for this is Nutribionics, Box 959, Washington, Utah, 847380, 800-852-8280. You may also wish to consult books in the Further Reading section at the end of this chapter for more information. Above all, concentrate on having the best, most wholesome and balanced meals you can.

After you get started on a better diet, you will find your tastes changing, and you will become more aware of what your body needs. Our bodies do know, and if we listen, they will tell us what we need. Cooking and eating can become a pleasant, restorative interlude in your day, rather than a "hurry up, grab a bite" affair. Susan Duquette, editor of the *Sunburst Farms Family Cookbook*, talks about the honor of cooking. She says that in the quiet of your kitchen you accept this honor and see yourself as the exchange between food and your family. She says, "What you give of yourself, to the food, is what others will receive. It is so important to prepare this food with care in order to sustain the life-force which is the nutrition in all foods."

Does it seem we have come far afield from habit control? Remember that you are a system, made up of systems, and that you exist in a series of larger systems. Like the bus, you need the right fuel in order to do your job. Many times I have watched clients improve in their ability to control habits when they began to pay attention to what their bodies need in terms of exercise and diet. Your improved health and feelings of strength and well-being are the most powerful internal reinforcers there are.

Exercise

You have been doing mental exercises to produce internal reinforcers. Now you need to do something more active. There is ample evidence to show that aerobic exercise makes profound and positive changes in a person's biochemistry.

Aerobic exercise means activity that improves *cardiovascular endurance*—the sustained ability of the heart and lungs and blood to take oxygen from the air and deliver it throughout the body.

Every cell in the body requires oxygen. If your heart is strong and your lungs elastic, your cardiovascular system will be able to deliver oxygen efficiently to every cell. That includes, of course, cells in the brain and nervous system. If the blood is delivering oxygen, it is also delivering nutrients that are needed for the brain to function at optimum levels. Aerobic exercise must be sustained for at least 20 minutes in order for you to achieve significant benefits. Golf won't do it—the exercise there is start and stop, it doesn't sustaining movement for a long enough period of time.

The best aerobic exercises are walking, cycling, swimming, cross-country (not downhill) skiing, running, rowing, aerobic dance, and jumping rope. The first three, walking, cycling, and swimming are the safest for most people. Walking has a special advantage, in that it is a low-impact, weight-bearing exercise that helps to increase bone density.

Most fitness experts agree that 20 minutes of aerobic exercise three times a week is sufficient for increasing cardiovascular fitness. Exercise of any kind should be preceded by a five-minute warm-up. It is also a good idea to check with your doctor if you have any health problems. If when exercising you become exhausted or feel ill, definitely stop until you see your doctor.

Walking

Because there are so many books written about exercise, I will confine the rest of this discussion to walking, which is generally safe for just about anyone. You don't need a lot of equipment—just good shoes. It's hard to damage yourself unless you decide to walk five plus miles the first day, or you take a bad fall. You also should not walk alone in deserted places. One of the nice things about walking is that you can do it anywhere, at any time you choose. You can also walk and visit with a friend at the same time, which is nice.

Nearly every shoe store sells shoes suitable for walking, and they need not be expensive. I prefer an athletic shoe that cushions my foot and provides support through the instep and arch. Try on a lot of shoes, and walk around the store several times. Be sure to try them on with the kind of socks you plan to wear when walking. Cotton ones are better than synthetic.

Before beginning your walk you need to determine your resting heart rate. After sitting for five or ten minutes, count your heart rate by feeling the pulse on the inside of the wrist at the base of the thumb, or in the carotide artery in the neck, just below the angle of the jaw. Make a note of that number. If you count for only ten seconds, multiply by 6.

Begin your walk with about five minutes of strolling, gradually increasing your tempo to a comfortable pace. The goal is to achieve a pace that increases your heart rate. Most people can exercise safely when their heart rate increases to between 70 and 85 percent of their maximum heart rate. Since maximum heart rate decreases with age, you need to use the following formula to determine your target heart rate:

1. Subtract your age from 220. This will give you your theoretical maximum heart rate in beats per minute.

2. Multiply that figure by .70 and also by .85.

The range between those two numbers is your training heart rate. The low end represents 70 percent of your maximum heart rate and the upper end 85 percent. Exercising so that your heart rate is between those two numbers will condition your heart.

About five minutes into your walk, stop and check your heart rate the same way you checked your resting heart rate. Do it as soon as you stop walking, because it begins to fall right away. If you are below the target rate, you can slowly increase the tempo of your walk, checking your heart rate again in five minutes. After a while you will know how fast you need to walk to maintain your training rate, and you will no longer need to check your pulse.

If you feel any discomfort in your chest, or you are too out of breath to talk, slow down and forget the target rate. Go home and make an appointment for a checkup. Do the same if after the walk you are inordinately tired and sleepy. Do not do anymore walking until you have discussed it with your doctor.

It's also important to warm up and cool down. Some people use stretching exercises for this. I use cat stretches, which take only a couple of minutes. Then I just walk slowly, gradually increasing speed, slowing down at the end and stretching again. Cat stretches are exactly what you see cats do—slow stretching of arms, legs, and torso to comfortable limits. Mainly just what feels good. These are gentle stretches, and because you are doing what feels right to you, they will not do harm. Watch a cat.

Exercise has been shown to be more effective than anti-depressants in the treatment of depression. It stimulates the release of endorphins and other biochemicals that make you feel good. Your brain works better when well supplied with oxygen and nutrients. When you feel really good, you tend to not do your habit. Exercise and diet are critical to the success of your treatment. Remember the bus? The driver has to see to it that the bus is tuned up; filled with gas, oil, and transmission fluid; and overhauled when necessary. If these things are not done the passengers may suffer. When the passengers suffer, the other people in the city become disorganized. The entire system is in a state of tension and dis-ease.

References and Resources

Albright, Nancy. *Rodales's Naturally Great Foods Cookbook.* Emmaus, Penn.: Rodale Press, 1977.

Duquette, Susan, ed. *Sunburst Farms Family Cookbook.* Santa Barbara, Calif.: Woodbridge Press Publishing Co., 1976.

Gregory, Richard L., ed. *The Oxford Companion to the Mind.* Oxford and New York: Oxford University Press, 1987.

Grinder, John and Richard Bandler. *Trance-Formations.* Moab, Utah: Real People Press, 1981.

Lowe, Abraham A. *Mental Health Through Will-Training.* Hanover, Mass: Christopher Publishing House, 1950.

Pritikin, Robert. *The New Pritikin Program.* New York: Simon & Schuster, 1990.

Rossi, Ernest L. and David B. Cheek. *Mind and Body Therapy.* New York and London: W.W. Norton and Co., 1988.

Segal, Bernard. *Drugs and Behavior.* New York and London: Gardner Press, Inc., 1988.

Sherman, Janette. *Chemical Exposure and Disease.* New York: Van Nostrand Reinhold, 1988.

Stuart, Richard B. *Act Thin, Stay Thin.* New York and London: W.W. Norton and Co., Inc., 1978.

Time-Life Books. *The Fit Body.* Chicago: Time-Life, Inc., 1987.

Reward Rating Worksheet

List all possible rewards here:	Easy to obtain	Difficult to obtain	Seems unobtainable	How much will it cost?	Will I have to work harder to get the money?	How would I get the money?	How long will it take to get the money?	What will I have to give up to get it?	Is physical strength a factor?	Is special equipment required?	On a scale of 1-10, how badly do I want this reward?*	On a scale of 1-10, how much do I want to stay free of my habit?*
Example: Complete set of woodworking tools		X		$450	yes	extra part-time job	3-4 months	Dinner at home 2 nights/wk	yes	yes	8	10

*If this column is less than 6, eliminate that reward. It is too weak to be effective.

9

Avoiding Regression

Athletes who have trained arduously for years to condition their bodies can never stop training if they want to stay fit. They have to continue in a regimen of exercise, diet, practice, and mental control. Recently there was a documentary about young gymnasts who had won medals in Olympic competition several years earlier. Most were now beyond the age of competition. A few had maintained their training regimen at a sufficient level to allow them to excel in other athletic activities better suited to their age. Then there were those who had stopped training of any kind. These young adults had gained weight, were no longer physically fit, and reported less satisfaction with their lives than those who continued to be active. They had regressed. One of those tiresome old sayings, which happens to be true, is "Use it or lose it!"

This maxim applies to all skills, such as the ability to read rapidly, do arithmetic, dance, do calligraphy, and so on. It certainly applies to habit control. By now you have developed a regimen of exercise, diet, relaxation, and techniques for maintaining control of your habit. You have many written records of your training. Those records will be useful to you as a resource when you need to refresh your techniques or when you just need to see how far you have come.

Spotting the Danger Signs

In order to avoid regression, a technique called *spotting* must come into play. You know that there are certain symptoms or signs linked to your old habit. The same way that the driver of the bus has to be constantly aware of what the passengers on the bus are doing, what the engine sounds like, and what the traffic pattern is, as well as her own degree of alertness, you have to monitor each of your systems. That sounds like a burdensome task, but a friend of mine, who really does drive a bus, tells me that all of this awareness becomes automatic.

Hopefully you still have the notebook you used for writing the trivia of your days, because you still have a use for it. In the back of that book, write a list of the signs inside yourself and around you in the environment that are warnings. At least once a day look at this list and give yourself a mental checkup so that you can spot trouble before it comes.

At this time you probably have two or three signs, or cues, that signal real danger for you. These are the cues to spot so that whenever they arise you can put into operation one or more of the techniques you have learned. At this point it may be helpful to look at some of the danger signs others have identified. But in reading these, remember: the only limit to solutions for danger signals is your imagination. Every problem has not only *a* solution, it has *many* possible solutions.

Overeating

Heidi's overeating habit had begun when she left home for the first time to attend college. Like most students, she kept a supply of snacks in her room for study hours. She tended toward high-fat, sugar-laden snacks like candy bars, potato chips, caramel corn, and cupcakes. Eating seemed to ease the pangs of homesickness, the anxiety of tests, and the anxiety of not dating. She hadn't realized how severe her habit was until her clothes became too tight.

After working on habit control for several months, she began to feel that she was making progress. She was feeling better and had substituted apples and oranges for the candy and cakes. In her hot-pink notebook, where she listed the trivia of the average college student's life, she had also made note of three danger signs.

The first sign was the appearance in her mailbox of a letter from home. As soon as she saw the familiar handwriting her eyes filled with tears, and the empty feeling in her stomach became acute. Formerly she had reached for a candy bar while she read a letter from home. Now when she spots a letter, she automatically breathes deeply, touches her left wrist, and lets the happy memory of being with Mom working on a new dress fill her mind. The empty space in her tummy is immediately replaced by warmth and fullness. She feels her mother's love stretching across the miles to comfort and dry the tears.

Heidi's second danger sign was the announcement written on the blackboard that a test was imminent. Just seeing the word *test* was enough to send her to the vending machine for an ice cream bar. She felt panicky, short of breath. She felt like running away. Heidi handles this now with self-hypnosis. She has an agreement with her roommate that when she's doing self-hypnosis the roommate will take phone calls and prevent others from entering the room. It only takes about 10 minutes for her to get into a trance state, visualize, and fully experience herself in the test situation calm and secure. She reminds herself that she has studied the materials and the knowledge is in her brain. She instructs her brain to let this knowledge flow as needed as she answers test questions. Sometimes this needs to be done more than once before a test. When she gets to the classroom and the test booklet is placed before her, she closes her eyes, takes three deep breaths to reactivate the trance, and proceeds to take the test. In this way she is able to dissolve anxiety and tension, and she always does well on tests.

The signal for no-dating anxiety was seeing her roommate dressing to go out and hearing her talk about her boyfriends. In the past Heidi had developed a stream of self-talk about this situation that was totally negative and self-demeaning. "No wonder she goes out," Heidi would say to herself, "she has all that luscious long hair and those big dark eyes. Look at you, Heidi Cramer, you fat slob. You have no personality...you're a jerk...a dope...you're no good!" This kind of talk escalated as she munched through three bags of caramel corn, two candy bars, and six cupcakes. Then she had more unkind things to say about her lack of control.

Heidi worked hard on correcting negative self-talk. She spent time evaluating her assets and liabilities. Things are different now. When she sees her roommate getting ready to go out she talks to herself in another way. "OK, Heidi, what's good about you? You look very nice now that you've lost some weight. Your skin's clear and you have perfect teeth. You know lots of interesting things to talk about, but you're just a little too shy. You keep to yourself too much. Come on, let's go out and mingle." So Heidi packs up her books and goes to the library to study. There are more than a few people there, of both sexes, who obviously don't have dates. She begins to feel more comfortable and even strikes up a conversation with a fellow who is having trouble with the computer. She doesn't feel anxious anymore.

Compulsive Spending

Whenever Gina awakened in the morning feeling uneasy or worried, her thoughts immediately turned to, "What can I buy?" Then she would get through the day sustained by thoughts of a shopping trip. She fed these compulsive thoughts by avidly studying ads in magazines and newspapers. If someone at work had a new sweater or a striking accessory, Gina delayed her work long enough to get the details of where the purchase was made, how much it had cost, and where the shop was located. Gina realized that she must learn to spot both feelings and things.

Going through her daily trivia book, she saw that some of these things had not previously been recorded, so she had to backtrack and make additional entries. Although her habit was now under control most of the time, she was still taking note of ads and thinking about shopping. She didn't act on these thoughts often, but she could see that she was headed for a setback. She made a decision to strengthen her program.

First of all she had to confront the feelings of uneasiness she often had in the morning. She began to take more care to do the things she had learned to do for changing feelings. As she began to emerge from sleep, she began saying to herself, "It's OK, Gina, you're OK." Then she began to talk to herself about what she would wear, and how good the warm bath would feel. She also took time for a few minutes of reading before she got out of bed. Just getting her mind stimulated in this way lessened the uneasiness. Then she remembered to take plenty of time in the bath, reveling in the luxury of hot water and scented soap. At this time she also practiced deep breathing, so that by the time she wrapped up in the warm towel, she was feeling fine.

Gina also remembered to remove all advertising supplements from the newspaper and dispose of them without looking at them. At the office, when she saw a colleague wearing a piece of clothing she said to herself, "I'm glad Mary has pretty clothes. She looks very nice." Then she complimented Mary, and went on with her work, concentrating on doing the best job she could. Whenever a thought of shopping came into her mind, she took out her checkbook and affirmed the reality of her financial status.

Gina also had something special she wanted to save money for. Several of her friends were into bicycling, and Gina longed to join them. It had never been possible before because she was too much in debt to take on the burden of a bike purchase. Now she had one on layaway, and she only had three payments to go. Her agreement with herself had been to make these payments in cash, which helped stem the urge to spend.

Gambling

Ted thought he had the answer to his gambling habit when he asked for a transfer to a state where gambling was illegal. To his dismay he found that gambling still existed, just in other guises. There were Bingo games, friendly poker games, and sweepstakes opportunities that came in the mail. "Anyone else could enter a sweepstakes just for fun, and not even think about it," said Ted to his wife, Angie. "Not me. When I enter a sweepstakes I become obsessed with it. I dream about the money, I spend it before I have it by using my credit cards, and I find myself looking around for more sweepstakes."

"I know you do," Angie agreed, "and it takes an awful lot of time, doesn't it?"

The danger signals for Ted were the monthly bank statement, the big green and white envelopes that came in the mail, and the smell of a new car. He handled the green and white envelopes by visualizing the word *Trash* stamped across them in big letters. The word was a cue to put the unopened envelope in the wastebasket.

The bank statement was a little harder. One of the negative memories that had come up when Ted was doing a memory search was a scene that had occurred in his childhood home. Ted's father always flew into a rage when the bank statement came, blaming Mom and all the children for the depleted state of the bank account. "You'd think he never wrote a check himself," said Ted. "Even the 3-year-old got blamed for having to go to the doctor." The tension created by this scene had been securely anchored in Ted by the sight of a bank statement. He felt an urgent need to make the balance bigger, just as he had felt as a child.

Ted successfully restructured this memory so that the coming of the bank statement was an innocuous event of no special significance. Lack of money was a challenge instead of a disaster. This didn't happen in one experience, of course. The restructuring had to be repeated and practiced, and each time anchored with a touch to his wrist. Now when Ted receives a bank statement he touches his wrist before opening the envelope, letting the tension dissipate, and calm everyday business feelings fill up the space.

When Ted spots the smell of a new car, which is often only in his imagination, he visualizes his wife riding her bike, enjoying the way her hair streams out behind, and the fresh glow in her cheeks. "That's better than a new car," he says to himself, "riding with Angie like that is lots better." This has led to the two of them doing more biking, a low-cost recreation.

Compulsive Stealing

Megan had gone over her trivia notebook and the Life Systems worksheets many times trying to sort out just three or four danger signs she could spot for strengthening her control. She finally settled on four that seemed prominent. The first was mirrors, any mirrors. Whenever she looked in a mirror or plate glass window, she was filled with discontent about her appearance. The second sign was shiny, brightly colored objects. The third signal was a feeling of reluctance to spend money, and the fourth was hunger.

Megan realized that her discontent when she looked in the mirror had something to do with feeling deprived. She always had money to spend, but she felt lacking in physical attributes, as if something had been withheld or taken away. When she paid attention to what she was saying in her mind at those moments, she heard words like, "I don't deserve to be pretty," "mouse hair," "horseface," and other derogatory comments. Megan had to change the mirror into a positive focus to help her keep emotional balance. At home she put cards on the mirrors with single words to say over and over in place of the negative self-talk. Some of the words were "bright," "kind," "stately," and "regal." As she practiced these statements, other self-talk began to take over, such as, "not bad," "good-looking" and even "kind of pretty." She is now able to spot mirrors and other reflective surfaces to keep a positive attitude about herself.

Bright, colorful objects were simply leftover childhood longings for pretty baubles. She realized this was tied closely to the third danger signal because she wanted pretty baubles, but she didn't want to part with money. As she again examined her Life Systems worksheets, she saw that one of her big assets was a substantial income. Money was not a problem. She had enough to buy anything she wanted. Megan reflected further about the times she had taken these baubles and simply tossed them into a drawer, never to be used. Many of them were not even appropriate for her. "OK," she said to herself, "from now on the red barrettes and gold earrings will be a cue to buy something for someone else. I can afford it."

The fourth signal, hunger, was again a relic from a period of poverty she had experienced in her first marriage. Of course the cookies and packages of cheese she took were never eaten. "Hmm," she said, "well, if I can buy baubles for others, I can buy food for people who are hungry. I can afford to do that more than most people." After some research she settled on the Salvation Army as a good place to donate funds for the poor, and after that, the sight of food packages in stores reminded her to write out a check.

Lying

Dale had two danger signals, both having to do with words. Newspapers, concert programs, magazine articles, letters from friends and relatives all prompted Dale to lie if they contained any account of some exceptional event, accomplishment, or performance. He felt compelled to top every story in some way. The same was true for conversations, TV documentaries, telephone calls, and any other verbal reports of accomplishments.

Dale expected to be exceptional. He was greatly disappointed at times with the averageness of his life. As an office manager his days were filled with trivia. Announcements about reducing worker turnover did not compare with stories about three-foot-long trout or a cruise to the Bahamas. He had a competent, attractive, average wife who never won a beauty pageant and was never voted woman of the year. He had three intelligent, good-looking children who were not piano prodigies or star athletes. Dale wanted excitement, attention, and acclaim. Winning $10 million would have been just the thing.

What Dale really needed was three things: acceptance of reality, a unique hobby, and a better opinion of himself. Three things. Dale went to a toy store and purchased three of those little marbles that are magnetized so they stick to each other: one red, one yellow, and one blue. Primary colors for primary things. Now, whenever he is assaulted with words about exceptionality, he reaches into his pocket for the marbles. As he rolls them around in his hand, he says three things: "I'm an excellent office manager. I keep things even and under control at all times," "My family is stable, healthy, and happy; a wonderful average family. I'm grateful for my average family," and "I have gifts and talents that I have not yet explored. I can now begin to develop some of these things, too."

Dale has now become involved in Boy Scout activities with his three sons and has found that he has a talent for working with young people. He derives a great deal of satisfaction from helping boys who may not be getting much support at home.

Fire-Setting

Wendy was introduced to fire-setting by her brother at the tender age of 5. Sandy soon quit, having more interesting things to do, but Wendy continued. She found it to be a potent treatment for tension.

Wendy knew right away that she had to do a better job of spotting the danger signals, and she knew what those signals were. First there was the belly-tightening feeling that presaged the buildup of tension. Once that happened there were other signals, such as the colors of fire—red, orange, and yellow. Seeing the matches in her purse added to the effects of the other signals.

Once she was able to spot the belly-tightening early on she could interrupt it with relaxation. She used the progressive muscle relaxation method described in Chapter 6. Wendy first taped her own voice reading the exercise, reading slowly, and pausing in the indicated places. By playing the tape and listening, she found that she could totally dissipate the tight feeling in her belly, thereby interrupting the generalized buildup of tension.

To be sure the tension didn't start up again, Wendy had to be wary of the other danger signals, too. She decided, first of all, to never carry matches. Then she looked for an activity that would make fire-setting impossible. She didn't want to be a fireman, although putting out fires is opposite to setting them. She was happy in her job as primary school teacher. "If I could just use the talents I have in teaching," she mused, and then an idea was born. There was a lesson in the curriculum about home safety and proper use of matches, so why couldn't she expand it and be able to use it at will, rather than just at set times?

Wendy developed a plan on paper that involved frequent visits from firemen for 15-minute presentations on fire safety, two or three visits from forest rangers, and a series of brief story and coloring activities centered around handling emergencies of all kinds, including fire. She presented the plan to her principal, who readily endorsed it. Wendy became so wrapped up in this program that it grew to include a children's drama, written and directed by the children, about a child setting a fire and the consequences he experienced. This led to learning projects about handling other kinds of life stresses.

All the projects involved coloring, painting, and cutting brightly colored construction paper. The parents loved it. Several of them told Wendy that they had been concerned about a child's fascination with fire and tendencies to play with matches. The fire department loved it, and the superintendent of schools presented it to the curriculum committee for inclusion in all primary grades.

Hair-Pulling

At first Louise said, "Everything's a danger signal—telephones, doorbells, kids, relatives, clocks, car keys—you name it!" She did finally settle on three signals that were consistent producers of tension. First, the telephone. "Every time I see it," she said, "I'm either worried someone will call with bad news or I'm worried that someone I want to hear from won't call." Louise searched her memory for times when phone calls had been fun and pleasant. She then chose the best one, and in a state of relaxation reexperienced all of the feelings, sights, and sounds present on that occasion. She anchored this by visualizing a telephone and touching her left wrist firmly with her right hand. Now when she looks at the phone, or hears one ring , she touches her wrist and is flooded with feelings of pleasant anticipation. This enables her to calmly handle any message she may receive.

Louise had always had poor communication with her in-laws, which led to many misunderstandings and hostile feelings. She had made many attempts to overcome these problems, and there had been improvement in the relationships. But she was still nervous before holidays because she was afraid she would be criticized about her cooking and the way she and her husband were raising their children. Her in-laws had also ridiculed her for her hair-pulling, and these memories still rankled. Louise had talked with her sister-in-law about it, but had been afraid to approach the others. As Thanksgiving approached, she decided to write a letter to her husband's parents, stating her regret for the embarrassment her problem had caused them and explaining her progress toward control. She followed the steps in Chapter 7, and mailed the letter, feeling good that she had made the effort to improve their relationship.

About a week later Louise found a letter from her mother-in-law in the mailbox. She opened it with some dread, but was relieved to read expressions of love and apology for not having been more sensitive to her problems. Now Thanksgiving is looked forward to as a pleasant time, and family communications are open and direct.

Louise had one more important danger signal...clocks. It seemed that her life revolved around deadlines and timetables. When the alarm went off in the morning, the tension began. From then on she was constantly checking the clock, hurrying to finish a project or go to a meeting. The clock seemed to say "Go on...go on...go on." The clocks in her home and in her car all had orange dots on them already. Something more was needed.

One day, sitting at her desk, she looked at the clock, watching the second hand telling her "Go on...go on," she realized that the clock said "Go on" because that is what she had decided it should say. The clock had no living brain to make it give her a message like that. "Well," she said to the clock, "from now on you are going to say what I want you to say. You are going to say 'Slow down...take time...slow down...take time'." Not only did Louise lose her urgent tension, she found that by slowing down and taking time she was still able to meet deadlines, but without the distress and fatigue she usually had.

Explosive Temper

Sven was well aware that the danger signals he needed to focus on were the sounds of children quarreling, traffic jams, and misplaced tools. All three were things over which he felt he had no control. It was unbearable for Sven not to be able to control everything and everyone.

He decided to pay close attention to the children's quarrels the next time it happened. He didn't have long to wait.

"You give that back!" Sven heard as he came in the door that evening.

"I had it first...it's mine!"

"Mine!" This was accompanied by sounds of scuffling and quickly followed by screaming.

Sven's heart began to pound, his fists clenched, and his shoulders went up. "Wait," he whispered to himself, "wait and see what happens."

"Big baby," he heard next, "I don't want that stupid truck, anyway. It's a baby toy."

"Is not!"

"Is too!"

"Not."

"Is." Sounds of giggling, then, "Hey, I know. Let's go watch Rescue Rangers!"

Sven smiled, shaking his head. "I can't believe they got over that by themselves." Always before Sven had rushed in to break things up and wreak a little violence while he was about it. "All I had to do was stay out of it and wait. Amazing!"

Sven decided to use the words "Stay out of it, wait and see" as a response to that danger signal.

The next day, on his way to work, traffic was piled up as a result of an accident about a mile ahead. "Oh damn!" he said, pounding his fist on the steering wheel. Suddenly the words "Stay out of it, wait and see" came into his mind. "OK, I guess that'll work here, too. 'Stay out of it' really means get detached, and all I can do is wait and see anyway." This worked very well. Sven leaned back, turned off the motor, and began to observe other drivers. Some were reading books, others were out of their cars, pacing up and down in an angry way. Still others were having quiet conversations as they leaned on their cars, apparently enjoying the sunshine. Sven got so caught up in observing the behavior of the other drivers that he was surprised when 30 minutes had passed and the traffic began to creep forward. "Aha," he said, 'Stay out of it, wait and see' is a good philosophy for tense situations."

That left the matter of the misplaced tools. Sven had thought he had no control over what other people did with the tools. It occurred to him that there was no clear policy in his workplace about care of the tools. He decided to ask for a meeting of all the workers in his division on the following Friday, their short day. Using his "Stay out of it, wait and see" approach, he presented the problem to his co-workers, and asked for solutions. As it turned out, several of them were as upset about misplaced tools as Sven was. Many ideas were presented, and after about 20 minutes of discussion one plan was unanimously accepted. It was a simple plan of having a tool placement map drawn up and mounted in the storage area. When a worker removed tools, he or she had to initial a tool list and check it off when the tool was returned. Now Sven no longer feels the need to be in control. If a tool is misplaced, he can look at the list and ask the person who last used the tool about its whereabouts. Gradually, the workers became more responsible about returning tools to their proper places, and Sven was a more peaceable man.

Misuse of Prescription Drugs

Pain was the major danger signal for Nikki. She was so frightened of prolonged, unremitting pain that any twinge of pain was a cue to swallow pills. She had gotten rid of unnecessary drug bottles, and kept others in a less inaccessible place, but the pain itself was a constant danger.

Nikki had learned many techniques for handling pain. What she needed now was some kind of quick fix that could be applied anytime, anywhere, at the first sign of pain. More than that, she needed to use this quick fix before the pain, when she felt warning signs such as extreme fatigue or emotional upheaval. A lengthy relaxation exercise would not do when standing on a crowded subway, yet that kind of thing was what she wanted. Short, inconspicuous self-hypnosis would do it, she thought.

Nikki practiced with various combinations of words and breathing until she found one that would get her over the first flash of fear and pain. This is what she did. At the first flash or premonition of pain, Nikki took a deep, deep, slow breath, saying to herself, "Breathe in peace, breathe out pain." Sometimes once was enough, but at other times it had to be repeated. She also had a backup plan for the times when she didn't catch it on the first flash. If the pain was already well established, she would begin slow, deep breathing, focusing on the pain, seeing and feeling the color of it, and saying, "Float through to the other side." She found that floating through was more effective than trying to get the pain to disappear. The reality of life is that you have to tolerate some pain. It is impossible to always be pain free. There is a sense of victory in calmly enduring pain, in not letting it defeat you. Nikki lost a lot of her fear when she realized that she could endure what she couldn't erase.

Irresponsible Sex

Phil had learned through sad experience that his danger signals were parked cars and loneliness. It seemed that he expected himself to "park" with his date at the end of the evening. His friends all did it. But it had become a major problem for Phil, not least because he had already contracted genital herpes because of his sex habit. He was afraid, though, that the girls he dated would be offended if he simply took them home after the movie or dance. One girl he had gone out with had started a rumor around school that he was gay because he never took her to the lake at the end of their dates. The harassment he'd taken because of it was really unpleasant.

He didn't want to stop dating though. He really liked girls and dating. How could he enjoy dating without getting trapped by his habit? He thought about all he had learned. Two techniques came to mind as being possible solutions: assertiveness and competing activities. He had some trouble imagining how he could be polite and assertive at the same time. He didn't want to hurt anyone's feelings unnecessarily, and he wasn't sure the girls he knew would understand. He felt pretty close to his sister though, so he asked her about it.

"OK, Sis," he said, "here's the problem," and he explained the situation to his sister. Then they role-played the following scenario, taking turns being Phil.

After a school dance, Phil and his date Toni, instead of driving to the lake, would go for a walk around the downtown, looking in the windows and talking. During the course of the walk Phil could tell her how he felt about having casual sex and make it clear it had nothing to do with her. If Toni was offended anyway, or thought it was funny, then she wasn't the kind of person he wanted to be with.

It was a totally new way of doing things for Phil, and not easy. He had those expectations to overcome, as well as a pattern of behavior that had become comfortable. And he was scared of what she might say. He and his sister practiced until Phil felt confident he could carry it off.

As it turned out, Toni was fine with it, and felt touched that he confided in her. They became good friends. Phil also found it easier to be friends with other girls. It was fun to enjoy activities and conversation without being burdened with a pressure for sex.

The idea of competing activities had worked for parking, so Phil thought maybe it would work for loneliness, also. He made a list of things he could do when he was alone and lonely. His parents were gone a great deal of the time, as was his sister as well. One of the items on his list was photography. He had a camera and liked to take pictures, but he didn't know much about it. He found an after-school photography class and asked his parents to let him set up a darkroom in the basement. Phil is not only not lonely anymore, he's also a fine photographer.

Overuse of TV and Video Game

Joyce's danger signals were feelings of boredom, fatigue, and, of course, the mere sight of the TV. Her job was such that she sat in an office and was involved with people's problems and personalities all day long. When she came home at night, she was tired; she just wanted to sit. Then as soon as she sat down, she felt bored, and she automatically reached for the remote control. Instead of defusing from her hectic day, she turned her brain and body off, effectively anesthetizing all feelings. She had tried substituting reading, but her mind would race on with the day's events and she wouldn't be able to concentrate on the book.

In talking it over with her teenagers, she realized she needed some time to unwind before coming home.

"I know, Mom," said Margaret, "why don't you go for a walk in Merriweather Park? It's right on your way home, and the view from the top of the hill is terrific."

Joyce was skeptical of the idea at first. She felt it might seem undignified for a woman her age to don athletic shoes and roam around the park. But she agreed to try it for a week.

At first it was really difficult to stop the car at the park, change her shoes, and get out. And then the first quarter mile loomed before her. But after she was warmed up she started to notice things outside herself. The air smelled of grass and trees. There were bird songs and breezes that seemed to lift away the day's events.

By the end of the week she felt stronger and began to look forward to her walk. Sometimes when things were particularly stressful at work, she took a mental "walk" there, and came back feeling refreshed. Joyce found that she often seemed to solve problems while she was walking, ones she'd been unable to find a solution to earlier.

After a month or two, Joyce had trouble imagining how she had ever done without the walking. When she got home she was able to enjoy spending time with her kids and reading. She started seeing some of her old friends again, and made a couple of new ones. The TV didn't get used much, and when it was on, Joyce found herself wondering how she could have spent so much time watching such silly stuff. And the commercials...

Teeth-Grinding

Vivian had learned to keep her teeth apart. She was skilled at relaxation. But she still had two danger signals she needed to be able to spot more readily. The first was when she was showering in the morning. For some reason, that was the time when she would fall into a depressing, ruminating state. She thought about how ugly she was. She worried about bad things that had happened in her life a long time ago. She ground her teeth at the thought of embarrassing situations she had been in. By the time she stepped out of the shower, she was feeling unhappy and angry. Her jaw hurt.

"I know I have to spot that first negative thought and stop the vicious cycle," she said to the person in the mirror.

"Well, do it," the image said back.

"I don't know if I can. By the time I spot it, there have already been several such thoughts."

"So think something positive before you get in the shower."

Well, of course. Her habit of depressing rumination was predictable. She could prevent it. The next morning Vivian stood before the shower door and said, "This is a new day. I can make it whatever I want."

As she stepped into the shower she said, "Now I'm going to plan my day. This is going to be the best day of my life."

Later, as she toweled dry before the mirror, she said, "I feel great. I know what I'm going to do today, and I know I can do everything well."

"I knew that," said the image.

Vivian's second danger signal appeared when she was under pressure to hurry, such as rushing to work, standing in line at the post office five minutes before closing, or answering the phone as she was going out the door to an appointment. At those times her teeth clamped shut, and she didn't realize what she was doing until she felt the pain. Vivian needed to analyze what came before the tension that brought her teeth crunching together. She found it helpful to review her Life Systems worksheets. As she did so, she noticed a comment under "Liabilities" that she had forgotten about. She had listed her mother among her assets, but she was also a liability in the way she criticized Vivian for being too slow, too late, too lazy. "So that's it," she thought. "When I'm in a time crunch I hear Mom saying I'm always too slow."

That very evening Vivian was getting ready to go to a committee meeting when her son cut his hand on a broken glass. Swooping him up to soothe him, she forgot that the hand was bleeding all over the front of her blouse. She cleaned the wound, put on a butterfly bandage, and only then saw what had happened to her blouse. Now she would have to change clothes and be even later than before. Rushing into the closet in a whirlwind of anxiety, she suddenly stopped. "Stop!" she said, right out loud. "Emergencies happen. Being late is not the end of the world. I do the best I can." Then she was able to relax and once again get ready for the meeting. The technique of saying "Stop!" became an automatic response to stressful situations.

Smoking

Keith sat in the waiting room looking at the ashtray. The smell was both unpleasant and inviting. "Why don't they clean these damn things," he said to no one in particular. The other man in the room looked up, shrugged, and went back to his magazine. Waiting was hard, Keith thought, it is the most tempting time. This began a train of thought that led Keith to analyze whether it was the waiting that was his danger signal or whether it was the sight of the ashtray. The smell of the ashtray?

He got out his little red notebook and studied the list of danger signs. Yes, there it was: "Waiting for anyone," he had written. "That makes sense," he thought, "I don't have trouble with ashtrays anymore in other places. So what can I do when I'm waiting?" He began to write down some ideas about what to do when waiting. He was still busy writing when his name was called to come in for the interview.

Later, when the interview was over, and he knew he had the job, he thought about the waiting problem again. "I wasn't tense at all when I was writing in my book," he thought. "I didn't even think of smoking. Maybe that's what I could do...carry a little book and do my journal writing whenever I'm waiting."

Keith had had a desire for some time to write a personal history. He knew that journal writing was the way to start, but he never seemed to have time for it. "I wait a lot," he thought, "I wait for Marta to get ready when we're going out, and I do nothing but wait on the bus going home. I wait for meetings to begin. That's quite a bit of time when I could be writing in my journal."

Keith grew to enjoy, and even depend on, his journal writing. Not only did it erase any tension he felt when waiting, he noticed that it was a good way to solve problems. Putting his thoughts down like that cleared up confusion and conflict.

He couldn't write in his journal when he was in the middle of a management meeting, though. Sometimes the arguments about policy got pretty heated, and that's when people started lighting up. Keith discussed it with another former smoker, who had trouble with being in a smoke-filled room.

"We have two problems," Rob said, "the smoke itself is a danger, and the tension of the arguments is another."

Keith agreed. "I think we need a no-smoking policy. Most companies have banned smoking except for certain places, and as long as there are nonsmokers in the room, we shouldn't have smoking. It's a health hazard for all of us, to say nothing of the temptation."

Rob and Keith agreed to approach the personnel manager with a proposal. "There's a nice courtyard right outside the conference room," Keith told her, "That could be a smoking area, and it wouldn't bother anyone." The proposal was readily agreed to, and a memo went out to that effect. One problem solved.

"Now what do we do about the tension?" Rob wondered.

Keith laughed, "How about a policy banning tension in meetings?"

"You'll never get that one, buddy."

Keith whipped out his red book. "Do you have one of these? It's my list of things to do when I spot a danger sign...something that will make me want to smoke."

Rob was interested in looking at this list, and found some things that he thought would help him. He also added a couple Keith hadn't thought of.

Finally, they agreed that when the arguments began to heat up, either Rob or Keith (whoever thought of it first) would look at the other, smile and nod, and place his pen on the table. At that signal they said in their minds, "What difference will all of this make in 100 years?" That was a cue to begin slow, deep breathing, and to focus on the facts of the argument rather than the emotional opinions. After that both Rob and Keith were able to participate in these meetings without becoming tense and distraught. In a calm state they did not desire to smoke.

Keith still had one more danger signal, one more problem to solve. It was the sound of his ex-wife's voice on the phone. She had legitimate reasons for calling, but there was something about her voice that grated across his nerves like coarse sandpaper. In the past he had used cigarettes to remain calm and endure the call. Because this event was so aversive, Keith usually responded in an abrupt, irritated way. He just wanted her to shut up and hang up.

He wrote about his feelings in his journal. The more he wrote, the more he began to see that the problem was his attitude rather than anything she was doing. "It's like I make up my mind right away that I don't want to deal with anything she talks about. I don't even listen to her, and that's why she has to call back about the same thing."

"Whew, that's a revelation," he said. "Looks like I could do two things. I can focus on the content of what she's saying, instead of thinking about how much I dislike hearing her. Or I can ask questions to see if she has all the information she needs. That way she won't have to call back as often."

Their next conversation went something like this:

"Keith, I went up to Randy's school, and for some reason they want your Social Security number. Why on earth do they need your Social Security number? You're not the one going to school. I can't believe the stupid stuff they want just to pay your kid's tuition. By the way, Randy said he'd rather go with you on Thanksgiving and me on Christmas. Now I know you're not going to like that, but that's what Randy wants. He wants..."

"Wait a second, Riva. I can hardly keep up with you. You need my Social Security number, right? OK, it's 555-46-3113. Do you have it? Want to read it back, just to check?"

"Yeah, I've got it...555-46-3113. Now about Thanksgiving..."

"Riva, Thanksgiving's fine. I'm just tickled to death to have Randy whenever he wants to be here. I know he likes seeing your mom at Christmas."

"Oh. Well, I just thought you wanted him for Christmas."

"I want what Randy wants. I'd love to see him every day of the week, but he's better off with you. He likes the school, and his friends are there. You're a good mom, Riva. Please don't worry so much."

Big silence. Then, "Well...thank you. Are you going to pick him up on that Wednesday then?"

"Yes, I'll be there at 4:30 and bring him back Sunday afternoon around 3:00. Will that be convenient for you?"

"Well, yeah...sure. Wednesday at 4:30 and Sunday at 3:00."

Keith felt good. When he listened to what Riva was saying, rather than the tone of her voice, he realized that she was just trying to do her best without offending him. He knew things were going to be better for Randy if he and Riva could communicate in a friendly way. He also no longer needed to smoke during phone calls with Riva.

Life Events

Be on the lookout for stressful changes in your life. Psychiatrist Thomas H. Holmes has devised what he calls a Schedule of Recent Experience—a list of events that happen to most people some time in their lives. On the schedule each event is given a number to indicate the severity of the stress experienced as a result. After checking off all the events you have experienced in the last year, you add up the numbers. Holmes's studies showed that a total of more than 250 points indicates a level of stress so high that physical illness can be expected.

Others have elaborated on this list in various ways, but the point is that we'd better know how to handle our stresses or we'll get sick. A version of this schedule is included in Appendix B for your interest, but I think it is more useful to make your own list. Decide for yourself which of your recent life events are most stressful, which are only moderately so, and which are least stressful.

Neurologist Oliver Sacks, in his delightful book, *A Leg to Stand On*, tells of a change in his life that upset his equilibrium a great deal. You would probably enjoy reading the book for yourself, but in brief, here is what happened. Sacks was enjoying his life as a doctor, taking care of patients with long-term illnesses, and feeling that he was physically and emotionally integrated. He felt good about himself. Then he went hiking alone in the mountains in Norway, ran into an irritable bull, and fell, injuring his leg so badly that he could not stand, nor did he have any feeling in the leg. He writes of how his response to this major stress was a complete mind-body-soul existential upheaval. His personality changed, his mental processes were disordered, and he had times when it seemed his very senses were playing tricks on him. It is the best description I have read of what I have begun to think of as the "bus syndrome." With this abrupt and frightening disruption of normal functioning, Dr. Sacks writes, "I felt myself burning and freezing. Obsessive fears gnawed at my mind. My perceptions were unstable." Is there something there that sounds familiar?

Taking Control

Any event that causes you to feel helpless, rejected, abandoned, out of control, or just not feeling good about yourself, is a red flag of warning. When that happens you always have a choice. You can choose to see yourself as a victim, or worthless, or you can choose to interpret this event as an unfortunate occurrence that could happen to anyone and let it go. You have the tools now to handle many kinds of stress. By reviewing your Life Systems worksheets, adding and deleting as things change, you can stay on top of and in control of the stressful events in your life, whether they are in the past or present.

Should you feel yourself escalating into angry, vengeful feelings and starting to fantasize about doing your habit, you can defuse by changing your fantasy. If you are fantasizing about setting fire to your girlfriend's car, say to yourself "Stop!" and then change the fantasy to something like running a marathon, with you leading, carrying a large flaming torch. People are yelling and screaming for you, and the end of the race, as you collapse on the ground with your torch burning brightly, your girlfriend flings herself down beside you, pledging love and loyalty forever. Not a bad fantasy. Better than committing arson. You can become very good at creating fantasies.

It Isn't Just the Hard Times

Positive, happy times also bring increased stress. Exceptional events like getting married, moving to a wonderful new home, or a dramatic job promotion can be sufficiently stressful to bring on increased temptations to resume old habits. You need to be wary of changes. Changes in relationships, financial status, trouble with children, run-ins with in-laws…the list goes on and on. The key is to monitor the status of your daily life and spot the changes before you react.

A member of my family had an experience with financial gain and loss. A combination of economic, political, and social circumstances allowed my cousin to become wealthy nearly overnight. Suddenly he was on a high of well-being. He dressed well, bought a new car and a fancy home, entertained lavishly, and smothered everyone in the family with gifts. He became a little smug and arrogant about his wealth, which was annoying to the rest of us, even though we were glad to see him having prosperity.

Then came big changes. Economic depression set it. Major companies abandoned the area. Banks foreclosed. People who owed my cousin money filed for bankruptcy. He was left with holdings he couldn't sustain. Eventually, he too filed for bankruptcy. He had virtually nothing left. The big house was gone, as were the cars. No more big spending sprees. It was painful to watch him sink into depression and despair, to lose interest in life. He became bitter for a time. We felt helpless, not knowing how to help.

That was dramatic change, sudden and unexpected. Other changes may be planned for, such as getting married or having a baby. You know your son is going to go to college, and yet it is stressful when it happens. You know everyone gets sick sometimes, but it is shocking when it happens to you or to your loved one. All parents die, yet you are never prepared for the death of your own parent. How many times I have seen people revert to a habit of smoking, overeating, or some other habit when a parent has died.

It has happened to me. When my son died I "handled" it by stuffing everything in sight into my mouth. It didn't take long to see that this was a poor way to grieve. I had to do some work on myself, which fortunately paid off, and when my mother died I was able to go about the business of grieving in a productive way.

The message I'm trying to give is that if you are aware that changes can be traps for tempting you to do your old habit, you will be prepared to use techniques you have learned to stay in control. The thing is, you can do it. You have learned much in your lifetime about control. That knowledge will now be a resource in times of stress.

Commencement

The word *commencement* implies both beginning and ending. When you graduate from high school or college, you have a commencement exercise to mark the place in your life when you have ended preparatory training and are about to begin the practical training of life. That is where you are now with habit control.

You bought this book because you had a habit that was disrupting your life. As you progressed through the book, you should have learned that there is no end. You can never say, "OK, that's it, I don't need to work on that anymore." You have to practice these skills all your life. Remember that the book is about habit *control*, not habit *cure*. At times of stress and tension, your old habit may want to reappear, but now you know what to do. You know the signs and signals, and you can take action.

Remember that all learning takes time. Nothing is instant. There is a story, told by Shinichi Suzuki, who developed the Suzuki Method of learning music, about a man who wanted to train a bird to say his name. The bird's name was Pico. The man wondered how long it would take to train the bird to say his name, so he decided to keep track of how many times the name was spoken before Pico said it. Every day the man said *Pico* over and over, until one day the bird said *Pico* back to him. It had taken 2000 times of saying *Pico* before the bird said it. Then the man wanted to see if Pico could learn to say his last name. Once again the man repeated *Pico Matsumato* every day, many times, until the bird said it back. But this time it took only 500 times before the bird learned to say *Pico Matsumato*.

This principle of learning holds true for humans, too. Each learning period is shorter than the one before. As you learn to control a habit, to change a liability into an asset, you will find that the next project happens more quickly. People are too quickly discouraged when they are first trying to change. They rush back to the doctor, counselor, or therapist, and say, "It didn't work. I'm still doing my habit." You have to have patience to change a long-standing habit or to change things in your life so that you can maintain mental, physical, and spiritual health. You can do it. It just takes time.

My final assignment to you is to buy a toy bus. Place it where you can see it every day. Remember that anything that happens in your life, at any level, affects all the other parts. As the driver of the bus, you are the one who makes the decisions. You are in control. You, the driver, can never quit or give up. This is a lifetime job. I've always wanted to write a book called *Never Give Up*. And now I realize this is it.

Further Reading

Sacks, Oliver. *A Leg to Stand On*. New York: Summit Books, 1984.

Appendix A

Resources

This is a partial list of the available resources—just to get you started—it's only the tip of the iceberg. Check your local phone directory and library for others. Talk to friends and service providers for ideas. If you can't find exactly what you're looking for, call an organization with a related purpose. They will probably be able to refer you to what you need.

Community Resource Center—Provides information and help with job rehabilitation, parenting classes, domestic violence, and other kinds of counseling.

Alcoholics Anonymous—A 12-step program for alcoholics and families. Look in your phone book or write:

> General Service Office of AA
> Box 459 Grand Central Station
> New York, NY 10163

Drug and Alcohol Rehabilitation Services—Provides programs for job finding and social adjustments of the recovering alcoholic or drug addicted person. Check the phone book or contact the Resource Center.

Child Protective Services—In most states it is required by law to report suspected child abuse. Protective Services is one arm of Social Services, and will be listed as such in the phone book. You can also call 911.

Domestic Violence Project—For people who are experiencing violent assaults at home. They usually have a safe house where the victim may live briefly while receiving counseling and making new living arrangements. Look in the phone book or call 1-800-333-SAFE.

Crisis Hotline—You can call for any crisis on a 24-hour basis. Look in the front of the phone book under Emergency Numbers or call 911.

Your Church—A good place to get pastoral counseling, fellowship, and support. There are usually programs for children, youth, singles, and single parents.

Someone Else's Church—Talk to your friends about what they like in their church, or explore the phone book and visit several churches.

Counseling Services—Ask your doctor for a referral or call the Mental Health Association (below). Specify what kind of counseling you want: behavioral, vocational, marriage and family, and so on.

Mental Health Association—Provides referrals and educational books and films to be checked out. They also have support groups. If not listed in your phone book, write:

> National Mental Health Association, Inc.
> 1021 Prince Street
> Alexandria, VA 22314-1932

Legal Aid—City or county offices provide free or reduced fee legal services. Check the phone book or call any attorney's office for the number. The Resource Center can also put you in touch.

Parents Without Partners—A support group for single parents. It is both educational and social. If not in the phone book, watch the newspaper calendar section. Resource Center or Social Services would also have information.

Widow-to-Widow—May not be in the phone book. This is primarily a social support group for recently widowed women. The Mental Health Association, the Resource Center, or a hospice can help you with information.

Hospice—Provides emotional and physical care for dying patients and their families and includes a bereavement program for one year after the death. Usually located in hospitals, they are always looking for volunteers.

Compassionate Friends—Provides education and support for those who have lost a child. Look in the phone book or call a hospice.

Home Health Services—Provides in-home nursing care, social support, homemaking service, and some equipment. Always looking for volunteers and provides training for those seeking employment.

Housing Authority—A good resource when you need low-priced housing. There are income restrictions. Check the phone book or call Social Services or the Resource Center.

American Cancer Society—Provides information, equipment, and support groups for cancer patients and their families. They welcome volunteers. See the phone book or write:

> American Cancer Society
> 1599 Clifton Road, NE
> Atlanta, GA 30329

American Lung Association—Provides information, equipment, support groups, and some physical or pydrotherapy for patients with lung problems such as asthma or chronic obstructive pulmonary disease. They also have stop smoking classes and sponsor the Great American Smoke Out every November. They welcome volunteers. Look in the phone book, call your doctor's office, or write:

> American Lung Association
> 1740 Broadway
> New York, NY 10019-4374

Arthritis Foundation—Provides educational materials, support groups, classes, and sometimes equipment for people with various kinds of arthritis. They also have information about organizations concerned with specific kinds of arthritis. Check the phone book or write:

> Arthritis Foundation
> 1314 Spring Street, NW
> Atlanta, GA 30309

Planned Parenthood—Provides counseling about birth control, physical examinations for women, education, and referral. It may or may not be in the phone book. Call the Resource Center or ask your doctor.

Lupus Foundation of America—Provides educational materials, support groups, and referrals for people who have lupus, an autoimmune disease. Check the phone book or write:
> Lupus Foundation of America
> 1717 Massachusetts Avenue, NW
> Washington, DC 20036

Citizens Advocacy—Provides information and support for the developmentally disabled and their families. Call 1-800-332-1716.

Epilepsy Foundation of America—Provides educational materials, support groups, and other assistance. Check your phone book or call:
> Epilepsy Foundation of America
> Suite 406
> 4351 Garden City Drive,
> Landover, Maryland 20784

National Multiple Sclerosis Society—Provides educational programs, support groups, clinics, equipment, and referrals. Look in the phone book or write:
> National Multiple Sclerosis Society
> 202 E. 42nd Street
> New York, NY 10017

National Alliance for the Mentally Ill—Provides information and support for patients and families. Write to:
> National Alliance for the Mentally Ill
> 1901 N. Fort Myer Drive, Suite 500
> Arlington, VA 22209

Aids Hotline—Provides 24-hour crisis support and referrals. 1-800-342-AIDS. (There may be a wait.)

You can also get printed materials about AIDS and about other diseases from state and local public health departments or you can write:
> U.S. Department of Health and Human Services
> Public Health Service
> 5600 Fishers Lane
> Rockville, Maryland 20857

Appendix B

Schedule of Recent Experience

Part A

Instructions: Think back on each possible life event listed below, and decide if it happened to you within the last year. If the event did happen, check the space next to it.

	Check here if event happened to you	Mean value (use for scoring later)
1. A lot more or a lot less trouble with the boss	_____	_____
2. A major change in sleeping habits (sleeping a lot more or a lot less, or change in part of day when asleep)	_____	_____
3. A major change in eating habits (a lot more or a lot less food intake, or very different meal hours or surroundings)	_____	_____
4. A revision of personal habits (dress, manners, associations, etc.)	_____	_____
5. A major change in your usual type and/or amount of recreation	_____	_____
6. A major change in your social activities (clubs, dancing, movies, visiting, etc.)	_____	_____
7. A major change in church activities (a lot more or a lot less than usual)	_____	_____
8. A major change in number of family get-togethers (a lot more or a lot less than usual)	_____	_____

9. A major change in financial state (a lot worse off or a lot better off than usual)   _____   _____

10. In-law troubles   _____   _____

11. A major change in the number of arguments with spouse (a lot more or a lot less than usual regarding child-rearing, personal habits, etc.)   _____   _____

12. Sexual difficulties   _____   _____

Part B

Instructions: In the space provided, indicate the *number of times* that each applicable event happened to you within the last two years.

	Number of times	X	Mean value	=	Your score

13. Major personal injury or illness   _____   _____   _____

14. Death of a close family member (other than spouse)   _____   _____   _____

15. Death of spouse   _____   _____   _____

16. Death of a close friend   _____   _____   _____

17. Gaining a new family member (through birth, adoption, oldster moving in, etc.)   _____   _____   _____

18. Major change in the health or behavior of a family member   _____   _____   _____

19. Change in residence   _____   _____   _____

20. Detention in jail or other institution   _____   _____   _____

21. Minor violations of the law (traffic tickets, jaywalking, disturbing the peace, etc.)   _____   _____   _____

22. Major business readjustment (merger, reorganization, bankruptcy, etc.)   _____   _____   _____

23. Marriage   _____   _____   _____

24. Divorce   _____   _____   _____

	Number of times	X	Mean value	=	Your score
25. Marital separation	_____		_____		_____
26. Outstanding personal achievement	_____		_____		_____
27. *Son or daughter leaving home (marriage, attending college, etc.)*	_____		_____		_____
28. Retirement from work	_____		_____		_____
29. Major change in working hours or conditions	_____		_____		_____
30. Major change in responsibilities at work (promotion, demotion, lateral transfer)	_____		_____		_____
31. Being fired from work	_____		_____		_____
32. Major change in living conditions (building a new home, remodeling, deterioration of home or neighborhood)	_____		_____		_____
33. Spouse beginning or ceasing work outside the home	_____		_____		_____
34. Taking on a mortgage greater than $25,000 (purchasing a home, business, etc.)	_____		_____		_____
35. Taking on a mortgage or loan of less than $25,000 (purchasing a car, TV, freezer, etc.)	_____		_____		_____
36. Foreclosure on a mortgage or loan	_____		_____		_____
37. Vacation	_____		_____		_____
38. Changing to a new school	_____		_____		_____
39. Changing to a different line of work	_____		_____		_____
40. Beginning or ceasing formal schooling	_____		_____		_____
41. Marital reconciliation	_____		_____		_____
42. Pregnancy	_____		_____		_____

Your total score   _____

Scoring

The mean values for each life event are listed on the following page. Write in the mean values for those events that happened to you. For items in Part B, multiply the mean

Life event	Mean value	Life event	Mean value	Life event	Mean value
1	23	15	100	29	20
2	16	16	37	30	29
3	15	17	39	31	47
4	24	18	44	32	25
5	19	19	20	33	26
6	18	20	63	34	31
7	19	21	11	35	17
8	15	22	39	36	30
9	38	23	50	37	13
10	29	24	73	38	20
11	35	25	65	39	36
12	39	26	28	40	26
13	53	27	29	41	45
14	63	28	45	42	40

of times an event happened, and enter the result under "Your score." Add up the mean values in Part A and your scores in Part B to get your total score.

The more change you have, the more likely you are to get sick. Of those people with a score of over 300 for the past year, almost 80 percent get sick on the near future; with a score of 200 to 299, about 50 percent get sick in the near future; and with a score of 150-199, only about 30 percent get sick in the near future. A score of less than 150 indicates that you have a low chance of getting sick. So, the higher your score, the harder you should work to stay well.

Stress can be cumulative. Events from two years ago may still be affecting you now. If you think this applies to you, repeat this test for the events of the preceding year and compare your scores.

Other New Harbinger Self-Help Titles